BASQUE FIRSTS

THE BASQUE SERIES

Basque Nationalism
by Stanley G. Payne

Amerikanuak: Basques in the New World
by William A. Douglass and Jon Bilbao

Aurrera!: A Textbook for Studying Basque
by Linda White

Back to Bizkaia: A Basque-American Memoir
by Vince J. Juaristi

*The Basques, the Catalans, and Spain:
Alternative Routes to Basque Nationalization*
by Daniele Conversi

*Chorizos in an Iron Skillet: Memories and Recipes
from an American Basque Daughter*
by Mary Ancho Davis

The Circle of Mountains: A Basque Shepherding Community
by Sandra Ott

Deep Blue Memory
by Monique Laxalt Urza

An Enduring Legacy: The Story of Basques in Idaho
by John Bieter and Mark Bieter

Gernika, 1937: The Market Day Massacre
by Xabier Irujo

The Good Oak
by Martin Etchart

Reclaiming Basque: Language, Nation, and Cultural Activism
by Jacqueline Urla

The Basque Language
by Alan R. King

BASQUE FIRSTS

FIRSTS

People Who Changed the World

VINCE J. JUARISTI

UNIVERSITY OF NEVADA PRESS

Reno & Las Vegas

University of Nevada Press, Reno, Nevada 89557 USA
www.unpress.nevada.edu
Copyright © 2016 by University of Nevada Press
All rights reserved
Manufactured in the United States of America
Cover photos (*top to bottom*): Edurne Pasaban, courtesy of Edurne Pasaban; Cristóbal
Balenciaga, courtesy of the Balenciaga Museum in Getaria, Spain; José María Arizmendiarrieta,
courtesy of the Mondragón Cooperative Corporation; St. Ignatius of Loyola, copyright 2013
Jesuit Institute London, used with permission; Santiago Ramón y Cajal, courtesy of Cajal
Legacy, Instituto Cajal, Madrid; Paul Laxalt, courtesy of the Ronald Reagan Library.

Library of Congress Cataloging-in-Publication Data
Names: Juaristi, Vince J., 1969– author.
Title: Basque firsts : people who changed the world / Vince J. Juaristi.
Description: Reno, NV : University of Nevada Press, [2016] | Series: The Basque series |
Includes bibliographical references and index.
Identifiers: LCCN 2016005518 | ISBN 978-1-943859-20-7 (pbk. : alk. paper)
    ISBN 978-0-87417-000-9 (ebook)
Subjects: LCSH: País Vasco (Spain)—Biography. | Basque Americans—Biography.
Classification: LCC CT1355.B37 J87 2016 | DDC 920.009299/92073—dc23
LC record available at http://lccn.loc.gov/2016005518

The paper used in this book meets the requirements of American National Standard for
Information Sciences—Permanence of Paper for Printed Library Materials, ANSI/NISO Z39.48–
1992 (R2002). Binding materials were selected for strength and durability.

This book has been reproduced as a digital reprint.

To Jacob and Alexis and
Other Basque children
Born and unborn
May these stories
Inspire them to
Change the world

Contents

Preface

IN THE THIRD GRADE, my *Weekly Reader* told of Ferdinand Magellan, the first man to circumnavigate the globe. I gobbled up the story—the wooden ships propelled by wind, the rowdy sailors, the dangers of storm and pirates and enemy vessels, and the sheer adventure of sailing into the great unknown. It was everything a third grade boy could want to fuel his imagination and eagerly finish his homework.

It wasn't until fifteen years later while reading economic history at Harvard that I learned that Magellan hadn't finished the voyage at all. He had died half-way round in the Philippines, his body left behind on the Isle of Mactan. What the hell, I thought? My *Weekly Reader* had been a big fat liar. An itty-bitty part of my academic foundation crumbled.

Naturally, I asked myself, if not Magellan, who was the first to circumnavigate the globe. I hunted for an answer and shocked myself when I found it. The first man was Juan Sebastián Elcano—a Basque man! My heart skipped a beat. I swelled momentarily with ethnic pride and then wondered why history had shrouded this beautiful historical nugget and not hoisted Elcano on a brilliant pedestal for blazing a trail that changed the world for all time. I was a little mad, in fact.

As my Harvard studies consumed me, the anger disappeared, of course, but the thought remained as a gnawing unanswered question. Years later it resurfaced with a vengeance during a most unexpected moment.

In 2013, Pope Benedict XVI resigned, and a few days later, Jorge Mario Bergoglio was elected as the new pope. To the world, he became Pope Francis, a man with soft eyes, a big smile, and a generous spirit. As a Catholic, I watched this happy warrior on a balcony at the Vatican turn to a crowd that desperately thirsted for a prayer and blessing; but before offering them, he asked the crowd first to pray for him. Here stood a humble man, I thought, and more so a man who could make a simple robe shine with grandiosity.

Reporters said that he was the first pontiff from the new world and the first Jesuit to hold the title. He surely was a Jesuit, I thought, a man of humble roots, one of the sack-wearers. They went on to describe the first Jesuit as St. Ignatius, a Spaniard they said, who had breathed life into the order nearly 500 years ago.

"What the hell?" I yelled at my television. "St. Ignatius was a Basque man!" I had known that fact since junior high. Dad had told me about him at some point, and the knowledge had stuck, just as his dad I'm sure had told him. I knew what I knew. That's the way it so often was with the Basque, one generation informing the next, like a grand chain of stories that linked the history and pride of an ancient people, father to son, mother to daughter, stretching over five hundred years into the past, maybe to St. Ignatius himself. I then looked him up to be sure, perused a couple biographies, and even read his autobiography, *Reminiscences*. All confirmed his roots in Loyola, Spain, a man of Basque origin. I wondered why the world didn't share this knowledge or simply chose to disregard his Basque identity. That's when Juan Sebastián Elcano returned to me. It was my big fat lying *Weekly Reader* all over again.

At that moment this book was conceived.

The Basque have long hoped for an independent country. Whether that will ever happen, no one can say. Yet if the Basque cannot gain geography, they can still invade and take territory in history that's rightfully theirs, especially in those instances where their achievements have so dramatically influenced the course of human progress. I wanted to contribute to that effort, if only in a small way. I started with these two figures—Juan Sebastián Elcano and St. Ignatius— whom I knew to be Basque and who seemed beyond reproach as worldly figures.

Before I considered others, I asked what it meant to be Basque. Ethnicity aligned easily with nationality: French from France, English from England, Mexicans from Mexico. But for ethnic groups without a country, like the Basque, swallowed up by other nations, their identity derived from factors other than national boundaries. Different people could produce different definitions and carve out wholly different subsets of demography, geography, or language.

My definition was simple. I considered someone Basque if he was born in or a resident of one of the seven provinces of the Basque country spanning Spain and France—Bizkaia, Gipuzkoa, Araba, Lapurdi, Nafarroa Garaia, Nafarroa Beherea, and Zuberoa. Anyone born outside the Basque country who shared the ancestry or spoke the language and self-identified as Basque landed inside the tent as well. If a person self-identified as not-Basque, I excluded him regardless of where he was born or raised.

This definition was straightforward, I thought, and let me investigate Basque contributors like Elcano and St. Ignatius who had left considerable marks on world affairs. Elcano and St. Ignatius served as important baselines. They were not only achievers but ultra-achievers, men whose contributions transcended the Basque community to benefit people everywhere. Elcano had circumnavigated the globe, confirming the Earth as a sphere and setting in

motion frenzied expeditions that would populate the newly discovered continents. St. Ignatius tenaciously established the Jesuits, placing education at the
top of his agenda, sending men worldwide to teach and open schools, thereby
educating millions from all nationalities over the centuries.

After these two, who would come next, I wondered? Narrowing the list
of potential candidates was not easy. In history, Basque men and women have
excelled in medicine, law, literature, science, business, and politics. They have
raised respectable families, started businesses, and fought wars. All they have
done in Spain and France, and in the diasporas of the Americas, has threaded
deeply into whatever community they have called home.

But I wanted more than the hard-working, thoughtful, decent Basque
citizen, of whom there are many. I wanted the Basque man or woman who (1)
contributed to the progress of all people everywhere, not only to other Basques;
(2) remained highly regarded and are likely to remain so for the rest of time; and
(3) achieved something remarkable—first. Being first mattered.

In the shadows of history, I found several extraordinary gems. After Elcano
and St. Ignatius came Santiago Ramón y Cajal, a Navarran, the first neurologist
and a Nobel laureate in medicine, who defined and drew pictures of the human
nervous system, setting the framework for all future neurological study of the
human brain. Cristóbal Balenciaga, the king of haute couture, followed. He
was a man who reshaped how women dressed, transforming Victorian stan-
dards into freer silhouettes that Western women still enjoy today. Christian
Dior called him "The master of us all." A contemporary of Balenciaga was José
María Arizmendiarrieta, a priest who found a poor, destitute, unemployed
congregation in Mondragón at the start of World War II. Over thirty years, his
work as the first social entrepreneur resulted in the Mondragón Cooperative
Corporation (MCC) with 257 cooperatives, nearly 100,000 worker-owners, and
over $24 billion in annual revenue.

These five figures are no longer living, though their achievements remain
vitally rooted in communities and countries worldwide. I included two others
still alive today. The first, Paul Dominique Laxalt, served as governor and later
as senator from Nevada. But his greatest influence came as first friend to President Ronald Reagan, guiding policy, offering advice, attending the president's
bedside after an assassination attempt, and helping to transform the economics
and security of the United States. The seventh and final profile is of a good
friend of mine, Edurne Pasaban, originally from Tolosa, Spain, who lives now
in San Sebastiáån. She is the first woman (Basque or otherwise) to summit
the fourteen tallest peaks in the world, a feat so daring and difficult that only a
handful of brave souls in all history have ever managed it.

Finding materials about these men and women was sometimes a challenge. Wherever possible, I relied on primary sources such as autobiographies, letters, interviews conducted by others, or diaries and journals. For Edurne Pasaban, I conducted several interviews of my own to dig into her rich life. Ramón y Cajal left a voluminous autobiography, St. Ignatius a treasure trove of thousands of letters, Arizmendiarrieta a portfolio of economic papers and legal artifacts still in use by the Mondragón Cooperatives, and Laxalt a documented political life at the University of Nevada, University of Virginia, and the Ronald Reagan Presidential Library in Simi Valley, California.

Other profiles were less easily researched. There is no evidence, for example, that Elcano kept a diary, though I suspect he did somewhere at some time, given the quality of his writing. Instead, his full voyage relied on the chronicle of a single scribe who, out of vengeance, omitted Elcano's name from the official record and then passed four copies of this record to various kings and queens in Europe. Ever since then, the historical truth has jousted with that flawed record. Only through scant eyewitness accounts, investigative material after the voyage, a coat-of-arms bestowed by King Charles, and other documents from the Spanish and Philippine archives can the official record now be corrected nearly five hundred years later.

Balenciaga was almost as mysterious. He was a recluse who sat for only one interview before his death. His aesthetic was revealed in his work, the dresses, which he viewed as a painter views canvas and color. Close friends filled in the blanks about his thoughts before, during, and after World War II, his influences from childhood, his anguish over losing his lover, and his struggles with Christian Dior and Coco Chanel.

Six of these seven hailed from the heart of Basque country, hugging the Atlantic coast or backing up against the Pyrenees. Across five centuries, they trod the same paths by foot, donkey, wagon, or car, saw the same blue skies and Biscayan vistas, spoke the same languages, and were wrapped in the same culture. The remaining one, Laxalt, was first-generation American, raised in Carson City, Nevada, his father a sheepherder from the French side of the Pyrenees.

These lives shared more than geographic ethnicity. What popped out immediately was that all seven were Roman Catholic. Most Basque are, of course, but I wondered if the affiliation had driven them in some special way. What I discovered instead was that they influenced the church more than the church influenced them. Through the Society of Jesus, St. Ignatius helped transform the church. Father Arizmendiarrieta defied church elders and spoke more of economics than Jesus's parables. Elcano led his men in prayer at the Santa Maria de la Vitoria to thank the Virgin Mary and Child, but his

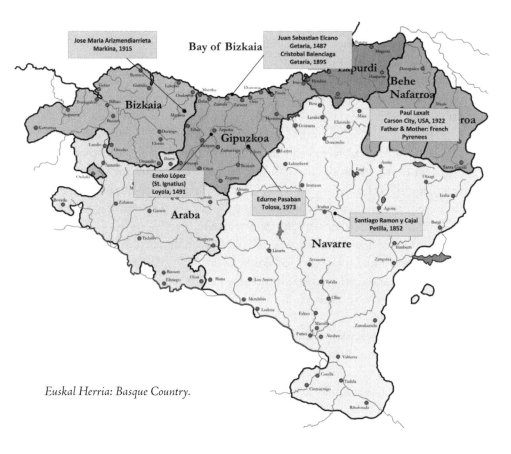

Euskal Herria: Basque Country.

successful voyage eviscerated the pope's Treaty of Tordesilla, which had defined how the world divvied up the seas between Portugal and Spain, the two great powers of the day. Even Balenciaga designed new cassocks for priests to bestow a shinier, more modern look. All they accomplished, it seemed, came about in spite of the church.

They shared other intangible qualities that went a long way to explaining their success. I marveled at their work ethic especially. St. Ignatius wrote thousands of letters, often by candlelight with a quill pen. His words stood in place of sword and shield. Ramón y Cajal wrote volumes on histology and neurology and then sketched thousands of pictures in pencil, pen, or charcoal to illustrate those texts. Laxalt visited nearly every state in 1976, 1980, and 1984 to stump for Ronald Reagan's election. Next to the president, he was the most widely known figure of the campaigns. Others showed equally indefatigable work habits, never confined to eight hours a day or the bookends of sun-up and sundown. Each burned the midnight oil, drawing more light from a lifetime.

Their work was never scattered either but rather was supremely focused, their goals clear. Toward the end of his voyage with the Portuguese pursuing, the ship leaking, and the men starving, Elcano had a singular determination: reach home. All other considerations melted away. Ramón y Cajal wanted to prove his neuron doctrine and dethrone the dominant neurological theory of the day. When not in the classroom, his every minute turned on this one ambition. Balenciaga tore ensembles at the seams and started over with needle and thread because an offending sleeve had turned a dress from a fashion showpiece to a rag fit for death. He would not stand for it. And St. Ignatius might have been describing all of them when he wrote, "One rare and exceptional deed is worth far more than a thousand commonplace ones." Each of them shared an intense focus often to the detriment and neglect of all else.

As much as I admired these incredible souls and hoped to emulate their traits, it sometimes felt like they had crossed a line from dedication to unhealthy obsession and still further to life-threatening passion. During a quiet meal with Edurne Pasaban one night in Amherst, Massachusetts, I probed her risky flirtation with danger.

"What compels you to climb?" I asked.

"I love the mountains," she said.

"I love mountains too, but I haven't climbed Everest and K2 and the other twelve. What makes you or anyone go to that extreme?"

"I don't think it's extreme," she said.

I chuckled at that. "Out of billions and billions of people who have walked the earth since the beginning of time," I said, "only 33 have climbed the 14 tallest peaks. I could do the math, but by definition, that's extreme."

"I hadn't thought of it like that," she said.

"So I ask again, what drives you? What makes you risk your life? What sets you apart?"

She puzzled over the questions, chewing one prawn after another down to the tail. There was silence between us. It was the first time, I thought, that someone had framed her behavior this way. An answer did not come, at least not quickly.

Then she said, "A big purpose fills up a life."

I liked the sentiment. It applied so very nicely to her, and to the achievements of the others. Inherent in this big purpose was big risk. Climbing an 8,000-meter mountain meant risking death with every footfall. Hoping to reach Jerusalem, St. Ignatius passed through villages beset by plague and crossed the Mediterranean swarming with pirates and enemy vessels. Elcano set out to circumnavigate the globe, a fool's errand almost certain to end in death. Although his predecessor had been shot for defiance, Father Arizmendiarrieta opposed his monsignor, the town council, and Franco's government to make possible the Mondragón Experience. In one case, he even forged documents, hardly the norm for a man of the cloth. Ramón y Cajal risked intellectual and academic obscurity by challenging so many renowned scientists who had staked their reputations on the prevailing neurological theory of the day. Big purposes yielded big risks for all of them.

Their tenacious work ethic seemed to push them past these risks, though not without tremendous setbacks. One thing I learned from studying these men and women is how history sometimes dwells on the achievement of a life while ignoring or skimming over the stumbles. Too often, the destination trumps the journey. The outcome may be grand, but what makes it grander, I think, is all that a person overcomes to achieve it.

From dire straits, fatigue, physical limits, even darkness and despair, there is born a deeper admiration. Edurne Pasaban suffered depression, attempted suicide, and received long-term care in hospital before out-climbing three other women for her coveted title. Trying to round the Cape of Good Hope, Elcano nearly sank his ship twice, killing all hands before succeeding on the third try. Laxalt failed to get his friend Ron elected in 1976 despite a Herculean effort, yet succeeded in 1980 and 1984. Ramón y Cajal lost out twice on a professorship and thought of leaping from a mountaintop before he made his breakthrough. These and other struggles made them human not super-human, flesh and blood not conjured spirits, real not phony. Their failings help us relate to them and ultimately heighten our feelings of awe at all they did and have done in a single lifetime.

Finally, these profiles motivated me as I hope they will motivate others, Basque and non-Basque alike. To fill up a life with big purpose, as Edurne said, sounds like a wonderful guiding star for every adult and child. Yes, you must work hard. Yes, there are risks. Yes, you will fall and fall and fall again. But it is in the getting up that these extraordinary Basque men and women demonstrated greatness and earned our eternal respect. Now, in return for that greatness, they deserve full recognition in history, credit where credit is due, for all they have given the world.

BASQUE FIRSTS

Juan Sebastián Elcano

Primus Circumdedisti Me

IT WAS SEPTEMBER 8, 1522, when the ship sailed up the Guadalquivir River into the Spanish port of Seville. Once a glorious 85-ton carrack with oak keel and pine masts christened *Victoria* at the Basque shipyards of Gipuzkoa, it was now only a ghost ship, low in the water, with tattered sails and battered hull. Aboard were gaunt survivors, starving, barely able to stand, covered in open red sores over their arms and legs, chest and back. Their teeth had fallen out from bleeding gums. Only 18 men and four captives remained of an initial crew of almost 270 who had sailed from this very spot three years earlier under a Portuguese captain named Ferdinand Magellan.

There were five ships then, dubbed the Armada de Molucca by Spanish King Charles I. It had the singular mission of sailing west (instead of east) to the Molucca Islands and returning to Spain with spices, thereby charting a path around the globe, if such a voyage were possible. None had done it before. Magellan and his crew would be the first. But on this day, it was not Magellan who led the *Victoria* into Seville's port but rather a lesser known man, a 35-year-old Basque mariner named Juan Sebastián Elcano who, against improbable odds, brought the crew home after Magellan's death to finish the first circumnavigation of our world.

The world that Elcano returned to had been divided for over 25 years between the great empires of Portugal and Spain. In 1494, a year after Columbus's return from his first voyage, Pope Alexander VI issued a papal edict calling for "a straight line be determined and drawn north and south, from pole to pole,

A statue of Juan Sebastián Elcano stands in the plaza of Getaria. Erected in 1934, the statue shows a bearded Elcano with his right hand on a tiller, his left hand holding a compass, and a foot on a coil of rope. The face reflects an early lithograph and painting of him from other sources. Photo by the author.

3

on the said ocean sea, from the Arctic to the Antarctic pole . . . at a distance of three hundred and seventy leagues [1,110 miles] west of the Cape Verde Islands." All lands west of the boundary belonged to Spain, those to the east to Portugal. It was called the Treaty of Tordesilla, and it defined where Spanish and Portuguese captains, sailors, and merchants could travel without encroaching on each other's territory.

Elcano knew of the pope's edict. He was born in probably 1487 in Getaria, Gipuzkoa, Spain, a coastal town, not much bigger now than it was then, with a proud tradition and livelihood derived from the sea that dated to the 13th century—of whaling and fishing, shipbuilding and manning crews. Today it has the same old world oaks overlooking a safe harbor as in Elcano's day, the same smells of fish and brine wafting through the marketplace, the same waves crashing on the promontory, and the same thunder and winds holding ships close to shore.

Basque fishermen in Elcano's day followed a ritual before boarding ships. They attended mass at the Iglesia de San Salvador where Elcano was baptized. It still stands today near the harbor as a magnificent ogival church made of sandstone. After confession, they headed out to sea and returned with anchovies, bass, bream, eel, herring, lobsters, sardines, and whale. They gave the first whale of the season, a gift of the ocean, to the king "from head unto tail, as the custom is."[1] Thereafter, the men cut out the whales' tongues and presented them at the church altar, a gift to God for the harvest. The priest ate some and returned some to the sea with a blessing of thankfulness, and there the circle of reciprocity allowed the Basque fishermen to thrive season after season. The local coat-of-arms still shows a harpooned whale flanked by sailors under a Spanish crown.

Elcano's parents, Domingo de Elcano and Catalina del Puerto, both native to Getaria, had eight children: Elcano, third among them; two older, Juan who married, and Domingo who became a priest; four younger brothers—Martin, Anton, Juan Martin, and Ochoa—who followed Elcano as navigators; and finally a little sister, Sebastiana, who married a Gainza. Through various marriages, Gainza became Lardizabal, the family name that represents the Elcano line today. Little more has survived of Elcano's youth: no diary or letters from family, no communion or confirmation records, no mention of formal education or posting as page on any vessel in or out of Getaria's port.

The record of his life picked up 20 years after his birth when empires, content with Tordesilla's distribution of the seas, fought bitterly to divvy up the land. By invitation of France, Spain sent troops to Italy to take the Kingdom of Naples in a joint campaign. In 1507, Spain emerged in glorious triumph with half

*This lithograph of Juan Sebastián Elcano pro-
duced in 1854 resembles an earlier painting from
a hundred years before. The painter indicated,
"This is what I imagine our great Elcano may
have looked like." In reality, we cannot be certain
of his appearance, though this visage has come
down through history as Elcano's likeness.*

of Naples as a prize. By age 20 Elcano had come to serve on one of the returning vessels, though in what capacity or for what duration is unknown.

No sooner had he returned to Spanish soil than a new war was declared. Spain needed war. Its regions—Aragon, Castille, and Granada—had been stitched together over several decades by the union of King Ferdinand II and the cunning Queen Isabella. The stitching between these kingdoms was not perfect, and feuds often erupted. The best way to quell these internal disputes, reasoned the crown, was to focus on external threats.

Even though Isabella had died in 1504, her strategy lived on. The duty to guide Spain after her demise fell less to Ferdinand, who had lost much of his authority, than to Jimenes de Cisneros, Cardinal Archbishop of Toledo. Cisneros was perhaps the most powerful man in the country, years before he had led the effort to vanquish the Moors and expel them from southern Spain. Within months of Elcano's return from Italy, Cisneros called for a new war against the Moors in Northern Africa.

In 1509, a fleet of 10 ships and 80 smaller vessels embarked for Africa. The 22-year-old Elcano was on board as chief mate, reportable only to the captain and responsible for all ship operations above and below deck. It was a position unusual for someone of his youth, which showed officials' respect for his talents. Young, energetic, a master in the mighty Spanish fleet, on the eve of battle— what youthful man's blood would not pound with the primitive passion of such a great mission? Cisneros was aboard. Elcano listened to his rousing speech to the troops, his powerful voice defying an aging body: "For many years you have seen the Moors ravaging your coasts, carrying off your children to slavery, and dishonoring your wives and daughters. The day you have long desired, the day for avenging these crimes has come!"

The fleet flew through the deep blue of the Mediterranean. It anchored off the coast of Africa and bombarded the Moorish town of Oran. The city burned. Elcano and troops went ashore, setting ladders to scale the city walls, advancing wrung by wrung beneath a barrage of stones and arrows from the other side. The Moorish opposition was futile. As the sun set across the yellow desert, over 4,000 Moors lay dead in Oran's dirty roads or in the cindered rubble of its buildings. Only 30 Christians died that day. One could scarce imagine a more lopsided battle in all the horrific annals of warfare. When Cisnero entered Oran, he first went to the prisons and freed over 300 Christian slaves who rejoiced at their renewed freedom. Elcano bore witness to these events, which proved so powerful, so memorable that he wrote of them decades later in his last will and testament.

Though still a young man, Elcano had gone where most from Getaria, Gipuzkoa, would never go in a lifetime, from the Italian campaigns to the siege of Oran, aboard the king's ships. Adventure coursed in his blood; adrenaline had become an addiction. He now yearned for a new adventure.

He did not wait long. The conquest of Oran opened Africa as a new frontier for territory, riches, and slaves. Cisneros convinced King Ferdinand to ready a larger fleet including 100 vessels from the Basque shipyards in Gipuzkoa alone. Their target was Tripoli on the coast of present-day Libya. To participate in this new adventure, Elcano bought a ship of his own. It weighed over 200 tons, larger than any that Magellan would eventually sail. The ship's name was not recorded.

The siege of Tripoli in 1510 did not go well. Spain suffered deep losses that compelled the king and archbishop to pull back and end the engagement. Returning home, Elcano discovered that Spain's booty from far-off conquered lands had become outstripped by its expenditures; the crown did not pay its bills on time, or ever. Unable to compensate his sailors, he borrowed from Italian merchants who soon called the loan, forcing him to sell his ship. It seemed to be a responsible course, but in Spain of the sixteenth century, selling an armed

Spanish vessel to foreigners, as Elcano had done, broke the law, subjecting him to arrest, a fine equal to the ship's value, and a summons to the king's court.

He fled Gipuzkoa for the anonymity of the much larger city of Seville, but the violation dogged him. He knew of no captains in the king's employ who would hire a man at odds with the crown. For a man who thrived at sea, it was a bitter punishment to be rooted on land. As a man of faith, he knelt for hours before Mary in various churches of Seville, moving from one to another to avoid authorities. He prayed for redemption, to not be forsaken.

A reply to prayer came on the wind. In Seville at the time, a lively buzz swept the streets about a new expedition, one of danger, perhaps stupidity, but certainly one of daring and intrigue headed by a Portuguese man named Magellan. Rumor told of a seemingly impossible mission: to sail a fleet west across the Atlantic to find a secret route to the highly coveted Spice Islands on the other side of the world. The Spice Islands, or Moluccas—a group of islands in what is now Indonesia—grew coveted plants such as nutmeg, mace, and cloves and had only been reachable by the arduous eastern route around the Cape of Good Hope. Few believed that a western route were possible; in fact, most expected a ship going west to be torn apart as it crashed into a continent or alternately to fall off the Earth if it sailed beyond the horizon. Rarely had anyone so profoundly pushed to turn Plato's Ship of Fools from allegory into reality.

It is hard for a person of the modern era to fathom why someone would travel by ship, risking life and limb, to procure a pinch of pepper. Nearly any spice that tempts or tangs the palette today is easily bought at a corner grocery store. But in Elcano's day, spices were in high demand—pepper, cinnamon, nutmeg, cumin, ginger, cloves, and others—and with their growing demand came higher prices and greater wealth. The man or nation that controlled land, villages, towns, islands, or countries with the proper climate and soil to grow and harvest these spices became the king among kings, the nation among nations, wealthy and powerful. In 1499, five years after the Treaty of Tordesilla, Vasco da Gama had navigated to India, giving Portugal an edge over Spain in the transport and trade of spices. Spain wanted to even the odds, which is why King Charles listened to Magellan's plan for a western route and, though finding it far-fetched and dangerous, agreed nonetheless to fund the expedition.

Elcano investigated these rumors and found the mission real, though hardly achievable. Feeling desperate, however, he pursued the opportunity. If nothing else, it offered a chance to put out to sea where he had spent so much of his life, where among waves and plumed sails, hard labor and adventure, things made sense and—more practically—where the law would have a hard time following him. He hoped that officials needing worthy, seafaring men would overlook his transgressions in favor of his experience.

In the royal offices that made appointments, most high-ranking positions were filled by Basque men, many from Gipuzkoa. One retired official, who had worked in the royal offices for years, was Elcano's relative and spoke on his behalf to the treasurer who controlled the king's purse for all vessels. By way, therefore, of familial connections and Basque nepotism, Elcano gained an appointment in Magellan's fleet as master of *Concepción* with the added duty of recruitment. At least 10 men of Gipuzcoa joined Magellan's fleet through Elcano's efforts, though 40 Basque sailed out of Seville who may have been Elcano's recruits as well. He could not have been more excited.

Having secured an appointment, Elcano now sought out the advanced education needed to help run such an expedition. The royal office ran a school of navigation where the headmaster was none other than the great seaman and navigator Amerigo Vespucci, after whom the continents of America had been named.[2] Vespucci administered Elcano's final exam on trigonometry, the use of the astrolabe for latitudes, and the mathematical artistry of measuring longitude by landmark, star, current, and wind.[3] Elcano received high marks and a certificate as an officer and was sent on to help prep the fleet at dock in Seville.

In July 1518, a year before launch, the five ships in Magellan's fleet had sailed from the Basque port of Lequetio to Cadiz in southern Spain. From there, the ships went on to Seville where retrofitting and stocking commenced: a tarring inside and out, a bubbling for leaks, a doubling of hull thickness, the stocking of sails, and the storing of food, water and wine. The most common food was a crunchy, high-carb biscuit called hardtack, made from flour, hot water, and sometimes a bit of salt. Elcano worked day and night in the retrofit, counting every item and controlling every detail as he had in Oran and Tripoli.

What he couldn't control were Portuguese spies who wanted to stop this voyage, and for good reason: It threatened the Portuguese monopoly over the Spice Islands. If the Spanish sailed west as allowed by the Treaty of Tordesilla, and by skill or luck found a way to the Moluccas, would Spain have claim by law to the same islands and spices that Portugal already claimed via their eastern route? No one knew, and the uncertainty worried the Portuguese. During the retrofit of the fleet, orchestrated riots erupted in the shipyards designed to derail the expedition. Portuguese influence, therefore, became a critical concern, worsened by the whispers of Spanish crew and commoners who noted Magellan's Portuguese ancestry and the 40 Portuguese crew members.

King Charles commissioned an inquiry to determine the extent of the Portuguese influence. Elcano testified saying that Magellan was "a discreet and virtuous man and careful of his honor." It was a note of praise that later in his dealings with Magellan must have curdled his blood. He went on to say that he was "well satisfied with the company of the ship in which he was master, because it was a good company, adequate for the cargo which his ship carried, and that he had also heard the masters of the other ships say that they too were satisfied with the company in their own vessels."

Content with the testimony, the King's commission approved the voyage and encouraged the Armada de Molucca to get underway with all deliberate speed. With orders to proceed, Elcano checked the stores of his ship, the *Concepción*, on the eve of launch. The cargo would last only two or three legs of the journey before needing to restock, he surmised. If the men squirmed with hunger and thirst, he knew they would blame him.

Being shipmaster was a station beneath his skill but still important, and he performed the role well. Yet no matter how important his job or how well he performed it, he received scant attention in official records or ship logs while crossing the Atlantic, or during any part of the expedition.

Antonio Pigafetta, a Venetian scholar and chief chronicler of the voyage who would write brilliant descriptions of local customs, plant and animal life, and religious ceremonies of the cultures they encountered along the way, did not mention Elcano a single time in all three years of his journal. The omission was not accidental. It confirmed instead how much Pigafetta, a Magellan loyalist, loathed Elcano, cutting him from official records and attempting to erase him from history. Where Elcano emerged for the first time, however, made Pigafetta's silence understandable, though no more truthful, for eyewitnesses of the expedition would later utter *Elcano* and *mutiny* in the same poisonous breath.

N O THREAT INSTILLED GREATER FEAR in the heart of kings and captains than the thought of mutiny, for if a crew took a ship by force to avenge grievances, word spread from port to port, ship to ship, undermining naval strength and the power of the throne. Yet from the outset, mutiny within the Armada de Moluccas seemed unlikely. Magellan's ships were nearly new or refitted from Basque shipyards, the most reliable in all of Spain; the expedition was large and well-stocked with food, water, and wine; the men had been handpicked by the king, Magellan, or Elcano; part of the trip was already charted and explored; and the mission was truly historic. This voyage, more than any other, began with every advantage.

Not long after leaving Seville on August 10, 1519, sailing south to the Canary Islands, and crossing the Atlantic, however, the men became restless. Their dissatisfaction was piling up. First, the five ships contained an enormous diversity of sailors—40 Basques, 120 Castilians, 43 Portuguese, 25 Italians, 17 French, 4 Germans, 5 Flemish, 6 Greek, 2 Irish, 1 British, 1 from the Azores, and 6 from Africa. Each man had his own language, culture, and naval background. Unifying this motley crew and getting them to cooperate was a constant challenge.

Second, the King's Commission about Portuguese influence may have satisfied the king, but it hadn't quelled suspicions aboard ship. Three of five captains, all Spaniards, believed that Magellan remained secretly loyal to Portugal. To allay these fears, King Charles had named Juan de Cartagena, who served as captain of the *San Antonio*, as Magellan's co-captain-general. Once underway, Cartagena demanded equal voice in all decisions. Outside Spanish waters, however, Magellan honored this demand by immediately relieving him of command and confining him to quarters, which intensified suspicions and split loyalties.

Third, for more than four months, in defiance of the king's orders, Magellan charted an equatorial path across the Atlantic that traversed long stretches of windless waters. The perilous calm tested the crew's patience, raised questions about Magellan's sea-faring wisdom, and convinced the men that God might indeed be frowning on this mission.

While crossing the Atlantic, Elcano managed to stay impartial in the growing partisanship of the crew for and against Magellan, but this indifference was tested as the fleet reached Rio de Janeiro and Magellan began his relentless quest for a route around South America. Although, according to Pigafetta, Elcano and other masters filled their hulls with "geese [penguins] and sea wolves [seals] in great numbers," Magellan reduced the men's rations, not knowing how long the armada would bump along the coast before finding safe passage. The decision enraged crewmembers who believed their performance and hardships deserved reward, not punishment. Elcano as shipmaster bore these arrows of anger.

Along with hunger, the men fought the elements. Between January and late March of 1520, six storms blew in, each worse than the one before, often battering the men for days with freezing rains, ferocious winds, and crashing waves. "We lost sight of the North Star," wrote Pigafetta. Even when the sea calmed, Magellan ordered one or more ships into dangerous capes and harbors and up shallow rivers to explore waterways that might circle round or pass through the southern continent to the great sea beyond. But no path was successful.

The failures of the search, the bitterness of gray skies, the onset of winter, the pangs of hunger, the lack of wine—all beat down and wrung out these men, weakening their resolve. Elcano's neutrality changed to suspicion. Whispers began that a strait did not exist, that to avoid certain death it would be better to turn now and go back to Spain. In this sullen atmosphere, on the last day of March, the armada sheltered in a cove named Port St. Julian off present-day Argentina where the five ships would wait out the winter.

To bolster spirits and suppress a brewing rebellion, Magellan spoke to the crews. The moment might have reminded Elcano of Cisnero's speech before Oran. No greater mission had befallen men, said Magellan, and duty demanded they see it through. Instead of finding fault, each should find new fortitude. Other men, Portuguese men, he said, had sailed farther south along the continental coast and had not complained of hardship, so why should they? In this great quest, he said, he preferred dying to returning to Spain a failure.

The do-or-die speech seemed thoughtful and courageous, the kind of speech that one expected from an historical leader, but it missed the mark with many, including Elcano. Rather than shore up courage, it hardened opposition. In the wee hours of a moonless night on April 1, 1520, Easter Sunday, a plan was hatched to strip Magellan of command.

Aboard Elcano's ship, the *Concepción*, the night buzzed with conspiracy, shifting allegiances, and talk of tactics. The ringleaders were Juan de Cartagena, former captain of the *San Antonio*, who had been relieved as co-captain-general, and Gaspar de Quesada, captain of the *Concepción*. The two invited Elcano into a longboat that stealthily rowed through cold black water to the *San Antonio*. Aided by about 30 co-conspirators, the trio climbed the hull like soft-pawed cats, and then one and all made their way to the captain's quarters. Captain Álvaro de Mesquita slept peacefully in his bunk, unaware that rebellion was in the offing. Soon enough, he was in irons.

The master Juan de Elorriaga, a Basque mariner whom Elcano had recruited, confronted the mutineers. Some accounts say Elcano had approached Elorriaga the day before hoping that he would help "prevent a mutiny." Whether the two had spoken before or he had encountered the mutineers for the first time on *San Antonio*, Elorriaga sided with Captain Mesquita and Magellan's mission. Would Elcano, who showed obedience to Captain Quesada, have expected anything less? Elorriaga's fight, however noble, failed. Captain Quesada pulled his dagger and ran Elorriaga through with four violent thrusts, leaving him for dead. He lingered in agony for three to four months before succumbing to his wounds.[4]

With Mesquita chained and Elorriaga subdued, the remaining crew offered little opposition. The conquest of the *San Antonio* was complete, and Elcano was asked to take command. Such was their confidence in him that Cartagena and Quesada would entrust Elcano with the largest ship in the armada. He barked orders to arrest the disloyal, guard supplies, and ready the ship for battle, arming men with crossbows and prepping reconnaissance to other vessels. The mutiny spread to the *Victoria* where Captain Luis de Mendoza, already predisposed against Magellan, eagerly joined Cartagena and Quesada in their quest.

As night turned to gray morning, crews woke to a new reality. With Quesada, Cartagena, Mendoza, and Elcano were the *San Antonio*, *Concepción*, and *Victoria*; and with Magellan were the flagship *Trinidad* and the *Santiago* under Captain Juan Serrano. Three ships against two—Magellan's back was against the wall. The mutineers demanded of Magellan: relinquish command and return to Spain. He dismissed them and then hatched a plan of his own.

Targeting the *Victoria*, Magellan sent a longboat of his most loyal men with a private letter for Mendoza who foolishly let them board. The letter demanded that Mendoza surrender to the *Trinidad*; anything less would mean his death. Mendoza crumpled the paper and tossed it overboard. Magellan's men lunged at him, plunging daggers into his head and throat and felling the mutinous captain to the deck. With "power of cord and knife," Magellan hung Mendoza's dead body upside-down from the yard arm for all to see, those aboard *San Antonio* and *Concepción* especially, and then drew and quartered the corpse, mounting the body parts on stakes.

What Elcano thought or felt as witness to this carnage, or if he witnessed it at all, was never recorded, but not long after, support for the mutineers fell away. Elcano's first command since owning a ship in the Tripoli campaign faded to nothing as the *San Antonio* and *Concepción* capitulated to Magellan.

Under a drumhead court convened on April 26, 1520, at St. Julian, Cartagena, Quesada and 40 others including Elcano received guilty verdicts and sentences of death. To Quesada's guilty servant, Magellan commanded, "lop off your master's head to avoid the same fate." The servant pondered only a moment then drew a sword and beheaded his kneeling master. The corpse was quartered with the parts mounted on stakes. Another mutineer was strung up by his hands with cannonballs tied to his feet as a rope raised and lowered to maximize the pain. Still another had his joints dislocated and was left to writhe on deck in excruciating pain until he simply suffered to death over several days of anguish. Magellan was an accomplished tormenter who seemed to crawl from the pages of Dante's *Inferno*. Cartagena and a priest loyal to him were banished to the St. Julian mainland to fend alone in the wilderness against storm, beast, and cannibals for the rest of their natural lives.

Elcano and others escaped such cruelties, their sentences reduced to hard labor in shackles. The armada weathered the winter at St. Julian another five months during which Elcano endured his punishment: scrubbing floorboards, butchering livestock, preparing meals, packing the riggings, manning the deck in storms of ice and wind and rain till his flesh blued and limbs numbed. The chains around wrists and ankles tore his flesh. For a man who had seen battle at Naples and off the African coast, and had owned a ship greater than any now in the armada, the humiliation must have overwhelmed him.

Five months later in August 1520, needing their skill to find the strait, Magellan restored Elcano and others to full service. Only four of the five ships got underway, with Elcano once again master of *Concepción*. He learned that during his hard labor, the *Santiago* had been caught in a storm, run aground, and broken up, though all crew had survived. So it was after five months, a mutiny, executions, and a lost ship that the Armada de Molucca raised anchor, never again to port at St. Julian.

Farther south the four remaining ships of the armada anchored at the Rio de Santa Cruz for seven weeks. Magellan sent vessels to explore surrounding waterways for the strait. The *San Antonio* and *Concepción* found a broad channel of great width and depth that did not dead-end inland. In exultant spirit, the two crews returned with the momentous news. Pigafetta wrote of the occasion: "We joined in their shouts of joy, and all gave thanks to God and the Blessed Virgin Mary." Both ships were dispatched a second time to the channel for reconnaissance of depth and width, reefs and shoals, and the tides. But only one came back, Elcano's ship, the *Concepción*. *San Antonio*, by a mutiny of her own, slipped away to Spain, leaving Magellan and the mission behind.

The three small ships—*Trinidad*, *Concepción*, and *Victoria*—sailed through this newly discovered channel on November 28, 1520. It would become the gateway from east to west christened then and forevermore the Strait of Magellan. Elcano ordered *Concepción*'s guns to be fired in salute, the blast rumbling the first echoes about the cape, the men gushing joy and relief. Through the continent they sailed, emerging after 350 miles into the great blue of the Pacific.

One could only imagine Elcano's heart and mind at this moment filled with memories of Getaria a world away, of battle and conquest in Africa, joining the voyage to escape the law, surviving a mutiny, weathering punishment, and reaching this place where no European before had come. For a second, it would be permissible to excuse him for thanking destiny, and in reply, destiny might have said, *ez bazaude amaitu*, "you are not finished."

F OR THREE MONTHS, nine days, and over 13,800 miles, the men journeyed the Pacific. Finally, in March 1521, a Basque from Navarre roared "Land ahead!" and the ships soon anchored in Guam in the Mariana Islands. The news could not have been more fortuitous. Pigafetta wrote of their grave plight:

We ate biscuit, and when there was no more, we ate the crumbs which were full of maggots and smelled strongly of mouse urine. We drank yellow water, already several days putrid. And we ate some of the hides that were on the largest shroud to keep it from breaking and that were very much toughened by the sun, rain and winds. And we softened them in the sea for four or five days, and then we put them in a pot over the fire and ate them and also much sawdust.

Nineteen had died of scurvy, another 25 to 30 hovered near death, Elcano included, whose gums bled and skin erupted with red sores.[5] Magellan was said to have tossed his maps overboard, declaring them useless. On the verge of giving up, helpless and hopeless, the three ships with bedraggled crews finally anchored and the native people swarmed the ships to barter food for iron, which the men eagerly obliged. Elcano replenished the hulls with enough fish, coconut, plantains, and sweet potatoes to last until the armada reached the Philippine archipelago.

They sailed on, beyond Homonhom arriving at Limasawa on Easter Sunday, a year exactly from the midnight mutiny at St. Julian. At Limasawa, the men unfurled a Castilian flag and erected a cross "at the top of the highest mountain, so that they [Limasawans] could see it every morning, and adore it, and so they did," wrote Pigafetta. The Europeans celebrated with a mass followed by a great feast, in which the Basque men danced, Elcano among them, displaying precision with a sword and fancy choreographed footwork. In time the armada moved on to the island of Cebu, where Magellan and the king made vows of alliance. "The Captain and the King called one another brother," said Pigafetta, "and within a week, the whole island was baptized." They continued their efforts at converting the islanders to Christianity, and Magellan declared Rajah Humabon the Christian King and ruler in King Charles' name over all surrounding islands. He promised Humabon that in exchange for his allegiance, should he ever need him, he would come to his aid, even smite his enemies.

No sooner had the promise come than an enemy appeared on the Isle of Mactan. A local chief Lapu Lapu refused obedience to Humabon and Humabon asked Magellan for help. Though Magellan's crew begged him to reconsider, "he did not want to abandon his allies," wrote Pigafetta. But for Magellan, a pledge was a pledge. Arriving three hours before dawn on April 26, 1521, 49 men dressed in helmet and breastplates, brandishing arquebusses and crossbows, waded a half mile into shore; the other 11, including Elcano, who still suffered from scurvy, stayed on ship. Magellan expected a disorganized rabble of cowardly savages as opposition. What he got instead was a well-led army of

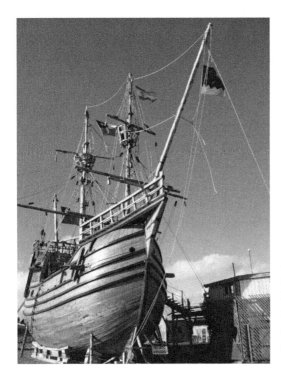

A replica of the Victoria, *an 85-ton Spanish carrack, on which Elcano finally became captain and the only ship that completed the circumnavigation while under his command. Photo by the author.*

1,500 tribesmen defending home and island, wives and children, with poison-tipped spears, arrows, and thick shields. The 49 men who had gone to shore were outmatched and outgunned. A poison arrow pierced Magellan's right leg and another his shoulder. Seeing him wounded, the natives lunged with ferocity: spears sailed, darts whizzed, and his helmet was knocked off. Then "the men had no hope of defense," wrote Pigafetta. Magellan was dead. The men who were not bleeding out or dead already dropped weapons and retreated into the water to reach the ships.

Magellan's sudden absence led to a week of chaos and tragedy. Humabon asked for the remains of Magellan and nine slain men, but Lapu Lapu refused. "They would not give him for all the riches in the world," said the chief. Without recourse, the crew departed Mactan leaving the bodies of captain and comrades on that Philippine island.

New co-captains were declared—Captain Serrano and Duarte Barbosa, Magellan's brother-in-law. Not all respected them, least of all Elcano, who thought his own skills superior to theirs and their reputations replete with poor judgment and missteps. It was in the treatment of Magellan's interpreter,

Enrique, where the new captain-generals made a fatal error. In a deposition after returning to Spain, Elcano explained: "Serrano, being unable to do anything without this intermediary, reprimanded him with bitter words, telling him that in spite of his Master, Magellan, being dead, he was still a slave and that he would be whipped if he did not obey everything that he [Serrano] commanded. The slave became enraged by Serrano's threats. Ire overtook his heart." Pigafetta attributed the vile treatment of Enrique to Barbosa, not Serrano. But whichever co-captain-general provoked the rage, the consequences proved dire.

Seeking out Humabon secretly, Enrique told him that the Europeans had malice and greed in their hearts, that to strike them first was the only way to ensure safety. Humabon believed him and invited the new captain-generals and 25 others to a feast on the island. It would be their last supper. Humabon, the Christian king, murdered them all.

In haste, the remaining men raised sail and escaped the island. By the next day, João Carvalho became the third captain-general in a single week. Gonzalo Gómez de Espinosa became captain of the *Victoria* and Elcano captain of the *Concepción*. How he must have felt: born among Basque whalers, of seafaring blood, on the shores of Getaria, now finally captain again of a ship so long after Tripoli! Sadly, the moment lasted no more than a day. The *Concepción* had sprung leaks. There weren't materials or a safe port to effect repairs or even enough men at this point to run three ships. Elcano advised with heavy heart on May 2 to scuttle and set fire to the *Concepción*. In sadness, Elcano watched his home for nearly two years burn and sink into the dark waters of the archipelago.

Two ships remained—the *Trinidad* and *Victoria*—each bearing tired, sick men and both led by a captain-general whom few admired. Elcano doubted Carvalho's navigational skill and found him morally unfit. An incident from months before had colored his opinion. In Brazil, Carvalho had reunited with a native woman he had known from a previous voyage and with whom he unknowingly had conceived a child. After learning of the son, he had tried to smuggle mother and child aboard, but Magellan had turned the woman away, permitting only the boy. As the ship set sail with her only child, the mother had watched from shore and wailed and tore out her hair. Elcano and others, though hardened by the salty sea and perhaps longing for the safe bosom of their own mothers, saw this as a wicked immorality. Pigafetta wrote of it in his journal, and sailors deposed after the journey mentioned the incident in testimony. The crew held Carvalho in low esteem.

The new captain meandered from island to island on a southerly course. Over the next week, Pigafetta cited at least five stops, each place a mix of great promise and mortal danger: natives holding "arrows poisoned with an herb," yet a tribal chief who "drew blood from his left hand, and sprinkled the blood on his body, his face, and the tip of his tongue, as a sign of the greatest friendship." After the massacres at Mactan and Cebu, Elcano no longer had confidence in conversion as a viable policy. He counseled a policy of trade only, which Carvalho and Espinosa heartily embraced.

The change was perfectly timed. On July 9, the two ships arrived at Borneo. In harbor, a proa glided alongside "with the bow and stern worked in gold" and topped with peacock feathers. A delegation of eight old men came aboard. Sitting on a rug, they presented Carvalho, Espinoza, and Elcano with betel leaves, areca nuts, and "two cages of chickens, a pair of goats, three vessels full of rice wine distilled by an alembic, and some bundles of sugar cane." Then after embracing the three leaders, the eight old men departed. By these gifts and the resplendent city before them, the men saw power and wealth beyond any the men had yet encountered.

Elcano and seven others were invited ashore. They brought gifts of their own: for the king, "a Turkish robe of green velvet, a chair of violet velvet, fine ells of red material, a red hat, a covered drinking goblet, five notebooks of paper, and a gilt writing case;" and, for the queen, "three ells of yellow cloth, a pair of silver slippers, and a silver needle case full of needles."

Within two hours of bestowing these gifts, Elcano, the Basque mariner, son of Getaria, heir to great whalers, climbed atop an elephant that led him to the house of the governor. More gifts were exchanged, and the men feasted and slept on soft mattresses. The elephant carried Elcano the next day to the king's palace, the route "full of men with swords, lances, shields." Inside he sat on a rug in a large room "full of barons" and "decorated with silken hangings." In front of him stood the king's guard, 300 in all, bearing naked swords. At the end of the room was the king sitting at a table with his young son, and behind them, a line of women, daughters of the chiefs, who by law were the only ones who could attend king and prince.

To talk to the king directly was forbidden. Elcano spoke first to a chief who spoke to a relative who asked a question through a tube. If he chose, the king whispered a reply and the answer followed the chain back to Elcano. The method was clumsy and made additionally comical by the regal protocol. Elcano had to clasp hands to head, raise his left foot then his right, and bow three times between sentences. Over several hours, he explained who he was and the distance he had traveled. He told of King Charles and how he sought peaceful relations and trade. According to Pigafetta's account, "the King had them told that since the King of Spain wished to be his friend, he was very happy to be his."

Gratified, Elcano and the seven men left the palace wearing "golden and silken cloth around their privates, daggers with golden hafts adorned with pearls and precious stones, and many rings on their hands." They feasted that night like kings themselves from gold plates, gold spoons, and porcelain bowls before returning finally to *Trinidad* and *Victoria* in the harbor.

During three weeks of such luxury in Borneo, Elcano set men fixing the *Victoria*. It needed new timber to stop leaks, and tar and wax to reinforce the hull, which the king had provided generously. However, as the ship was slowly returned to its formidable form, the captains became suspicious of the king's hospitality. Each day, more of the proa gathered around *Trinidad* and *Victoria*, until one morning, over 100 surrounded them like alligators circling wounded ducks.

A messenger climbed aboard Trinidad telling the crew that the king's son wanted to play with Carvalho's son. Everyone was apprehensive. Reluctantly, Carvalho, who needed supplies, agreed but only if Elcano, Espinosa, and two guards went along as proper security. What smelled like a trap proved correct. The king kidnapped the boy, killed the two guards, and let Elcano and Espinosa return only after three days. Though no ransom was ever recorded, it was reasonable to believe that the king coveted the ships, larger and more powerful than any proa in his fleet.

Recalling the men and armaments at the king's court, Elcano knew that rescuing the child was impossible and advised Carvalho against it. Desperate and hoping for a prisoner trade, Carvalho nabbed the king's chief bodyguard who sat unprotected on a proa. The move enraged the king who, if he sought to retaliate, could have raised an army to dwarf the 1,500 warriors of Mactan where Magellan had died. Carvalho had little choice but to release his prisoner and, at risk of being overrun, raise anchor, which the men did on July 31, leaving Carvalho's Brazilian-born son in Borneo.

Soon after, Carvalho lost his command. The men unanimously chose Espinosa as captain-general and Elcano as captain of the *Victoria*. Under their leadership, the ships arrived three months later on November 6 in the Moluccas, the great prize that the Portuguese had long monopolized.

In a sense, their mission was now a success, proof that a ship could sail west to reach the Spice Islands. For Elcano, it was a personal triumph of rising, once again, to the rank of captain, so long after his youthful days off the coast of Africa. Yet the new title must have come with an unenviable foreboding. With a hungry and diminished crew, the chance of evading the Portuguese and surviving countless unknown perils was not very good. It would call forth every vestige of his seafaring skill to reach Spanish waters and once there, hopefully, cast weary eyes on his beloved Getaria.

THE *Victoria* WAS ELCANO'S SHIP NOW. The hull was bleached by the sun, the once-white sails brown and torn. The 44 Europeans and 13 natives of Africa, Brazil, and various Indonesian islands were hungry and sick. Yet as bad as the *Victoria* was, the *Trinidad* was worse. At Tidore, the first of the Spice Islands, Elcano and Espinosa agreed to part ways. *Trinidad* would stay in port to carry out repairs and then sail east, retracing the voyage across the Pacific. Elcano would sail the *Victoria* west through the Spice Islands, around the southern tip of Africa, and then north to Spain.

At Tidore, the chief who was old and wise welcomed the men. "He and all his people," wrote Pigafetta, "wanted to be true and very faithful friends to their king, the King of Spain, and that he received them as his sons, and that they could go ashore, as though they were in their own houses." He fairly traded, asked that more Spaniards visit in the future, and then signed a letter vowing his allegiance to King Charles.

The moment was auspicious and telling. Clearly the Portuguese already operated in these waters. The chief knew them well and hoped an alliance with Spain would protect his island, or at least balance the two great powers of Europe. Moreover, Elcano and Espinosa learned that the Portuguese knew of their arrival and had given orders to capture or sink their vessels. Whether sailing east or west, the two captains had to avoid a confrontation that neither ship could win against well-armed Portuguese vessels with well-fed crews of greater numbers.

Elcano traded anything and everything to fill *Victoria's* and *Trinidad's* hulls with spices, particularly cloves. One hundred pounds of spice cost a half ducat or sixteen yards of ribbon or mirrors and combs or shirts off their back. Nothing of value remained that could be done without, though Elcano heeded royal instructions that "ships must not be heavily laden, in order that their sailing quality may not be impaired." So he lightened the load, which angered some crew, who did not want to forfeit profit. The crew yielded, nonetheless, to Elcano's experience and decision. One chronicler called him the "Governador," and before leaving Tidore the crew voted him the *tesorero,* the man who handled ship finances. He was the most trusted among them.

Elcano raised anchor on December 21, 1521, blasting artillery as the crew waved a final farewell to their sister ship, *Trinidad.* How or what Elcano and his men thought or felt at this moment was not recorded. In the face of so many unknowns—the Portuguese on the hunt, the unpredictable island kings, the potential for pirates in search of booty—Elcano and his men had to feel some trepidation over what predators might lay just beyond the next isle ready to steal their cargo and sink their ship. Whatever their anxiety, it did not deter their mission.

The *Victoria* passed nearly thirty islands, stopping at several to skulk ashore quietly and load mace, nutmeg, sugarcane, pepper, white sandalwood, camphor, cinnamon, and ginger. If invited ashore, Elcano rarely accepted. The massacre by Humabon still held a fresh place in his mind and in the minds of his men. The only island that he skipped was Ternate where the Portuguese had a known stronghold.

Equal in value to the spices were signed letters that Elcano received from each chief whom he invited aboard the *Victoria*. The letters pledged friendship and allegiance to King Charles and a solemn wish to trade with Spain. At least on paper, these commitments would please King Charles, though practically a question remained whether they violated the Treaty of Tordesilla. Such a legal issue did not concern Elcano, and if it had, the answer would have come from the king's diplomatic core, not from the deck of *Victoria*.

Tired and weary, Elcano wanted only to fulfill the mission and return home. To do so he would have to evade the Portuguese who patrolled these waters around the Spice Islands. Elcano charted a course south—terminally south, in fact—to Timor for restocking, and then to unchartered waters where he knew the Portuguese would not tread. It would give him, he reasoned, a better chance of circling the Cape of Good Hope at Africa's southern tip where storms and cross currents wrecked the most seaworthy vessels and shamed the most arrogant captains.

Nearly to the bottom of the world he sailed, reaching what is known today as Amsterdam Island, a sub-Antarctic land mass with year-round cold and wind. Having traded clothes, shoes, and blankets for spices in the tropics, the shirtless, barefooted men now suffered mightily. Their plight was worsened by a storm of ice and wind that rocked the ship, crashed waves over broadside, and splintered the foremast. The exhausted, cold, hungry men manned the pumps night and day, and even when the waters calmed, the *Victoria* sailed against the wind with only two masts, not three. Few challenges were spared the company.

Turning northwesterly after nine agonizing weeks of Antarctic cold, the men pled with Elcano to stop off at Madagascar for food and repairs. He refused, being "more desirous of their honor than of their own life, determined to reach Spain, dead or alive." Here was a brave decision. Among starving men, cold, near death, the Basque mariner went against the grain of the crew's opinion, knowing that food in their bellies counted for little if the Portuguese captured them at port. He risked a general mutiny to be sure, just as Magellan had, but still the crew sailed on, honoring royal instructions that "on no pretext whatever is the Captain-General to attempt to discover, or to touch at land within the limits of the King of Portugal."

On May 8, over three months after Tidore, Elcano anchored at the mouth of the Great Fish River or Port Elizabeth, on the easterly shore of what is present-day South Africa. The men were able to scavenge for food, but the stop revealed an unfortunate reality. Despite the excruciating southern route—longer in fact than their Pacific voyage—the *Victoria* had not yet circled the Cape of Good Hope, falling short by nearly 500 miles.

Efforts to find food failed, and *Victoria* could not stay longer to search for it. The Portuguese had doubled their hunt. Elcano had to round the cape or risk capture. He thrust and tacked into the treacherous swirling waters off of South Africa, the westerly winds pushing hard against him. His first attempt ended in failure. The starving men bore the frigid waves and the brutal onset of scurvy. With so few alive, every sailor manned the pumps night and day without rest or food to keep the *Victoria* afloat. Elcano tried a second time, nearly crashing on the shoals, but failed again. Then a third time, and the *Victoria* nearly sank. "Finally with the help of God," said Pigafetta, "we passed within six leagues of the cape." It was May 19, 1522.

If miracles exist, then this moment counted among them. Another 22 seamen had died from starvation or sickness. Without food, the rest would soon follow. Elcano convened his officers for an important decision. Should they anchor at an African port for food and supplies, most likely coming up short but evading the Portuguese, or sail to Cape Verde where food and supplies were abundant, risking a run-in with the Portuguese?

The decision was notable, for after all the crew had endured, it would have been for naught had the Portuguese captured their cargo, sunk their vessel, and killed them. Equally important was the way in which Elcano went about the decision. In the past, he had been content giving orders, even when such orders had run contrary to the wishes of his crew. In this case, he posed a question to his officers, allowing a consensus to form about the next steps in the voyage. No record explains this change in approach. Was he worried about mutiny? Was he uncertain about the way forward? Did he see virtue in democratic rule, even aboard ship? Any one of these might have been the case. Or maybe he knew, as most men know, that in grave moments of life and death, when the trappings of social order no longer hold sway, all voices gain equal timber and strength, and every man deserves a say in how he shall live or die.

Whatever the reason, the men opted to sail to the Cape Verde Islands, a distance from Tidore twice as long as the anguished voyage across the Pacific. When the *Victoria* dropped anchor 148 days later, only 31 men were alive, and yet immediately another dilemma presented itself: what to use as barter. Shirt-less and shoeless, the men had exchanged all they had owned of value for spices in their hull. The only logical course was to use the spices for trade.

To do so risked the Portuguese discovering who they were and where they had been. Elcano, therefore, planned a ruse. He siphoned cloves from the cargo, loaded them on a skiff, and sent thirteen men as escort to sell or trade them at market. On shore if anyone asked, he instructed them to say that they had come from America, lost a foremast, and now needed rice and repairs. The ruse worked twice, giving Elcano the food and supplies that ship and crew needed for shear survival. "With those good words and with our merchandise," rejoiced Pigafetta, "we got two boatloads of rice."

On the third trip to the market, however, the skiff did not return. Elcano waited a day, then another, in breathless anxiety. Clearly the ruse had been undone, but how or by whom remains a mystery. One account blamed a Por-tuguese man who had pretended to be Spanish to join the expedition, but now, among his people, betrayed the mission. Another said that natives privately traded cloves and in the process revealed the names Magellan and the Armada de Molucca. Regardless, the Portuguese boarded the skiff, confiscated the cargo, and held the 13 men as prisoners.

Four Portuguese boats then approached the *Victoria* demanding that Elcano surrender ship and crew. He refused outright. He countered that his vessel, the skiff, and the 13 men were protected by King Charles of Spain. By nearing his ship with hostility, he said, their actions were an act of war. If they failed to withdraw, they and Portugal would incur the wrath of King Charles, the most powerful sovereign in the world. The bluff worked. The Portuguese consulted their superiors. In that moment of hesitation, Elcano gave orders to lift anchor, raise sails, and race home.

The Portuguese pursued. Even though Elcano and his men had a head start, their condition only worsened, and they'd be no match for the Portuguese with fresh ships and crews. The loss of 13 men on the captured skiff had put *Victoria*'s numbers at 18 European and four non-Europeans: one-third fewer to raise sails, man pumps, rebalance cargo in storms, and operate a vessel of *Victoria*'s size with only two masts, not three. What little rice they had procured at Cape Verde was depleted quickly, and hunger returned like a grim friend.

With the Portuguese on his tail and still 3,600 miles from Spain, Elcano charted a course for home. It was not, as the Portuguese might have expected, a strictly northern path, the shortest route. Rather, by another sleight of hand, Elcano plotted a northwesterly route to the Azores, which added distance but tapped the powerful westerly winds that Columbus had used on his return from the Americas. *Victoria's* sails plumed, and her speed quickened. The Portuguese had been outmaneuvered.

Just when grace seemed to smile on them, another storm hit their rickety ship in August. It tore the sails in strips, cracked the hull, and stole whatever strength and health remained in the flesh and bone of Elcano's men, who appeared better suited for a life hereafter than a life here and now. How the *Victoria* survived, leaking badly, laden with spices, with a skeleton crew of starving sick, freezing, water-logged men, remains a marvel still today.

Yet survive they did, and a month later, safe in Spanish waters, a day from the Bay of San Lucar, Elcano penned a letter to King Charles. As if he knew already that his return was a historical achievement, he carefully laid down each step of the voyage: finding the channel, crossing the Pacific, Magellan dying in the Philippines, reaching the Spice Islands and the cargo they carried, rounding the Cape of Good Hope, and confronting the Portuguese. He wrote of the 13 men taken prisoner and asked that the king secure their release and that all his men benefit fairly from the cargo now in *Victoria's* hull. "I close herewith," he said, "kissing your Majesty's hand and feet. Written in the ship *Victoria*, in San Lucar, a.m. 6 September, 1522."

Two days later, a ship that had been presumed lost with all crew dead sailed up the Guadalquivir River into Seville. Elcano ordered artillery fired. They were scraggly, skinny, bleeding men. Their ship looked more haunted than seaworthy. They passed the church of Santa María de la Vitoria, their namesake, where they and their comrades had prayed and asked the Virgin Mary for her blessing three years before. They now bowed their emaciated heads, blasted artillery again, and dropped anchor at port for the last time. They were home.

Eʟᴄᴀɴᴏ ᴀɴᴅ ʜɪs ᴍᴇɴ touched ground on September 8, 1522. In a candlelight vigil, the 18, like walking dead, dragged body and limbs to Santa María de la Vitoria to thank the Virgin Mary and Child. Among the survivors were four Basque, of whom Elcano was the only Gipuzcoan, three Galicians, one Andalucian, one Castillian, one Estremaduran, one Mallorcan, one Portuguese, one native of France, two Greeks, one Lombard, one Ligurian, and one German.

Word spread of the ship's return. In reply to his letter, King Charles thanked Elcano and invited him and two fellow seamen of his choosing to appear at court in Valladolid to present their account of the voyage. Elcano chose Alvo, the pilot, and Bustamente, the barber and ship surgeon. Each appeared separately on October 18 before a board of inquiry where they answered 13 questions about the St. Julian mutiny, Magellan's death in Mactan, the punishments administered, and the actual weight of the spices in the hull.

Conspicuously omitted was Pigafetta, the chief chronicler. It showed the great animosity between him and Elcano that still shapes history nearly 500 years later. Eventually, King Charles invited Pigafetta to court, and Pigafetta presented the monarch with "a book, written by my hand, concerning all the matters that had occurred day to day during our voyage." Pigafetta shared the manuscript with the kings of Portugal, France, and Italy, each version omitting the name Juan Sebastián Elcano. Though the original was lost, four hand-copies—three in French, one in Italian—survived. The king's inquiry had to reconcile Elcano's testimony, Pigafetta's journal, and the depositions of the crew from the *San Antonio* who had returned to Spain in May 1521 after abandoning the armada. These sources gave greatly divergent accounts of who did what and when, leaving the official record conflicted, then as now.

Despite these conflicts, the expedition altered our understanding of the world. It proved the Earth to be a sphere, clarified proportions of land and water, and showed that sailing west gained a traveler 24 hours. If these findings emerged as certainties, the line of demarcation from the Treaty of Tordesilla produced only controversy. Delegates from Spain and Portugal convened in Badajoz, Spain, near the Portuguese border to agree on a new line. For Spain, Elcano appeared as a commissioner with eight others including Don Hernando Colon, son of Christopher Columbus, and Giovanni Vespucci, brother of Amerigo Vespucci. But the proceedings degenerated into absurdity, both sides claiming the Moluccas as their domain. From then on, the Treaty of Tordesilla ceased to function as a viable arbiter of territorial and naval claims.

The *Victoria* carried over 52,000 pounds of spices, which, at market values of the time, paid for the whole expedition. Pleased by this lucrative haul and the signed letters of allegiance from kings and chiefs in far off places, King Charles rewarded Elcano with an annual pension of 500 ducats. In response to Elcano's request, the king secured the release of the 13 men who had been taken prisoner by the Portuguese. He pardoned Elcano in writing for his role in the St. Julian mutiny and for selling his ship earlier to Italian merchants. Finally, he bestowed knighthood on Elcano with a coat-of-arms that shows, still today, a castle, spices, two kings, a globe, and the words:

Primus Circumdedisti Me
"Thou First Circled Me."

With his pension in hand, Elcano started a new chapter in his life. He had relationships with two women: María de Ernialde, who gave him a son, and María de Vidauretta, with whom he had a daughter. He did not marry either,

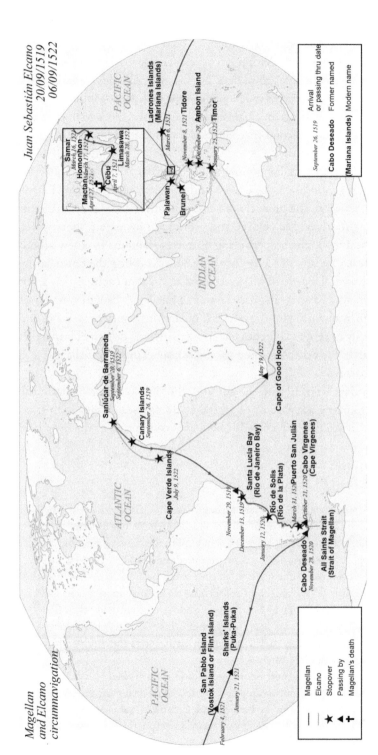

Magellan
and Elcano
circumnavigation

Juan Sebastián Elcano
20/09/1519
06/09/1522

This map of the first voyage around the world distinguishes between Magellan's command and Elcano's command, showing key dates along the route. Magellan died on the Isle of Mactan in the Philippines. He never completed a circumnavigation of the globe. Derived and adapted from "Magellan Elcano Circumnavigation-en" Licensed under CC-BY-SA-3,0 via Wikimedia Commons.

but he cared for both and hoped his earnings would help defray the cost of two families; indeed, they would. Within a few years, however, Elcano sought yet another command in the king's royal fleet. In 1525, King Charles commissioned the second Armada de Moluccas to follow the same path and establish a permanent base in the Spice Islands for Spanish trade. It consisted of seven ships and 450 men with Elcano as second-in-command under Garcia Jofre de Loaisa, a Basque of Biscayan ancestry.

The expedition met challenges not unlike the first. Crossing the Pacific, men died of scurvy including Loaisa, the captain-general, which elevated Elcano to the rank of admiral, the pinnacle of achievement for a Basque mariner of Getaria, or any mariner. He enjoyed the promotion for only a short while, however, as creaking joints and erupting blisters, symptoms he knew all too well, signaled that he was not long for this earth. Knowing the excruciating miles still to travel, the new admiral retreated to his dim cabin to pen a last will and testament. He wrote in great detail in a fine hand, bequeathing funds for his children, accounting for every article of clothing, every possession, and giving generously to several churches including the Iglesia de San Salvador, his baptismal church. He called on seven men, all Basque, to witness the will and affix their signatures.

Then five days later, Elcano the admiral, the first to circumnavigate the globe, a hero to many, a navigator of all the world's seas, a Basque man from Getaria, died. In solemn ceremony, his body was committed to the deep blue of the Pacific.

Notes

1. In the Old Testament, the Lord tells Moses in Exodus: "Consecrate to me all the first-born; whatever is the first to open the womb among the people of Israel, both of man and of beast, is mine." This passage refers to fertility, which was a gift from the Lord to the people, and in return, the people promised the first born. Not willing to sacrifice children, however, this first gift broadened to use livestock as a substitute for offspring, as the Lord told Aaron: "You shall sprinkle their blood upon the altar, and shall burn their fat as an offering by fire, a pleasing odor to the Lord; but their flesh shall be yours." In Basque fishing villages like Getaria, this tradition manifested with the first whale going to the king, the divine here on earth, and to the church, where at the altar the priest accepted the tongues.

2. Amerigo Vespucci was a contemporary of Elcano, though older by a little more than thirty years. He was an Italian explorer who studied finance, navigation, and cartography. After returning from the New World, Columbus had posited that Brazil represented the eastern shores of Asia. It was Amerigo Vespucci, by drawing the first

maps of the New World, who demonstrated that Brazil was not Asia at all but rather a separate landmass, a new continent that had been undiscovered heretofore by the Old World. Initially, many in Europe had coined the phrase "New World" to describe this land of Columbus. Once Vespucci showed the land to be different from Asia, however, it gained a new name—"America"—derived from *Americus*, the Latin version of Amerigo Vespucci's first name. It's fair to say that he is the only human who has had not one but two continents named after him.

3. At the time, no one could compute longitude with accuracy. Elaborate efforts had been created to calculate it by the placement of stars. But these methods often resulted in ships losing their way or crashing into rocky shoals and sinking. Scientists from Galileo to Sir Isaac Newton wrestled with how to calculate longitude. A solution would not come until 1760 when a lowly clockmaker—John Harrison—introduced the chronometer, changing how men and women would forevermore sail the seas.

4. In reading multiple versions of this event, one wonders what passed through Elcano's mind. Elorriaga was a fellow Basque from Gipuzcoa, whom Elcano had recruited for the voyage. Although we cannot know for certain, it is not unreasonable to believe that Elcano had known Elorriaga for years before the expedition given the tight relationships within small fishing villages in the Basque country. With the mutiny ending so soon after it started, did he ever think of what he had done vis-a-vis Elorriaga? There's no way to know. But Elcano's last will and testament indicates that he had a conscience. One wonders if Elorriaga's ghost haunted his conscience.

5. Scurvy is a disease that afflicts people deficient in vitamin C. Its name comes from the Latin for ascorbic acid, *scorbutus*, the chemical name for vitamin C. A sufferer feels fatigue and lethargy during early symptoms, followed by spots on the skin, spongy gums, and bleeding from all mucous membranes. In advanced cases, scurvy causes wounds to erupt, teeth to fall out, skin to turn yellow, hallucinations, and finally death. During the 1700s, 200 years after Elcano's day, scurvy was still killing sailors. During the Seven Years' War, for example, the British enlisted nearly 185,000 sailors. Of those, nearly 134,000 ended up missing or dead of disease, and scurvy was the leading cause. Interestingly, one admiral in 1740 changed his men's recipe of rum to include lemon or lime juice because the water tasted so terrible. Both the admiral and his crew remained healthier than the rest of the Royal Navy with no incidence of scurvy among them. It raised eyebrows. Not until the end of the 18th century, however, was scurvy eliminated as knowledge of its cause and a robust supply of limes spread around the world. It was through the consumption of limes in the fight against scurvy that British sailors acquired the acidic nickname—Limeys.

6. The *Trinidad* finally departed the port of Tidore after three months of repairs, weighed down by 50 tons of spices, on April 6, 1522. The ship encountered a severe storm and the crew suffered a deadly bout of scurvy. Espinosa turned back to Tidore, only to learn that on May 13 a squadron of seven Portuguese ships had arrived at Tidore to capture or sink Magellan's fleet. Eventually, the *Trinidad* was captured, and the crew killed or forced into hard labor.

St. Ignatius of Loyola

The First Jesuit

A SOLDIER IN ARMOR with sword and dagger lay in blood on a dirty table in the conquered citadel of Pamplona, Navarre, the Kingdom of Spain. It was 1521, and there was war all around. Though fighting for Spain's king, the soldier had won the admiration of the victorious French who had carried him from the battlefield to French physicians. A cannonball had shattered his right leg and tore flesh from the left. As doctors set the bones, stuffed muscle and tendons under skin, and wrapped the bloody limbs, this 30-year-old soldier bore the pain in anguished silence. To do less would have been unworthy of earthly honor, especially for a man such as he, christened Eneko Lopez, of noble birth.

After 12 days, the French let Eneko go on a shiny black steed to his family home, the Castle of Loyola, near the town of Azpeitia in Gipuzkoa, Castille in the heart of Basque country. The leg hadn't been set right. By time he reached Loyola, a bone poked two inches through the skin. Not willing to abide the deformity, he ordered family physicians to saw it away, all without being anesthetized or tied down. An infection developed with high fever, chills, delirium, and risk of gangrene, and Eneko teetered between life and death for nearly three days. All expected him to die, but then the infection broke. He woke to one leg shorter than the other, giving him a lifelong limp and ending his days of soldiering. For service and duty he would have to look elsewhere.

During his convalescence, Eneko turned to reading. From an early age, he had immersed in stories of chivalry and fantasy: *El Cid*, the legendary hero who vanquished Moors in the eleventh century; King Arthur and his knights; and the *Song of Roland*, which ends tragically with a military leader who cares

The Vision at La Storta, outside Rome, November 1537. In 1904, the master Albert Chevallier-Tayler (1862–1925) completed 10 paintings of the life of St. Ignatius. They now hang in the St. Ignatius Chapel of the Church of the Sacred Heart, Wimbledon, England. Photo copyright 2013 Jesuit Institute London. Used with permission.

more for glory than faith. With none of these books available, he turned to the popular *Golden Legend* by the Dominican Jacobus de Voragine and to *De Vita Christi* by Ludolph of Saxony. Together these books chronicled the life of Christ and the saints and let Eneko imagine himself in key moments of Christianity: the birth in the manager, the crucifixion at Golgotha, the resurrection.

Transfixed by the stories, he had found his mustard seed and with it, an internal struggle.[1] He had been born into nobility, wealth and power, castles and coats-of-arms where men earned stripes by strength of blade, victories in battle, and contests of honor. From the age of seventeen, he had dueled and beaten men who questioned the Christian faith, not for faith itself or devotion to God but to fulfill soldierly duty. Reading now of Christ and the saints, eyeing his useless legs, and feeling gallantry slip away, new thoughts crossed his mind: something as simple perhaps as *What now?*; or more specifically, *How would it be if I did this which St. Francis did, and this which St. Dominic did?* Then after these saintly thoughts, he thought again of battles waged or unwaged, or of a certain lady whom he fancied in the flesh. The two sides, Earth and heaven, struggled evenly.

Eneko noticed a difference between them. When he thought of noble battle and clashing swords, of such "worldly deeds which he wanted to do," a delight came over him, but after a little while, the delight faded to desolation. He described it as "dry and discontented." Of saintly deeds, of going to Jerusalem barefooted, of fasting, of giving and sacrificing, of doing all that St. Francis and St. Dominic and Christ Himself had done, he felt a similar delight, a deep happiness and contentment, yet these feelings did not fade. He reflected on this difference, even marveled at it. Some delightful thoughts left him sad, others happy, the spirit of each coming from different places, one from the devil, one from God.

Lying in bed, he resolved that once able to travel, he would set aside the soldier and go to Jerusalem as a pilgrim without possession or title. He suddenly felt a loathing for his past, remorse for the dark sensations of glory dipped in blood, and of flesh and fancy that had governed his life. From these he could find no reprieve until one night, he "saw clearly a likeness of Our Lady with the Holy Child Jesus," which gave him peace. It was his first vision. He felt the pain lessen in his legs and heart. Later in life, he would say, "Oh, how vile this earth seems when I look on heaven," and it would bring him to this vision and to this time of convalescence when his mustard seed had taken root and begun to blossom.

His family noticed the change in him. He was one of 13 children, and the youngest son, born in October 1491. His name, Eneko, meant *My Little One* in Basque. His brothers had always looked after him and sensed that he now verged on transformation. They begged that he "not throw himself away" by disregarding the great hope they had for his future, and they warned against insulting the family honor. On such matters he prayed, though nothing discouraged him from his path. Days later, able finally to limp with a staff, he climbed on a smelly mule and rode from Loyola toward Barcelona, and from there, hopefully, to Jerusalem to do as saints do.

A FTER DAYS astride a dirty mule, he learned that the plague had closed Barcelona to outsiders. He took the delay as a good sign. It allowed a stop at the Monastery of Our Lady of Montserrat where a Benedictine abbey stood atop a mountain beyond a saw-toothed ridge. As a student of King Arthur, Eneko might have known that the monastery had been reputed a sanctuary for the Holy Grail, which as a knight he might have defended unto death. This fact came from his old life. Now, however, he sought this refuge for its seclusion and for a confessor who could hear and absolve a lifetime of sins. He hoped to purge his inner conflict before limping into Jerusalem.

A few miles before arriving at Montserrat, he encountered a Moor who highlighted this inner turmoil. Mary conceived as a virgin, said the Moor, but after Christ's birth, she lost all claim to virginity. Despite his counter arguments, Eneko failed to change the Moor's opinion, and so the companions parted, the Moor riding ahead, leaving Eneko angry and despondent and wanting to give chase with a sword. He pulled back his anger, however, seeing it as earthly, not heavenly, though wondering still if he had done honor to Mary, the Christ Child, and God. To resolve the dilemma, he loosened the mule's reins at a fork in the road, letting the beast follow the Moor on the left, or continue to Montserrat on the right; inspired by God, believed Eneko, the mule chose the latter.

For three days at Montserrat, Eneko confessed his sins in writing to the oldest and wisest monk. He knelt and prayed and wept and ate and drank sparingly. Unburdened, he shed his valuable armor, giving it to a beggar, and handed sword and dagger to his confessor who placed them on the altar. He then dressed as a pilgrim in coarse cloth that draped down to his shoeless feet. His dark hair receded from a broad forehead; a cropped beard and mustache framed a narrow face and pursed lips; his eyes were sad yet honest; his nose, prominent and wide. He stood no higher than five feet two inches and still walked with a heavy limp. Nobility had fallen from him, and he looked small. Few had given up so much in so short a time; word spread of the sacrifice.

Appearing as a saint, he knew, did not make one saintly. As much as he wanted to emulate St. Francis, St. Dominic, and Christ Himself, the real chore was turning the soul from earthly glory to the greater glory of God. Barefooted,

A likeness of St. Ignatius derived from his
death mask. The statue stands in the Jesuit
Institute of London. Photo copyright 2013
Jesuit Institute London. Used with permission.

holding a staff for balance, he walked about 20 miles from Montserrat to Manresa. There he found St. Lucy Hospital, which cared for the poor and indigent. He insisted on tending the sickest patients, often cleaning them of blood, urine and feces. These lowly duties suited him. Each day he attended Mass, Vespers, and Compline, prayed seven hours, and took communion with a glass of wine on Sundays. He slept on the ground using stones as pillows, drew blood by lashings, and begged for the worst food, eating once daily and adding ash to vegetables to worsen their taste. His hair, beard, and nails lengthened, making him look like a primitive. Over four months Eneko endured these hardships, though *endured*, for him, was not a proper word, for the humility gave him unexpected contentment. Suffering cleansed; charity redeemed; from both he took peace.

Yet he regarded his faith as wanting. Two hundred feet from St. Lucy Hospital, in a valley called the Vale of Paradise, near the stream of Cardenero, a cave opened on a rock wall, its face concealed by bramble. Eneko limped through the thorny brush and there in secluded repose communed on his knees with God well into the night. He stayed in the cave for 11 months, often fasting for three or four days, taking only a cup of water, and sleeping little. And when he did sleep, the cave's rocky floor was his bed. He lashed his back until strips of blood welted and oozed and then beat his chest with stones as St. Jerome had done to expel demons from the heart.

He lived these days more in darkness than light. Nothing from his personal account, or from contemporaries, spoke of joy during this extreme penance. On the contrary, the evidence pointed to temptation and despair. An inner voice rose up questioning, "How canst thou endure this kind of life so austere for the 40 years which mayest perhaps yet have to live?" It invited him to surrender to heaven. Frightfully, he fumbled for an answer. He yelled into the cave, "Wretch, canst thou promise me with certainty an hour of life?" The inner voice fell silent for a time and then returned with a new argument: "You have done enough to merit heaven." It was vanity telling him to take pride in austerity itself. The devil came with a bag of tricks.

Eneko countered the treachery with faith until, quite unexpectedly, God left him. It was his greatest trial, an infinite darkness. All destined for saint-hood speak of it, a time when their thread to God snaps, casting them alone into a spiritual void. Eneko prayed all the more, and panicked too, believing that his written confession had been inadequate, even untruthful, and needed to be amended lest he prove permanently unworthy of God's grace. His confessor accepted the changes, yet still the darkness persisted as an unquenchable longing: the more he drank by suffering, the more he thirsted. In horror, an inner voice told him to end his life. He yelled again into the cave, "No, I will not; Never, O my God, never will I offend Thee so!" He resolved to fast, as other saints had done, to draw God's faint whisper, yet nothing came of the effort. After seven days without a hint of divine breath, his confessor threatened to withhold absolution unless Eneko, now near death, took bread and wine, and so he did.

After months of despair, starvation, and illness, he felt a new feeling, one of disgust at seeking martyrdom or believing that his paltry deeds could shape God's actions. Grace was God's gift, not compensation for self-inflicted suffering. The anxiety of so long a time then left him gradually, like fog burned away by morning sun, and the darkness lifted, and the light returned, and so too the divine whisper. His novitiate had come to a close.

His time in the Cave of Manresa laid the groundwork for the Spiritual Exercises, which he would refine over the next 30 years to guide his own life and help others meditate, pray, and commune more closely with Christ. Much of his life's work emanated from them and bound him to his disciples, and all to each other. He would later be investigated for the document and then celebrated by the Vatican. For now, with a deeper faith, the pilgrim looked to Barcelona, where the plague had subsided, and then to distant Jerusalem.

Twenty months had passed since the cannonball at Pamplona. Though the limp remained, he stood now on stronger legs, purposeful and strong; he was a different soldier to be sure. He set out from Manresa in January 1523 for Barcelona wearing sandals and beret and with only "charity and faith and hope" as companions. His begging yielded food for which he bestowed a blessing, though if asked, he never divulged his destination lest it be seen a vainglorious conceit. His journey was that of a solitary pilgrim, though he never felt that he walked alone. If he fell, God would lift him; in hunger, He would provide food; in thirst, water. Eneko would have it no other way. To want for nothing in poverty was one of his virtues.

He spent 20 days in Barcelona before gaining passage to Italy and walking 100 miles to Rome. The going was slow, often lonely, though prayer offered strength and happiness to stave off the pain in legs and belly. On the path, he befriended many who unloaded their problems, and then as quickly as they matched his limping pace, told their stories, and received his counsel, they moved on. To the end of his life, he would show an uncanny habit of attracting wayward souls like frantic moths to humble light. He spoke not of himself, ever, in his countless letters. Perhaps this selflessness, so rare then as now, gave off its own illumination.

Before reaching Rome, a trio of fellow travelers stayed with him: a mother, a daughter dressed as a boy, and a young man. By nightfall, they arrived at a farm-house where soldiers, warming by a campfire, put the mother and child in a loft, and he and the young man in the barn below. After falling asleep, screams came from above. Eneko woke to see the woman and her daughter barreling down, weeping, and pleading for him to intervene, for the soldiers, seeing through the mother's ruse, had tried to rape the pair. Had it been 20 months earlier, the soldier of old might have pulled a sword and lopped off their heads, but such a thought did not occur to him now. He protected mother and child, spoke of men's evil and the treachery of these men particularly, and beseeched them to leave, which they did. Eneko escorted the mother and daughter up the road to sleep in a church. At sunup he continued on his own to Rome.

He arrived in the Italian capital on Palm Sunday, the day of Christ's entry into Jerusalem. He had no money, which made passage to the Holy Lands unlikely. Undeterred, he received a blessing from Pope Adrian VI. To gain access to a pope, even a pope of the 16th century, was not an easy undertaking, which suggests that Eneko stood apart from other pilgrims. The Vatican archives described him as a "cleric of the diocese of Pamplona," suggesting that he had a tie to religion prior to defending the citadel in 1521. In whatever manner he gained access, his personal wherewithal secured bread and money through alms that would take him to Venice nine days after Easter Sunday.

On his first night there, a rich Spaniard whom he knew invited him home. At dinner, he did not speak unless spoken to, and then by the close of evening, after one or more glasses of wine, told the Spaniard of God and the salvation of souls in a soft powerful tone, which so impressed his benefactor that he introduced him to the Venetian doge the next morning. As one of his duties, the doge scheduled travel for the governor's party and other dignitaries and agreed to grant Eneko space on the next ship to Cyprus. However, almost immediately Eneko fell ill. The Spaniard, in his kindness, summoned a physician and asked if the pilgrim could get on the boat the next day. The doctor replied, "He could get on the ship if what he wanted was to be buried there." Eneko ignored the warning and boarded anyhow.

To reach Jerusalem in the 16th century required an uncompromising resolve. In Eneko's case, he passed through towns infected by plague, yet avoided the disease; cared for the sick at St. Lucy's, and contracted no illness; suffered hunger or thirst, and gained benefactors; needed a ship, and found one at port. In 1522, the Turks captured Rhodes, which disrupted travel, yet Eneko's vessel, traveling across the Mediterranean, was never attacked. When storms rose, other ships sank while his made it safely to shore. From all over Europe, pilgrims set out for Jerusalem, first to Rome then Venice then Cyprus and finally to the Holy Lands; but only the strongly persistent made it and returned to tell their tales. What appeared as lucky or miraculous by some was the stubborn determination of a special man who would not be deterred from his devotion to God or his personal mission to save souls.

In August of 1523, Jaffa, that ancient town of Solomon, Jonah, and St. Peter, came into view. Eneko had made it, and it filled his heart with joy. He went ashore joyfully on August 25 and from there over land by donkey to Jerusalem, 40 miles away.

After a kind welcome by the Franciscans who oversaw the holy places, he wanted only to see the Mount of Olives. East of Jerusalem's Old City, amid olive groves sloping up hillsides, a sea of 150,000 graves dotted the landscape. It was here that the resurrection of the dead would start when Christ returned. Here Jesus had wept over Jerusalem, taught disciples the Olivet Discourse, returned on the night of His betrayal, and ascended to heaven at the foot of the mountain in the Garden of Gethsemane. Eneko bribed sentries with a penknife and scissors to let him pass. He wanted to feel every grain of sand between his toes.

Praying and weeping at Christ's footprints, Eneko felt a wave of faith like an ocean of love. It was infinitely grand yet still his heart could hold it and in his soul the joy grew and grew. He knew a oneness with God that he had not known before. He "wanted to stay forever," for every part of him "wished only to help souls."

Noticing his absence, the Franciscans dispatched a Christian of the cincture, a Syrian, who finding him, gripped his arm in a severe vice and dragged him on limping legs from this happy solitude. Eneko would say later with a deep contentment that being pulled in pain from that place gave him certainty that "he was seeing Christ always over him."

Presenting letters of recommendation (though how many and from whom are unknown), he pled with the Franciscans to let him stay. The chief guardian resisted, claiming the order had not enough food. He'd provide his own, he said. But if he were nabbed by Turks, said the Franciscan, then they'd be strapped with a ransom. Not of their order and asking for no special treatment, Eneko said he'd bear the risk. Frustrated, the guardian finally threatened to excommunicate him if he did not accept the decision. It was an unfortunate and heartbreaking checkmate for a man who had longed to fulfill a dream only to have it dashed so soon after realizing it.

Forced to depart in the morning, he retraced his steps by donkey to Jaffa and tearfully said goodbye from the deck of a ship, never knowing if he'd see Christ's prints again. On the return voyage to Cyprus, he resolved that strength of faith needed strength of mind, for the Lord willed it. Only by education could he "give himself with more ease to the Spirit, and even to be of benefit to souls," all for the greater glory of God.

IN EARLY MARCH 1524, Eneko accepted private study with Jeromi Ardevol who agreed to teach him grammar for free at the Barcelona Estudi General. The pilgrim's commitment was unwavering. He said to Ardevol: "I promise you that I shall never fall short in paying attention to you in these two years as long as I can find bread and water in Barcelona on which I can survive." He kept this promise through every year of study. Yet however divine his inspiration, he worried that his faith might wane, so he took up daily penance and active salvation of souls. Though required to wear shoes, he tore holes in the soles, widening the gaps a little each day, until by winter no soles remained, only the tops, so his bare feet trod the cold hard ground. As at Manresa, he prayed for hours each night and fasted. During the day, he spoke in public squares.

More activist than scholar, he learned of a Dominican convent called the Holy Angels north of Barcelona that had become a house of ill-repute. No better challenge for the reformation of souls could have presented itself. After his lessons, he visited the wayward nuns daily, oversaw prayers, and gave the Spiritual

Exercises. Over several months, he restored the nuns' vows and their deeper faith in service to God. The men who had turned the convent to a brothel angrily denounced and threatened Eneko for returning it to a convent, but the pilgrim stood unfazed.

One day, a good priest, Puyalto, begged Eneko to let him help save the sisters' souls. Thankful for the company, he happily accepted the request. On the path, a bedeviled man jumped from the shadows to beat the two, leaving both in pools of blood, Puyalto dead and Eneko near death. By the kindness of a passing miller, the pilgrim was taken to a bed where strangers who heard of the attack wept at his bedside, sponged his forehead, and prayed for his eternal soul. His survival was in doubt. After a month of delirium, to the great astonishment of all, he rose and took food and drink and went immediately to the nuns whose salvation lay in wait. Though weakened and hardly recovered, he met another man on the path, a merchant named Ribera, who admitted that it was he who had paid the assassin and now asked for Eneko's forgiveness. Without hesitating, the pilgrim bestowed it and continued to the Convent of the Holy Angels.

Far from slowing his work, the attack seemed to strengthen his resolve and deepen his faith. Returning one day from the Holy Angels, he passed through the streets of Belloc where to his shock, a man named Lissani hung by a swinging rope, his body limp. A crowd wailed beneath the dangling feet. All wondered how anyone of such promise could take his own life. Lissani was cut down and laid in the dirt. Dropping to his knees, Eneko tried to revive him. He wept and prayed over the body; others wept and prayed with him. Then yelling as a man possessed, he commanded in Jesus's name that the man come back to them. The witnesses would later testify that Lissani opened his eyes and expressed deep sorrow for his actions but then closed them again and died on the spot. In this moment of repentance, he earned salvation and the right to rest eternally in consecrated ground. Later, the event emerged as a documented miracle for Eneko's canonization as St. Ignatius of Loyola.

During these episodes and his two years of study with Ardevol, the pilgrim gained his first disciples: Calisto, Juan de Artiaga, and Diego de Cáceres. These men owed no obedience to him, only to God, vowing poverty, chastity, and the salvation of souls. The foursome became a kind of theological fraternity of devout men who bonded not in hierarchy but through a singular commitment to serve God by whatever special gift each had to offer. From this point on, the pilgrim would leave disciples behind him like bread crumbs.

In 1526, following a successful exam, he enrolled at the University of Alcala to study the logic of Soto, the physics of Albert, and Peter Lombard's theological *Sentences*. He prayed often, spoke in public squares, and gave his Spiritual

Exercises. But he sought no converts; they sought him. Once converted, they gave up possessions, donned the sacks of coarse cloth, and took vows of poverty and chastity.

News traveled to the Office of the Inquisitor in Toledo about these "sack-wearers" or *alumbrados* (illuminati), a term used at the time for heretics. Vicar General Figueroa investigated, interviewing many and reviewing the Spiritual Exercises. His findings proved contradictory. He found no wrong-doing, but ordered the men nonetheless to dye their sacks different colors and wear not just the tops of shoes.

The pilgrim obeyed, though retorting, "But I don't know what good these inquisitions do. We'd like to know if they've found any heresy in us."

"No," said Figueroa, "if they had found it, they'd have burnt you."

"And they'll burn you too," said Eneko, "if they find heresy in you."

Eneko's growing reputation attracted the venom of men who preferred the status quo and who used the mechanisms of church and government, often one and the same, to investigate and tear him down. But each time, he resurrected the fighting spirit of the Basque soldier, never acquiescing; he demanded that accusations be presented in writing and that the verdict likewise be in writing for the sake of truth, his own reputation, and the good work of his disciples.

Figueroa proved to be his first nemesis. Watching Eneko for fault, he investigated the pilgrim again four months later. Three women had been seen entering and exiting his quarters at different times, a level of impropriety worthy of expulsion if not a finding of public indecency. In their interrogation of March 6, 1527, however, the women testified that the pilgrim had been

> teaching us the commandments, and the mortal sins, and the five senses and powers of the soul, and he explains this very well. He explains it through the gospels and St. Paul and other saints, and he says we should examine our consciences in front of a holy picture every day, bringing to mind things in which we have committed sin; and he advises us to go to confession every week and receive the Sacrament at the same time.

With no findings, Figueroa dropped the investigation. Yet a mere four months later, he sent the magistrate to arrest Eneko. In jail, the pilgrim continued his studies, received visitors, and taught the Spiritual Exercises. One benefactor tried to get him out. In response, he said, "He for whose love I came in here will get me out if this will serve His purpose." Eneko stayed in jail.

But what, after all, were the charges? For 40 days, he had not been told until finally, Figueroa revealed that a mother and daughter had disappeared and

Eneko had been implicated. Yes, he knew of them, explained Eneko; they had wanted to go abroad to help the poor, but he had discouraged it believing that they, by their beauty, might attract marauders who would do them harm. He encouraged them to stay in Alcala where much work remained to be done. "Preposterous!" said Figueroa. Two days later, the mother and daughter returned and confirmed the story, prompting the inquisitor, reluctantly, to release Eneko. As the pilgrim left the jail, Figueroa demanded that he and his followers dress as other students, stop talking of faith, and discontinue the Spiritual Exercises or risk excommunication and banishment. "This is blocking the door against helping souls," concluded the pilgrim. And so with heavy heart, he left Barcelona with Calisto, one of his three disciples, for Salamanca.

He arrived in Salamanca in October 1527, and there his zeal returned boldly. After only 12 days, however, he attracted the attention of the Dominican order and they summoned him and Calisto to a meeting.

"How is it that you preach?" asked the Dominicans.

"We do not preach," said Eneko, "but we hold spiritual conferences on the virtues and vices, and we endeavor to excite those who hear us to the love of the one and the hatred of the other."

"But to speak suitably of the virtues and vices one must have either studied in the schools, or must be taught by the Holy Ghost Himself," said the Dominican. "Now you have not been taught in the schools, you must be therefore taught by the Holy Ghost."

Eneko did not accept the notion that to be a good Christian one must attend a school, so he spoke as he had in public of virtue and vice, of good deeds and bad, of love and hate, and of service to God and to others as a basis for the Christian soul. Rejecting this reply, the Dominican repeated his earlier claim.

"I have already said enough," retorted Eneko, "and I will say no more except before my superiors, who have a right to interrogate me."

"Well, since it is so, you must remain here," said the Dominican, "We shall know how to oblige you to speak."

The Dominican locked the chapel gates and confined Eneko and Calisto in separate cells. After three days, the local magistrate arrested and imprisoned the pair, shackling their ankles and chaining them to a post at the center of the room. Then Cáceres and Artiaga, his other disciples still in Alcala, were summoned and imprisoned as well. For 22 days, the foursome prayed, ate sparingly, and gave the Spiritual Exercises to visitors. Many came with bedding or food, offers of legal counsel or political influence, yet all assistance was turned away.

After three weeks, either as a test or a twist of fate, the jail doors flew open, and all prisoners escaped—all except Eneko and his disciples. When the guards returned, they found the foursome still in their cells, the doors ajar. Seeing that these men were cut from different cloth, the magistrate's verdict came back in their favor: "No error could be found either in their way of life or in their doctrine." It said they could teach and speak on godly things, but not adjudicate between mortal and venial sin.

Feeling limited once again, Eneko put the question of what to do before God. The answer came to depart Spain and complete his education in France. Leaving Calisto, Cáceres, and Artiaga in Salamanca, he arrived alone and on foot in Paris in February 1528 to study at Montaigu, one of 60 colleges at the University of Paris. The Almshouse of St. Jacques became his home. During his years in Paris, he was so short of money that he traveled to Flanders for two months each year where he begged daily, and then returned for 10 months to Montaigu for school. In this way, he raised enough to live and study, graduating 30th out of 100 with a Bachelors of Arts in 1532. Eighteen months later, he received a Masters of Theology.

It was a momentous year, 1534, not only for his becoming a Master, but for a group of friends coming together after the achievement. During six years in France, Eneko gave the Spiritual Exercises to many, but six men in particular did more than listen: They became disciples. The six men—Faber, Xavier, Laynez, Salmeron, Rodriguez, and Bobadilla—met with Eneko at the Church of Our Lady of Montmartre, two miles from Paris, where Faber gave mass and all took vows of chastity and poverty. They made a written record of this bond of brothers; regrettably, it has been lost to history.

They agreed to meet again in January 1537 in Venice after all had become Masters. From there, they would go to Jerusalem to live forever as devout pilgrims and win the souls of people who now languished as children of Mohammed. Each took their vow in tears. They all held advanced degrees, placing them among the most educated in all of Europe, and perhaps their studies tempered what might have been misguided passion or zealotry. The moment was rare: seven men, kneeling, intending only good, wanting to change the world, believing their success inevitable, all for the greater glory of God.

THE BAND OF BROTHERS reconvened in Venice in January 1537. Eneko had spent time in Loyola to visit family, staying at an almshouse, not the castle. He spent time teaching children the gospels and convincing officials to forbid gambling, set up welfare for the poor, and expel concubines from the chambers of priests. He even settled a longstanding dispute between local clergy and a convent of Franciscan nuns. The other brothers had been occupied similarly in Portugal, France, or other parts of Spain before arriving in Venice.

Now in Venice, three others—Le Jay, Brouet, and Codure—who had taken the Spiritual Exercises joined too as the newest disciples. Those who hadn't been ordained, including Eneko, entered the priesthood.

The legate of Venice noticed these men in sacks. Asking around, he was told that the leader, the Basque pilgrim, had been burned in effigy at Alcala and Paris. Wasting no time, the legate brought charges, but whatever their nature, they lacked enough severity to survive to the present. Eneko turned over his Spiritual Exercises and demanded a written verdict. It came back in his favor, but the legate encouraged him and his disciples to leave Venice as soon as possible.

They would have liked nothing better, but the journey to Jerusalem was delayed. A battle had been waging in the Mediterranean that limited travel to the Holy Lands even for men who felt divinely protected. Hoping to cross in spring or summer, they divided into groups to wait out the months in different towns: Eneko, Faber, and Laynez to Vicenza; Xavier and Salmeron to Monfelice; Le Jay and Rodriguez to Bassano; Brouet and Bobadilla to Verona; and Codurino and Hozez to Treviso. A year would pass and still the war raged worse than ever, closing any hope of seeing Jerusalem.

The trip was not meant to be, so they agreed to fulfill their vow to obey as divine will any wish the pontiff might command of them. Worried of raising suspicions if all went to Rome, only Eneko, Faber, and Layez would go, and the others would travel to surrounding towns where their work would show the virtue of the sack-wearers. Eneko told them to live on alms, lodge in hospitals, care for the sick, and serve as alternating superiors of one another. And if anyone asked whom they represented, say that they belonged to the Society of Jesus, for it was in His name that they performed their good works. It was the first time that any of them had heard the title, and it derived exclusively from Eneko. No one objected to it.

Eneko traveled with Faber and Laynez to Rome, and it was a memorable moment for him and vital for the Society of Jesus. Outside the city limits, Eneko knelt in the Chapel of La Starta to pray. He felt moved by a force stronger than any he had felt before, and he knew, he later said, that God had whispered to him: *puso con el hijo*—Put him with His Son. Laynez reported the occasion thusly:

> He told me that God had imprinted on his mind these words—'I will be favorable to you at Rome.' As our Father did not comprehend the full meaning of these words, he said to me, 'I do not know what is reserved for us, perhaps we shall be crucified at Rome.' He told me, moreover, that

Jesus Christ had appeared to him, carrying the Cross aloft in His arms, and that beside Him was the Eternal Father, Who said to our Lord, 'I will that Thou take this man for Thy servant.' Jesus took him and said to him, 'I will that thou serve Me.'

The three brothers took the vision as a happy sign, one of good fortune, not doom. It felt familiar somehow, trustable, like an old friend. When they thought on the episode years later, they marveled at how closely it paralleled a key memory of St. Francis, who had entered the church of St. Damiano, knelt at an image of the Crucified to pray, and heard a voice from the cross whispering, "Francis, go and repair my house which, as you see, is falling into ruin." St. Francis had then set out to obey the command. With the same fervor of St. Francis, Eneko and his brothers entered Rome around Christmas 1537.

They received an audience with Pope Paul III to tell of their vows—chastity, poverty, obedience in His name, and good works for the salvation of souls. The pope received them favorably and assigned Faber and Laynez to teach in the University of Rome, while Eneko gave Spiritual Exercises publicly, drawing crowds and converting several prominent, educated men of the Vatican.

No sooner had they begun than a disparaging campaign started against them. In one of his letters, Eneko described it: "During eight whole months," he wrote, "we have had to sustain the most terrible persecution which we have ever experienced in this life. I do not mean to say that they have troubled us personally or dragged us before tribunals, but by reports spread in public, and by denunciations the most unheard of, they have rendered us suspected by the Faithful, to their great disedification." Had the charges been clear, specific, and formal, Eneko and his disciples could have fought them, as they had in the past; but whisper campaigns thrive best in shadows and draw strength from half-truth, innuendo, and gullible listeners who pass what they hear to other gullible ears. Only by pulling it into light and bringing truth against half-truth could such a campaign be defeated.

And that was how Eneko fought this battle. After four months, the band of brothers came together in Rome, all but Hozez who had died of natural causes in Padua. Eneko called for a tribunal where accusers might come from the shadows and state their charges. Before three cardinals, two men showed their faces, both of wealth and stature, who on flimsy evidence and personal bias railed against Eneko's different path, his contempt for the cloth, and his steps at forming an order without the approval of the pontiff. The cardinals judged the arguments meritless, yet not wanting to offend the accusers, they left the outcome open, neither indicting nor exonerating. Such a verdict served only to fuel the whisper campaign and spread more rumor.

Not content, Eneko called on the pope at his residence. Speaking with him for more than an hour, he did not ask to be pardoned outright; rather "I begged of His Holiness in the name of all my companions that He would be pleased, in order to remedy the evil, to charge an ordinary judge, whom He should choose, to make inquiry into our doctrine and lives, that we might be blamed and punished if they were found fault with—at the same time, asking his protection if they were found to be without blame." Had Eneko not pressed the pontiff, the Society of Jesus might never have been. History so often turns on single moments.

Paul III appointed the governor, who served as bishop and the highest judicial authority, to preside over the matter. The proceedings drew on names and faces from Eneko's past, men who had once opposed him and now came to his defense. Figueroa, who had imprisoned him at Alcala, spoke of his virtue, and the legate at Venice, who had pushed him from town, offered praise. For the work of the disciples, officials from Sienna, Bologna, and Ferrara sent messages of admiration and good tidings for these men of the sack who had visited their towns, tended the sick, and saved souls. No one stood that day against them. More than exoneration, this company of men received formal absolution and gained a stronger, broader reputation too, one that made recognition of the Society of Jesus, at least in hindsight, a *fait accompli*.

OVER TWO DECADES HAD PASSED since Martin Luther penned the Ninety-Five Theses that railed against clerical indulgences and the corruption of Rome, launched the Protestant Reformation, and frayed Catholic devotion in the northern countries of Europe. Paul III had formed a commission to investigate the clergy's trading of absolution for money and sexual favors. Many in Rome hoped to rein in religious orders, not add to them.

Yet that's what Eneko and his disciples aimed to do. Not all agreed at first, but after three days of prayer for clarity and wisdom, the brothers vowed to retain their loyalty to each other and to this Society of Jesus that Eneko had so aptly named, even if the pope dispatched them to far off lands. Their next decision grew from the first: Under what governance would this society form? They had promised poverty and chastity but never obedience to any man in their group. Meditating separately on the idea, each returned to give an opinion of the pros and cons of appointing a single leader. Against selecting a leader, they argued that resembling other orders would be a strike against them, requiring obedience might turn new members away, and appointing a head disliked by the pope might derail the whole Society now or in the future. In favor, they reasoned that the Society of Jesus favored Christ, not any man; no current order spoke to the needs of the time; and the Society linked the laity directly to the pope without corrupt clerics as middlemen.

After several days, the brothers unanimously agreed to choose a leader and add obedience to their vows, and so it was, at this moment, that the Society of Jesus came to be. The Jesuits were born of these founding fathers. During mass and before communion, they each affixed their signature to this declaration:

> I, the undersigned, declare before God Almighty, the Blessed Virgin Mary, and all the Court of Heaven, that, after having prayed God and maturely weighed the matter, I have voted with my whole heart for the vow of obedience being taken in the Society, finding it more conducive to the glory of God and the preservation of our Society. I declare also that I have freely decided, but without vow and without any obligation, to enter into this Society, if God permit it to be approved of by the Pope. In proof of this resolution, which, by the grace of God, I have taken as I here declare, I go now to Holy Communion, though unworthy, with this same intention.
> On Thursday, 15th of April, 1539.
> J. Codurius
> Laynez
> Salmeron
> Bobadilla
> Paschasius Brouet
> Francis (Xavier)
> Peter Faber
> Ignatius
> Simon Rodriguez
> Claude Le Jay

They debated and added other points to their charter: namely, that new members must complete the Spiritual Exercises, vow to obey the pope, and accept any assignment to foreign lands; that the Society should elect a superior general, who shall serve for life; and that any decisions shall pass by a majority of votes.

Eneko sketched five chapters, which he named the Formula of the Institute of the Society of Jesus, and presented it at Rome for consideration and approval of the Holy See. In its opening lines, the heart of a soldier joined with the soul of a pilgrim, and it deserves lengthy treatment here:

Whoever desires to fight as a solider of God beneath the banner of the Cross in our Society, which we desire to be designated by the name of Jesus, and to serve the Lord alone and the Church, his spouse, under the Roman pontiff, the Vicar of Christ on earth, should, after a solemn vow of perpetual chastity, poverty and obedience, keep what follows in mind. He is a member of a Society founded chiefly for this purpose: to strive especially for the defense and propagation of the faith and for the progress of souls in Christian life and doctrine, by means of public preaching, lectures and any other ministration whatsoever of the Word of God, and further by means of retreats, the education of children and unlettered persons in Christianity, and the spiritual consolation of Christ's faithful through hearing confessions and administering the other sacraments. Moreover, he should show himself ready to reconcile the estranged, compassionately assist and serve those who are in prisons or hospitals, and indeed, to perform any other works of charity, according to what will seem expedient for the glory of God and the common good.

After hearing the five chapters, Paul III remarked, "The finger of God is here." In the Bull, *Regimini Militantis Ecclesiae*, dated September 27, 1540, the pontiff confirmed the new order, the Society of Jesus, though he limited membership to 60, a restriction lifted by a second bull of March 14, 1543.

The pope lost no time dispatching these learned men to do his work, calling them "reformed priests," a first wave of divinely inspired soldiers to counter the Protestant uprisings in Northern Europe. Before they traveled too far, Eneko summoned them during Lent of the next year to Rome to elect a superior general. He gave each the constitution to read and study, establishing a seven-day process that included three days of prayer, a sealed vote, and three days of reflection. The brothers put their votes into an urn, each one including a lengthy recitation of why he chose the person whose name appeared on the slip of paper. On the seventh day, in view of all, Eneko pulled the votes from the urn and read each aloud. By unanimous consent, the brothers had elected him their first superior general.

The only one who opposed him was himself. He cast no vote and immediately after hearing the outcome refused the charge. He called for a new vote after three more days of prayer, but the votes, and the reasons for each, turned out the same. He again refused. Laynez then stood to address him directly: "Submit, my Father, to the will of God. If you do not the Society will be broken up, for I am resolved to recognize no other head than him whom God has chosen." Eneko yielded on April 9, 1541, perhaps conceding the only fight of his life.

FIFTY YEARS had taken its toll on Eneko. Never healthy, he suffered gall-stones and liver pains and continued to limp from the bone shards left by the cannonball. Administering the Society through its most formative years only aggravated his condition, but he did not shy from or diminish the zeal with which he confronted each mounting challenge.

The king of Portugal, John III, delivered the first of these challenges. He petitioned the pope directly for six of Eneko's flock to go to the East Indies where the Portuguese had enjoyed a monopoly for decades over the spice trade. The pope kindly deferred to Eneko's judgment. Not wanting to upset one of the Society's closest allies, the pilgrim selected only two disciples—Xavier and Rodriguez—saying with diplomatic care, "If out of so small a Society you take six for one kingdom, what will be left for the rest of the world?" Appreciating this ambitious vision, the king gave in, keeping Rodriguez in Portugal to start a seminary and sending Xavier to India.[2] It would be the last time that Eneko and Xavier would see each other.

This missionary model came to define the Jesuits. Eneko operated from the church of Santa Maria Della Strada, a headquarters ironically named—*of the road*—for no Jesuits would live in monasteries. They would go where the pope commanded and use their natural talents to educate, tend the sick, and minister to the needs of the poor. "The true and primitive spirit of this company," wrote Eneko to King Ferdinand of Germany, "is, in all simplicity and humility, to go from city to city, and from country to country, for the greater glory of God and the salvation of souls, and not to confine its actions to any one particular province."

After Xavier left for India and Rodriguez for Portugal, he dispatched Le Jay to Germany, Faber to Spain, and others to the Americas, France, or elsewhere in Italy. By Eneko's deft hand, princes of Europe took Jesuits as confessors, strengthening the Catholic resolve of these royals, who in turn influenced the laity. It served as a first bulwark against the deterioration of Catholic faith since Martin Luther's Wittenberg declaration and John Calvin's Catholic denunciations in Geneva.

These influences of royalty, though valuable, compared little to Eneko's crusade for the education of children and adults. His enthusiasm shows in the Spiritual Exercises, his Spiritual Diary, the Constitutions, and his hundreds of letters to kings, queens, princes, princesses, dukes, duchesses, popes, and clerics across the world. It stemmed naturally from his life: his joy in reading, public sermons, education of nuns at Holy Angels, and spiritual exercises sketched at Manresa. More perhaps than any policy of the Vatican, his commitment to education breathed new life into the tired faith of congregants and clerics alike.

Pope Paul III approves the Society of Jesus, September 27, 1540. Photo copyright 2013 Jesuit Institute London. Used with permission.

In Gandia, Spain, he saw a first opportunity to shape this mission of education. Francis Borgia, viceroy of Catalonia and a trusted advisor to the king of Spain, witnessed the work of Faber and Antonio Araoz in Barcelona. A solemn, devout man, Borgia vowed to build a university to advance their work. In May 1546, Faber and Araoz would lay the cornerstone of the Society's first college in Gandia. Two years later, Borgia would undergo the Spiritual Exercises secretly and become a Jesuit himself, eventually joining Eneko in the rare pantheon of sainthood.

This early success in Gandia led to colleges elsewhere: in Messina (1548), Palermo (1549), the Roman College (1551), Vienna (1553), and French Billom

(1556). The movement caught fire. Locals wanted schools. Through congregants, the Jesuits raised money, built them, and served as teachers. Even in Luther's Germany, the heart of the Reformation, the duke of Bavaria requested two Jesuits for teaching positions at the University of Ingoldstadt. The Vatican, once resistant to this new order, saw education as a tool for extracting public loyalty. By contrast, Eneko saw education as an end unto itself, a divine good.

When an opportunity arose to start a seminary in Portugal, for example, he seized it. By 1549, it had grown from one Jesuit, Rodriguez, to over 250 men whom the king could send, by the consent of the pontiff, to any one of the lands under his dominion. As Eneko saw them, these men were not religious zealots. They were men of substance, well educated in logic, philosophy, and theology. Only by education, thought Eneko, could men exercise their unique talents, whatever they might be, for the greater glory of God.

During his tenure as superior general, he codified this idea into the Society's constitution. "The aim which the Society of Jesus directly seeks," he wrote, "is to aid its own members and their neighbors to attain the ultimate end for which they were created." This end was salvation by the fulfillment of one's own gifts. Where others confined knowledge to scripture, he incorporated a curriculum of "foreign languages, logic, natural and moral philosophy, metaphysics, scholastic and positive theology, and Sacred Scripture."

In a letter to Araoz, working now with Faber in Spain, Eneko showed a vision of education that reached beyond the Vatican and the walls of the church:

> From among those who are now merely students, in time some will emerge to play diverse roles—some to preach and carry on the care of souls, others to the government of the land and the administration of justice, and others to other responsible occupations. Finally, since the children of today become the adults of tomorrow, their good education in life and doctrine will be beneficial to many others, with the fruit expanding more widely every day.

All of this work, so many hours of toil, wore down this five foot, two inch man of poor health, now age 65. After 15 years, he had presided over the construction and administration of 33 colleges with six more approved. He had published the Spiritual Exercises with the consent of the Holy See and finalized the Society's constitution. Of greater demand was overseeing the more than 1,000 Jesuits now scattered across Europe, Asia, and North and South America.

By 1556, his body was tired out. He could no longer fulfill the duties of superior general and wished to be relieved of the burden. No one of the Society would think of accepting his resignation. To help with operations, three close friends, including his assistant, Polanco, bore his responsibilities though none would accept title of any form lest it cast Eneko in an unfavorable light. The pilgrim retired to a public house in Rome where he lay among others who suffered near death. Polanco sat at his bedside. Physicians came and went tending to his comforts, and he would send them away, saying others needed them more.

He would not think of death, for it was too happy a thought, a selfish indulgence he believed, to be with his God, his Father, and to know such contentment and joy. Friends prayed with him and wept. He would pat their heads and say a blessing, and the friends would smile through tears, feeling joy not sadness, knowing that he would soon be in the bosom of the Father. He was surrounded by peace and warmth and loving visitors every day.

In the early dawn of July 31, 1556, word went to the pope that the time of Eneko's end was near, but the message would not arrive soon enough. Without last rites, this Basque pilgrim of Gipuzkoa, this noble soldier of God, died.

Polanco delivered the news to the pope, to the Society, to men and women of good conscience, and to history:

> God has broken the bonds which kept him prisoner in this mortal flesh, in order to admit him to the liberty of the elect, having thus heard at last the prayers of his servant. For although he bore with much patience and courage the pains of his pilgrimage and the burdens which he sustained upon his shoulders, nevertheless he long since desired to praise and contemplate in the heavenly home His Master and Creator, Who, by His divine providence has left him to us up to this time, that his little Society which He Himself begun by his means, might enjoy the benefit of his example, his wisdom, authority, and prayers. But now that its roots have to all appearance struck deep, He has removed him to heaven, that being more closely united to Himself, the Plenitude of all Good, he may obtain for us a more abundant measure of grace, and that this plant may increase and grow abundantly, together with its fruit, in the various countries of the world.

Without the little lion protecting the pride, the Society came under attack, but the roots of Eneko's mustard seed had spread deep into worldwide soil. No charges stuck for long or caused irreparable harm. The brothers would elect another founding father, Laynez, as a successor.

Sixty-six years after his death, Eneko was canonized as St. Ignatius of Loyola on March 12, 1622.[3] The fruit of his mustard seed had stretched over four continents, the number of Jesuit colleges exceeding 300 with an additional 130 seminaries, and thousands of Jesuit devotees. Up to the present, these men of the sack, all disciples of a Basque pilgrim, would educate millions of children and contribute significantly to the fields of literature, physics, chemistry, mathematics, genetics, seismology, theology, and philosophy, all without title or honors, all for the greater glory of God.

Nearly 475 years after Eneko breathed life into the Society of Jesus, the world waited as it had 265 times before for the archbishops, gathered in the Sistine Chapel, to select a new pope. The last, Benedict XVI, had resigned nearly two weeks before on February 28, 2013. Thousands of faithful congregated two weeks later in St. Peter's Square on a cold, rainy night, training their eyes on a small chimney above the chapel, waiting for the archbishops to make their historic vote. The media turned the verdict into a simple formula, "White Smoke Pope, Black Smoke Nope." Everyone shivered in the rain under umbrellas, thankful perhaps for the close quarter of warm bodies.

It was 7:06 in the evening when the white smoke billowed. The bells of St. Peters chimed their deep bass. The crowd cheered and roared, waved flags from around the world, clapped and danced and stamped their feet. Amid this raucous throng, other quiet souls with solemn expressions and sleepy eyes simply prayed or recited the rosary. The excitement crescendoed, growing as a tidal wave, in anticipation of the man who would come forward very soon to bless the masses. The media speculated about whom it would be, yet no guess was better than any other.

Then came the moment. The man stepped on to the red-velvet balcony, and the crowd, seeing him for the first time, found a higher exhilaration and a treble of volume that rose into the heavens. The opulence of the palace contrasted brilliantly with this man's white cassock, simple and plain, free of regalia or finery.

His name was Jorge Mario Bergoglio, the first Jesuit pontiff, a man educated as a chemist. He would be the first pope from the Americas, born in Buenos Aires, Argentina, a man who loved the poor, lived in an apartment not a palace, cooked his own food, and rode public buses not private limousines. Like Eneko, and every Jesuit since, the man honored vows of poverty, chastity, and obedience to find God in all things. The world would know him as Pope Francis, the very first with that saintly name.

He looked out over St. Peters Square where the faithful, stacked half a mile deep, waved and cheered louder and louder, bouncing umbrellas, flashing cameras, climbing on shoulders, yelling, clapping, and crying. All awaited the first prayer from this man dressed in white. Yet rather than bestow his blessing outright as all popes before him, he did something extraordinary. He asked the happy, giddy masses to pray for him first, and as though on cue, all the heads bowed and all the eyes closed and a brilliant hush fell over the multitudes. All prayed in the rain for this first Jesuit pope, this humble servant of God, this one disciple among thousands from Eneko, a Basque pilgrim.

Notes

1. The reference to a mustard seed comes from a parable of Jesus. Though the parable is relayed in three Gospels of the Bible—Matthew, Mark, and Luke—the version is best described, in my opinion, in Matthew 13:31–32. It says: "He set another parable before them, saying, 'The Kingdom of Heaven is like a grain of mustard seed, which a man took, and sowed in his field; which indeed is smaller than all seeds. But when it is grown, it is greater than the herbs, and becomes a tree, so that the birds of the air come and lodge in its branches.'" In the Bible, the parable shows how the smallest faith can grow into something strong and powerful, yielding Heaven itself. In secular terms, it demonstrates how the smallest action in a person's life may grow over time to produce a large and important outcome, good or bad.

2. As the first Jesuit missionary, Xavier is worthy of a profile of his own. He was a Navarrese Basque, born Francisco de Jasso y Azpilicueta in Xavier, Kingdom of Navarre. Responding to the king of Portugal, and by order of Eneko and the pope, he set out for India on his thirty-fifth birthday. He started a seminary and built nearly 40 churches along the coast of Southern India and Ceylon, converting many. The Portuguese soldiers gave him fits. Those who were already Christian acted less Christian than the natives—drinking, stealing, and destroying local homes and farms. Many of the Portuguese, hailing from the spice trade, were once prisoners who had been granted amnesty in exchange for sailing aboard dangerous ships and settling in distant lands. Xavier's hands were full. He preached in Japan and the Moluccas and had hoped to do the same in China before his death in 1552. Xavier was beatified in 1619 and canonized in 1622. He gained the nickname "Apostle of the Indies" or "Apostle of Japan," arguably one of the greatest missionaries since St. Paul. Today he is the co-patron saint of Navarre with San Fermin, and the Day of Navarre (Día de Navarra) in Spain is celebrated on St. Francis Xavier's death, December 3, 1552.

3. The Catholic Church has established a process for a man or woman to gain sainthood. If a person has "fame of sanctity" or "fame of martyrdom," an investigation begins into the person's past. The first test is whether the person, by his or her intervention, has likely performed a miracle or by mere presence had a likely miracle performed. The second test is a review of the candidate's writing to confirm "purity of doctrine," which eliminates the chance of heresy or charges against the faith. This information is gathered and catalogued, authenticated and sealed, and then submitted to a special council called the Congregation for the Causes of the Saints.

The next stage determines veneration. If the person is virtuous, the Congregation determines if his or her deeds are of such a profound and heroic nature that they warrant recognition as venerable. If the person is construed a martyr, the Congregation determines whether he offered his life for the faith, for Christ, and for the Church. Throughout this process, a "general promoter of the faith," or a devil's advocate, pokes holes in the testimony, doing his best to discount the claims of veneration.

If deemed venerable, the Congregation next tests for beatification, or blessedness. A martyr may be beatified outright. If the candidate is not a martyr, then the Congregation determines if the person truly performed a miracle or by his or her intervention had a miracle performed. If confirmed, a person may gain beatification. Several have reached this point. The honor of beatification remains at a regional level or within a religious family. The Congregation must confirm a second miracle of the person to bestow canonization and then receive the formal favor of the pope to bestow sainthood. St. Ignatius was credited with many miracles during this process.

Santiago Ramón y Cajal

The Father of Neurology

THE 54-YEAR-OLD MAN fidgeted in his red velvet chair. It was so unlike the smooth wooden chair in his laboratory back in Spain. Bald with a wrinkled forehead, he had a narrow face, sad eyes, and steel wool beard, more white than black. He did not want to be amid this pomp. He preferred solitude, his lab, the microscope, drawing pens, staining agents, and slides of brain tissue. He felt embarrassed and unworthy to be in this place, but he had come for Spain, a country needing to think better of itself.

In this great hall of the Royal Academy of Music, more majestic than any in Spain, a great gathering of intelligentsia and the wealthy, ambassadors and ministers, scientists and men of letters from all parts of the world focused their eyes on him. Not far away sat the King of Sweden robed in black with gold epaulettes, the resplendent queen next to him, and then by her the descendants of Alfred Nobel. Across the way, ready to accept a peace prize, sat the US President, Theodore Roosevelt, a "man of the most impetuously warlike temperament," he would later write.

The king went to the podium. He looked so like a king, regal with a stout bearing. In his bold, elongated vowels and commanding voice he read off a long list of neurological accomplishments, as this little Basque man of Navarre squirmed in his red velvet chair. He anguished over what this pageantry was likely to bring—the letters to write, the banquets to attend, the speeches to give, the honorary degrees to accept. His life had been quiet and full of painstaking, beloved hard work. This whole affair was a great thorny distraction. "I had to

Santiago Ramón y Cajal would spend countless hours alone with an eye to his microscope and a hand around a pen or pencil to render whatever he saw through the lens. In his life, he drew thousands of pictures that defined and illuminated the human neurological system. This picture is from 1915, nine years after he won the Nobel Prize for Medicine. Photo courtesy of Santiago Ramón y Cajal. Cajal Legacy. Instituto Cajal. Madrid resign myself to it," he later wrote, "with a smile on my lips and sadness in my heart." After the king called out his name that day, December 10, 1906, Santiago Ramón y Cajal rose with grace to accept the Nobel Prize for Physiology and Medicine, sharing the distinction with an Italian rival, Camillo Golgi, whose work had been indispensable to his own.

Two thousand miles and a full lifetime from Sweden, Santiago Ramón y Cajal[1] had struck no one, especially not his father, as a future Nobel laureate in medicine. Born May 1, 1852, in Petilla, Navarre, Spain, Santiago moved soon after to Larrés, his parents' native village, then to Luna, and finally to Valpalmas where he formed his first memories. Those recollections were overwhelmingly of his father, Justo Ramón Casasús, a stern, hardworking disciplinarian, and hunter who, as a medical doctor, cared for the townspeople.

By age four, Santiago attended the local school, but his real education came from this firebrand of a father. As a first lesson, Don Justo took Santiago to a shepherd's cave to drill him in French, month after month, in heat and cold, on a rocky floor. Santiago never learned the language well, but whenever he spoke it as an adult, a dark and damp cave would pop into his head, forever linking solitude with the duty of learning.

By age six, a rift opened between him and his father, two people very much of equal will and temperament. His father emphasized books and study in reading, writing, geography, and arithmetic. But Santiago discovered "nature's gaudy festivals," the streams and flowers, fields and mountains, animals and birds, especially the birds. He traced their V in flight. He would lie on his stomach to follow chains of ants or study tints and shades of light, the blending of colors, the angles and lines of rocks. He imagined beauty; his father, logic and science. Nature was a kindly old man, he thought, with the heart of an artist—wonderful, dreamy, idyllic—nothing like his own father at all.

Two episodes crushed this innocent perfection. In Valpalmas's one-room schoolhouse, Santiago finished morning prayers with "Lord, deliver us from evil." Just then, lightning struck the bell tower, sending everyone into frenzy. Running outside to safety, he saw the priest bent at the waist over the railing, his clothes and flesh burned and the church bell melted. It frightened him. Nature had an unpredictable dark side. Not long after, the solar eclipse of 1860 excited people. They counted down the days and then hiked to a mountain peak to witness the celestial event. It fascinated Santiago, then age eight, that in science, humans had tools to unlock, predict, and understand the secrets of nature and the universe.

When he recalled this scientific discovery, he fondly remembered a patriotic fervor then sweeping Spain. Queen Isabel II, long criticized for infidelities in the bedroom and mismanagement of public funds announced victory over Spain's old rival, Morocco. The nation rejoiced, and her popularity soared. In Valpalmas, people danced *jotas* in the town square, drank wine from leather bags, slaughtered lambs and cattle, and forgot their poverty and lackluster lives. Forevermore, love of nature and science joined in his mind with love of country. He would never again think of one without the other.

In the same year, his father took the family to Ayerbe, a larger town closer to the Pyrenees, where most of his patients lived. By then, Santiago's mother, Dona Antonia, a beautiful woman, cared for him, his brother Pedro, and two sisters, Paula and Jorja. His brother and sisters received their father's lessons with joy, while he tilted further away. The move brought him misery.

In Ayerbe, the local boys did not accept Santiago with his different clothes, dialect, and mannerisms. In the town square, they bloodied his nose, made fun of his parentage, and ostracized him. Not shy of competition and desperate to fit in, he eventually bested them in their games, races, and jumping contests. To gain their esteem, he threw rocks through windows and stole from peach orchards. His escapades grew so daring that he rose to lead the group, crafting cudgels, arrows, and slingshots; stealing ever more bunches of fruits and vegetables; shooting rabbits or birds that he had once loved so much; or fashioning the helmets and breastplates for epic games of war. Each transgression, day after day, brought endless whippings from his father who still pressed science, math, and reading and dreamed that this rebellious son might follow his footsteps one day into the medical field.

Santiago pulled in the opposite direction. If not practicing anarchy, he took up his new passion: art. It combined two things he loved: nature and his father's opposition. Any blank surface—school books, desks, newly painted town walls—became welcoming canvas. Often he'd sit in a field to draw or paint farmers stacking hay or brooks gurgling over rocks or any horse, dog, cat, or sheep idling in a field. He wadded paper for brushes and chipped paint from fences and buildings to liquefy and mix colors to match evening light or flower petal or autumn grass. More than a knack, Santiago had a gift for seeing details that others easily overlooked.

What a waste of time, thought Don Justo. Whenever he found his son's drawings or paintings, he tore them up or burned them and gave out a beating. He forbade paint and art pencils or anything resembling canvas. His son had to smuggle and hide the materials. If discovered, there was another whipping. With this artistic rebellion came a growing truancy, which attracted even more vicious thrashings. Every missed schoolday was a personal defeat for his father.

One day he and brother Pedro skipped school and, knowing the punishment, hid in the forest instead of going home. By the second night, Don Justo went searching and found them asleep. He rousted the pair, tied them arm to arm, and marched them home through the public square to the jeers of Ayerbe's residents. Neither son went truant again, though Santiago, in defiance, stepped up his artwork. "Certainly without the mysterious attractiveness of forbidden fruit," he would later write, "the wings of my imagination would have spread, but they perhaps would not have reached the overdevelopment that they attained."

At wits' end in September 1861, Don Justo—who loved his son and wanted only a bright future for him—packed up the boy's few belongings and an old mattress and enrolled him with the Dominican fathers in Jaca 40 miles away. Certainly no unruly boy could withstand the discipline of these masterful, God-fearing educators.

FATHER JACINTO, a burly barrel-chested friar with a voice of Zeus, taught Latin in Jaca and enjoyed petty torments. He thrashed Santiago with verbal abuse or a backhand, cudgel, or ruler. For every misdeed, he withheld food for a day, locked the boy in a classroom overnight, or dressed him in a robe and feathered headdress. How else might he learn humility? Santiago lost weight and good health but never gave in. His stubborn streak ran deep. Yet with every punishment, his art flourished in landscapes, portraits of historical and religious figures, and caricatures of professors, earning him admiration and popularity among classmates. The friars of Jaca had failed.

Don Justo gave up on the Dominicans and enrolled Santiago at a school in Huesca. Once again he had to earn his stripes. Not strong enough to defend himself, he took beatings for a year from local boys who called him *Dago* for dressing like an Italian organ grinder. It was intolerable, so during summer break, he climbed trees, chopped wood, and lifted rocks, anything to improve strength, his *muscle years* he would call them. He mastered the slingshot and cudgel too. "If you wish to succeed in difficult undertakings," he wrote, "put your whole will into your purpose, preparing yourself with more time and effort than are actually called for." When the new school year started, a bigger kid threw a first punch. He returned two punches of his own, then pulled his sling and shot the kid between the eyes. He was no mere hooligan. He had become leader of the gang, the other boys nicknaming him the *Crazy Navarran*.

Mischief at school and during summer breaks lasted years, tearing down his father's ambitions. Don Justo tried everything, apprenticing Santiago to a barber as he himself had been, then to a shoemaker where his son's creative shoe designs unexpectedly drew him a following. That, of course, was not the intent.

All seemed hopeless. The despair he felt over his son amplified the despair he felt for his country.

In September 1868, growing discontent with Isabel II exploded into national labor strikes, riots in Madrid, and violent clashes. The liberal towns of Valpalmas and Ayerbe that had once celebrated Isabel's victory in Morocco now rejoiced at her imminent downfall. Prices rose, food became scarce, and unemployment layered gloom upon gloom. Revolution was in the air. By June 1870, the queen abdicated and fled to France where she'd live out her final days.

Amid the revolts from his son and the revolts in his country, Don Justo did something uncharacteristic. He enrolled Santiago at Zaragosa in a pre-med curriculum, as he had always wanted, and allowed him to enroll in a single art class too. It made all the difference. Santiago, now age 16, took a sudden interest in chemistry, physics, and natural history. His love of nature and art combined with a powerful curiosity to explore and measure scientific mysteries like the lightning at the church or the eclipse from a decade earlier. "The whole universe, both in the realm of the infinitely great and in that of the infinitely small," he said, "is constructed in accordance with the formulas of a sage geometry and an admirable system of dynamics."

Don Justo moved his family to Zaragosa, accepting a professorship in anatomy while serving as town doctor of the poor. After teaching in the morning and visiting patients in the afternoon, as if all the stars had now aligned, he and his son worked side-by-side in the basement of the Hospital of Santa Engracias, dissecting cadavers and identifying every organ by the latest French texts. Santiago's artistic gifts now were invaluable. He made drawings of every sawed, cut, or chiseled piece: striations of muscle; artery, capillary, and veins; endocrine and exocrine glands; and major organs from brain to eye to kidney to liver. "I saw in the dead body," he said, "not death with its host of melancholy thoughts, but the marvelous workmanship of life."

Santiago blossomed. Within a year, he became an anatomy assistant and tutored other students. He even competed for an anatomy prize. He was asked to describe and draw the inguinal ring around the groin. After writing at length and drawing in detail, a fight broke out among the judges, one storming out saying, "You are not pulling the wool over my eyes. Your paper was copied." But, of course, it hadn't been. Santiago took first place. To draw or paint was to know and understand. It flattened the world, reducing the most incomprehensible biological sciences to blocks of color and ink on paper. It set him apart from classmates and later from his colleagues of anatomy, histology, and neurology, who used words in place of Santiago's pens and brushes.

By the time he finished his education at Zaragosa, he hardly resembled the boy who had started five years earlier. Always a hard worker, he showed in his final years a shocking capacity to absorb material. He studied and drew with pens, pencils, and charcoal into early morning hours, often with little sleep or food. He had a worker's constitution imbued with a strong mind and artistic hand. So rarely had these triple gifts rested so gently in one body.

In September 1873, he earned a degree in medicine as Don Junto had always wanted, and now it really seemed that Santiago wanted it too. The celebration was short-lived. In search of a new monarch, Spain's political turmoil had continued: the prime minister was assassinated; a new republic was voted; Barcelona demanded independence; Catalonia and Valencia seceded; troops killed their officers; and the treasury had no money. It was during this national chaos that Santiago was drafted into the army.

Lieutenant Santiago Ramón y Cajal, second medical aide, looked dashing in army blue, so new and clean, brass buttons up the front, gold stripes on short legs and broad shoulders, a pill-box hat of blue and yellow, and a rifle at his side. Parading with pride before family and friends, he yearned for adventure away from Zaragosa, the cadavers in the basement, the classroom, books, and tests.

His first orders came on September 3, 1873. He would join the Regiment of Burgos to keep order in Lerida, Catalonia, against supporters of Don Carlos, who claimed the Spanish throne. His was a tired, complicated, cumbersome skirmish, with its origins in the First Carlist War of 1833. In that year King Ferdinand VII died, leaving his wife, Maria Cristina, to serve as regent over their infant daughter, Isabella II, until she could come of age and assume the throne. The king's brother, Carlos V, wanted the throne for himself, and the country was split between traditionalists and Catholics who sided with him, and liberals and republicans who sided with Maria Cristina. The fighting spanned the country, with supporters of Carlos concentrated in the Basque Provinces, Aragon, Catalonia, and Valencia. After seven years, the uprisings were put down, only to rise a second time six years later when rabble-rousing groups in Catalonia and Galicia called for the heirs of Carlos V to take their rightful place as rulers of Spain. Following a quick military intervention, nothing came of the demand, and a sense of quiet and calm washed over the troubled areas.

In 1868, when Isabel II had grown into her crown, a group of liberal generals overthrew her, leaving the country rudderless. The parliament installed a caretaker monarch pending elections in 1872, which resulted in violence against Carlist-leaning candidates. The grandson of Carlos V—Carlos VII—decided that his only recourse was to take up arms to fight the violence and overturn what he saw as a fraudulent election. And it was this battle into which Santiago had now been thrust.

Nothing in his writings suggested that Santiago favored one side over another or that he retained any strong political feelings for or against the crown. What he yearned for, more than anything else, he said, was close combat, an opportunity to test his mettle in worthy combat. But if action he sought, he would be disappointed. During his eight months in Lerida, he never treated a bullet wound, or even saw one, never slung a broken limb, never fired a weapon or heard one discharged. The whole affair was a dud. Instead of firefights, his memories were of the Catalonians and their zest for life, love of freedom, and devotion to beloved soil and sea. It was uncompromising, contagious, and long-lasting. Santiago had not experienced anything so intense, not even in Navarra among the Basque. He would remember the feeling and write of it for the rest of his life.

After the disappointment of Lerida, his number came up for an expeditionary force in Cuba: finally, adventure, and with it, a promotion to first medical aide. He was overjoyed at the chance to see the great territories of the Spanish empire—Cuba, Puerto Rico, Guam, Philippines—and the Americas too, the land he had dreamed of from romantic novels in his youth, the bright and beautiful landscapes of jungle, oak and pine, and the villages of scantily clad tribes. His father asked him to petition for a discharge so his studies would not languish. Santiago refused. Adventure was his lodestone; the Americas, his promised land.

Aboard the *España*, this exuberance strengthened while crossing the Atlantic. The water, he said, "glowed with mysterious refulgence" in the "phosphorescent wake of noctilucas." The sea was the "cradle of life," he said, and the "rhythm of the waves evoked the throbbing love of the mother embracing her children." Since the thirteenth century, so many Basque on whaling vessels had felt the same, even if they hadn't articulated it as he had. "I was a little afraid," he said, "feeling as if I were floating between two infinities." There was little doubt that he embraced his adventure with a full heart, clinging to every detail, building each moment to an epic climax of Homeric scope on Cuban soil.

Havana came into view after 17 days. After anchoring, he took to the land to walk a stream and an overgrown forest as he had at Ayerbe or Zaragosa. He found only shrubs and small patches of mahogany and cedar. Four hundred years of colonial life had decimated the jungle. Havana was dirty with shacks, animals living with humans, and snaggle-toothed Creole engaged in alcoholism, gambling, prostitution, bribery, rape, and murder. The Cubans relied on the labor of Chinese and black men, wrote Santiago, to make up for their own poor work habits. Of all the glamour in his dreams, only the Cuban women with brown skin, soft seductive voices, and bodiced bodies met his expectations.

Before Santiago left Spain, his father had asked friends to write letters of introduction to help him curry favor with commanders for plum assignments at hospitals. Santiago tucked them in his pocket, but when assignments were handed out, he kept them there, believing their use would be unbecoming an honorable man. Others had no such qualms. They used every scrap of influence to gain appointment to one of the few slots in Havana.

Santiago became director of the infirmary at Vista Hermosa in the District of Puerto Principe, the worst of Cuba. It had been devastated by war and crawled with armed rebels who had killed countless Spaniards already. Atop a hill surrounded by jungle, Vista Hermosa included a log fort as garrison, cramped barracks, and a thatch-roofed shack as hospital. Behind the two structures were ramshackle huts for Chinese and black laborers who built and maintained roads and railways. The little hospital held 200 beds, all occupied by men with malaria or dysentery. Caring for them engaged Santiago night and day. His untrained nurses often fell sick themselves.

In a small room separated from patients by a couple boards, he kept a bed, library, and photography lab side-by-side with muskets, bullets, quinine, biscuits, and sugar. It was less than a cubby hole, smaller than the cave in which his father had taught him French; he called it home. Every day he tried to draw, but mosquitoes—swarms of them—interrupted continually, leaving a number of unfinished sketches. Not surprising, he contracted malaria and, within a month, dysentery, yet as terrible as he felt, he continued to tend the men in the ward.[2]

The mosquitoes were as constant as Cuban rebels who leapt from the jungle like lions from tall grass. During one ferocious attack, Santiago lay sick in bed. He pulled himself up, stood on wobbly legs, and grabbed his gun. Then he handed out guns and bullets to his patients who knelt by their beds, their faces pale, eyes bloodshot, clothes matted with sweat, speech incoherent. They were armed zombies ready to defend the hospital and each other. Fortunately, soldiers outside repelled the assault without a breach of the hospital, but several patients died nonetheless from exertion. Overcome himself, unable to stand or perform his duties, Santiago was transported to a hospital in Puerto Principe where he convalesced for weeks, ate full meals, and enjoyed sleep without the suck of mosquitoes.

He recovered and hoped for a discharge to Spain. He received instead an appointment as director of San Isidro Hospital where his two immediate predecessors had died. He called it the "queue of death," far worse than Vista Hermosa, for two reasons: first, it was surrounded by swampland with never-ending mosquito hatcheries; and, second, a nearby railroad that brought regular supplies turned San Isidro into a larger target for Cuban rebels. The hospital had 300 beds, all filled, and a greater variety of maladies: smallpox, ulcers, malaria, dysentery, dropsy, bullet wounds, and broken bones.

Most of all, San Isidro suffered from a moral illness. Soldiers and hospital employees had been stealing patients' food and medicine, bribing officers, and operating an underground market. When Santiago discovered it, he confronted the major in charge who said past directors had gone along and advised him to do the same. Never one to go along, Santiago inventoried all supplies personally and, with lock and key, controlled their distribution, which escalated the battle with the major. In retaliation, the major installed two horses in the hospital. Santiago removed them.

"How dare you disobey me? I am in command here!" yelled the major.

"I beg your pardon," replied Santiago, "Inside this hospital there is no authority above mine."

The major brought charges for insubordination. If he had known of Don Justo and the stubborn battle between father and son for so many years, he would have known this act to be futile. Santiago countered the charges with a detailed account of theft, bribery, and corruption, the cost of all, and the black market, which the major by a dereliction of duty had allowed on his watch. Outmatched after one volley, the major withdrew the charges and let the matter drop.

For seven months, the corrupt practices melted away until Santiago, ill with malaria, dysentery, and dropsy, requested a discharge due to poor health. He transferred to San Miguel for recovery and then to Havana before earning an honorable release on May 15, 1875. An adventure it had been, but not the one he had expected, not even close.

While Santiago was away, Spain had gained a new monarch, Alfonso XII, son of the reviled Queen Isabel II. Aboard the *España*, Santiago wondered if this new king would lead Spain to a new day. He read an old newspaper where the king's premier, Antonio Canovas del Castillo, defended the battle in Cuba with a vow—*hasta el último hombre y la última peseta* ("until the last man and the last peseta"). Santiago had his answer. He only cared now for his medical books, experiments, and the feel of pens and brushes in his hand. Sated of adventure, a world of science and solitude awaited him. He slept most of the way home.

" I ASPIRED TO BE SOMETHING," said Santiago, "to emerge from the plane of mediocrity, and to collaborate, if my powers permitted, in the great work of scientific investigation that I hoped might bring some glory to my sad country." That ambition drove his career from 1875 on as he returned to Zaragosa as a temporary assistant in anatomy earning 1,000 pesetas annually (about $200). Don Justo encouraged him to take the exam for his doctor's degree, which he did in June 1877, passing comfortably.

During his exam in Madrid, he saw for the first time a microscope, that taboo instrument thought to be a purveyor of "celestial anatomy." There was nothing like it in Zaragosa. It enthralled him. He scraped together 700 pesetas (about $140) over four installments to buy a used one, and he set up a lab in an old attic stocked with staining agents, chemicals, slides, beakers, and a host of pens, pencils, and brushes. Never were his tools of science divorced from his tools of art. There in the small attic, he peered into the eyepiece, and oh what a world! "A fascinated spectator," he wrote, "I examined the red blood corpuscles, the cells of the skin, the muscle fibers, the nerve fibers, pausing here and there to draw or photograph the more intriguing scenes in the life of the infinitely small."

From his initial discoveries, he published in 1880 two pamphlets of original research in histology.[3] He included lithographs that he had engraved himself and printed 100 copies for friends and colleagues. Neither produced significant results, both going unnoticed, in fact. But he found the experience rewarding and illustrative of the kind of researcher he was—patient, scrupulous, humble, persistent, and open-minded—the last most of all, for if a claim failed experimental proof, he said so regardless of the author. He realized too that the language of science was French or German, not Spanish, so he subscribed to foreign journals, brushing up on French and learning German for the first time.

With the inquisitive nature of Socrates, he shored up weaknesses in physics, chemistry, and the natural sciences and filled gaps in his knowledge of histology from other countries. He yearned for the next test, a chance to prove his bona fides, which came soon enough. Two professorships—one in Granada, one in Zaragosa—opened for competition. He breezed through the material, dazzling the judges with colored diagrams on the blackboard. But in the end, he lost out on both.

The outcome was crushing, a personal failure and a failure in the eyes of his father; nothing could be worse. The ambition of fathers for sons is often greater than the ambition of sons alone. Adding to his misery was a bloody cough. It turned out to be tuberculosis brought on by unremitting malaria. He had reached a low point. Even when strong enough to climb from bed, he said, "This is only a reprieve. New attacks will come and then death." He thought of suicide, of climbing a mountain in the Pyrenees and hurling himself from the top. His career felt stagnant, his life lonely.

He could not shake the darkness. After months in the lab or confined to bed, he finally left both behind to walk in the forest among the oak and pine, along rivers and streams, beneath clear sky or sopping rain. There he rekindled his love of nature, snapping pictures or gliding pens and pencils or lumps of coal over tissue paper to capture the same oak or pine or field of flowers in different light or shade, and rejoicing at each picture as a unique scene. The gloom lifted, slowly, yet certainly.

With new enthusiasm, he returned to the lab with an eye on the microscope, escaping the big world for the small. There he found the magic of the stain, a new kind of tool for revealing or accentuating detail. Different chemicals highlighted different tissue or cells. One combination illuminated the cell wall, but not the nucleus; another mixture, the nucleus, not the mitochondria; and so on. By experimenting, he gained perspective at the microscopic level, not unlike the way a camera, by manipulating light and shade, could emphasize different aspects of nature. It gave him a new avenue of study, improved his skill with slides, and filled volumes with new drawings from the infinitely small world under the lens. His work intensified; his confidence grew.

In 1879, another position opened in Granada. Though advertised widely, friends said the slot had been promised to someone else. If professors favored the familiar over the learned, his only hope he thought was becoming familiar, even by losing again and again. To prepare, he studied the pathology of Ranvier, the natural history of Darwin, and the embryology of Haeckel.[4] Yet in the end, he finished second to the favored candidate. As consolation, Zaragosa named him the director of the university's anatomical museums. His spirits soared.

With a new salary, 125 pesetas per month ($25), and newfound poise, he courted Silveria Fañanas Garcia. "I was attracted no doubt," he said, "by the sweetness and gentleness of her features, the slender beauty of her figure, her great green eyes framed with long lashes, and the luxuriance of her fine hair." It was not the first he had seen her either. Years before in Ayerbe, she had been a petite, shy girl with pigtails. For reasons lost to history, though well known among rambunctious boys, Santiago had hit her with his sling shot; the rock, unlike cupid's arrow, would take longer to bear the fruit of love. All who knew the couple would say that "half of Cajal is his wife," and perhaps his only disagreement would have been that it was more than half. He loved her dearly.

Santiago felt good and whole, and for once so did Spain. King Alfonso had been recognized by Pope Pius IX, ending the Carlist Wars and sending Don Carlos fleeing for France. Although Alfonso's wife had tragically died of fever, he soon married Maria Christina of Austria, a beloved queen if there ever was one. In this new life of love and peace, Santiago tested a third time in 1883 for a professorship in Valencia. An independent panel of judges presided. By a unanimous vote, he won the position, and he moved his family to Valencia.

Three events propelled Santiago from a hardworking, brilliant, reclusive researcher of histology into a renowned scientist of neurology. The first came in 1885 when a cholera outbreak swept Spain. His alma mater, Zaragosa, asked him to investigate the disease and the claims of a new vaccine. It was a chance to help Spain. He threw himself into the opportunity. Confirming the findings of German biologist Robert Koch, Santiago's experiments showed the disease to be caused by the *comma bacillus*, but he found that the much hailed vaccine offered no protection from it.[5] For his brilliant thoroughness, the fathers of Zaragosa gave him a new microscope with more power than his antique. He accepted it with tearful gratitude.

Over the next two years, he put this fine gift to extraordinary use with his greatest publication to date: *Manual de histología normal y técnica micrografía* ("Manual of Normal Histology and Micrographic Technique"). It cataloged his own histological findings and confirmed or corrected findings of other scientists, especially from Germany and France. It ran 692 pages of small type including 303 drawings. The first edition, published in 1889, sold out immediately, as did the second, and soon scientists in foreign lands began speaking his name. Pictures transcended language. All who saw the book marveled at the countless hours and meticulous detail that went into its production.

This success convinced Santiago that he needed to reach foreign academia. As much as he loved Spain, the language of science still was German or French and increasingly English, not Spanish or Basque. He wanted to test himself against the best, as he had as a boy in Ayerbe and Zaragosa. Any articles he published from then on would be translated to French or German. He would have to step out of the cave and leave the quiet behind.

Santiago had gained a maturity in life and research. A new position opened in Barcelona that offered a higher salary and more equipment. With a fifth child now added to the family, he needed the financial boost. He had received lucrative invitations into the new field of bacteriology where Koch and Pasteur were thriving, but he stayed faithful to histology, the tissues of life, and his new interest, the human brain. He told his wife that he would never travel in a "luxurious carriage, but would always be enraptured from the eyepiece of the microscope, to the hum of the restless beehive which we all have within us." He accepted the professorship in Barcelona, packed the family, and settled among the Catalonians, that raucous bunch, to do some of his greatest work.

T WO THEORIES of the human nervous system, one dominant, one a weak rival, jousted for supremacy in the late 1880s. The reticular hypothesis, or network theory, from the German anatomist Joseph von Gerlach, held that nerve fibers from every muscle, skin cell, and sensory input were infinitely crossed and connected in a magnificent web or net within the gray matter of the brain. It was the dominant theory of the time and was defended most ardently by the Italian anatomist Camillo Golgi, who had devised a silver-staining technique to distinguish and study parts of it.

A competing theory, the free-ending hypothesis, from German embryologist Wilhelm His and Swiss psychiatrist Auguste Henri Foral, held that nerve fibers end freely in the brain but do not form a continuous web or network, rather branch like leaves on a tree. Unlike the network theory, which at least explained (without proof) how impulses reach the brain, the free-ending theory offered no explanation of how, if fibers were unconnected, impulses traveled from sensory input to the brain, or from the brain to muscles.

Neither theory offered much evidence to support its claims, although Golgi with microscope and stains had given the network theory some semblance of validity. Santiago, from his early investigations, felt different. He sided with His and Foral, saying, "The reticular hypothesis, by pretending to explain everything, explains absolutely nothing." His challenge now was turning instinct into thought, feeling into experimental proof.

A great scientist often has a propitious year, one that catapults him from a mediocre mind among millions to a rare achiever on a pedestal of distinction and honor and sets a framework for all his later work and the discoveries of so many others. Santiago's propitious year was 1888. In reviewing arguments for the network theory, he stumbled on Golgi's staining method—the *silver-stain*—which had yielded important findings early in Golgi's career until, mid-career, Gogli had abandoned the technique.

Santiago experimented with the silver-stain. He hadn't invented it, but he refined the technique: hardening nerve tissue in osmic-acid and potassium dichromate for several days, transferring it to a silver-nitrate solution for a day or two, dehydrating it with alcohol, clearing it with clove or bergamot oils, and washing and mounting it. Under the microscope, the nerve cells stood out in a silvery-black; hence, the name.

Golgi had accomplished the same on his own, but Santiago took the technique two steps further. Using birds and small mammals, he first applied the method to the whole nervous system—brain, spinal column, and tissue. He saw the panorama, not the snippets, revealing a pattern of connectivity and branches from which his artistic eye discerned logic and mapping, not a random network of fibers.

His second action, more profound than the first, was to use the silver-stain on the nervous system of embryos. When he observed the cross-section, it was unlike the nervous system of adults, as if someone had removed the curtain in the embryo to reveal a world of secrets. He asked himself, "Why this difference?" It was a good question.

The reason was due to a fatty substance called myelin. It protects nerve tendrils like insulation around a live wire, but the sheath is unformed in the brain tissue of embryos. When applied to adult tissue, the silver-stain cannot outline the myelin. It leaves the area blank. When applied to the brain tissue of embryos, the naked tendrils of the nerve brilliantly appear etched in silver-black. The result was a shocking discovery of an unseen world.

For months Santiago studied this new world culminating in his greatest achievement—the neuron[6] doctrine. It repudiated the network theory and gave proof for the free-ending hypothesis. The basic unit of brain tissue, he said, is not fibers, but the nerve cell, each independent of the next. The cell has a nucleus that feeds the cell and regulates inputs and outputs. It *receives* sensory inputs such as touch, smell, sight, taste, or sound from fibers called dendrites that branch at the ends like leaves, bringing impulses into the cell. The cell then *sends* signals by a different fiber called an axon. At the end of each axon, the fiber meets another cell at a point called a synapse where signals are carried by direct electrical connection, or more commonly, by chemical neurotransmitters, to dendrites of other cells. He called this the *law of transmission by contact.*

A cell links with other cells, he said, in a chain from the central nervous system—brain and spine—through a peripheral nervous system of skin, muscles, glands, and organs. Supporting and feeding the nerve cells, though distinct from them, are *glia* or glue cells that act as protective mothers: forming the myelin sheath around the axon, warding off pathogens, holding nerve cells in place, and guiding signals from point to point.[7]

It was a shocking body of work in a single year. He had revealed, for the first time, the human nervous system and dealt a crushing blow to the network theory. He would add detail and clarity to his neuron doctrine for the rest of his life. More importantly, he had ushered in a new framework within which other scientists, even to the present day, could investigate how the human brain sends and receives electrical and chemical signals, maintains muscular control, or suffers and recovers from degenerative neurological diseases.

He now wanted to tell the world. Unwilling to wait for German magazines, he created a journal of his own, *Revista trimestral de histología normal*

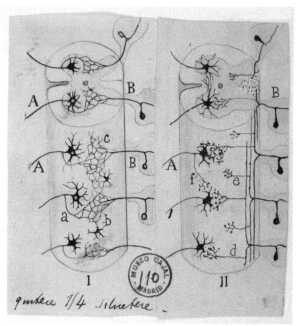

Santiago Ramón y Cajal captured in this drawing a comparison of reticular theory and neuron theory in the spinal cord. In the late 19th century, scientists believed the nervous system was a net or "reticulum," as shown in Part I above. The Italian anatomist Camillo Golgi subscribed to this theory; Ramón y Cajal disagreed. He believed the nervous system consisted of "neurons" contacting each other at precise points. These were called synapses. Ramón y Cajal's understanding is shown in Part II above. Ramón y Cajal used a staining technique that Golgi had developed to prove him wrong. The two, nonetheless, shared the Nobel Prize for Medicine in 1906. This drawing clearly set the two competing theories against one another. Both could not be true. Photo courtesy of Santiago Ramón y Cajal. Cajal Legacy. Instituto Cajal. Madrid

y patológica ("Trimonthly Review of Normal and Pathological Histology") in which he printed six articles in May 1888 and another six in August 1888. Each explained a different facet of his discoveries with intricate drawings by his own hand. He distributed the journal to foreign scientists and waited for a response.

Over several months, he received no feedback. Frustrated, he decided two things: first, to translate the articles into French and print them in German magazines; and second, to demonstrate his findings before scientists in his field. His first opportunity, at a meeting of the German Anatomical Society, became available the next year. He spoke in stilted French before scientists of 10 countries, displaying large hand-drawn sketches of the nerve cell with each fiber labeled in exquisite detail. All gave him polite attention, but no one expected anything of value from a man of Spain. In some cases, participants refused to hear any views that were contrary to the network theory.

But thankfully, Santiago earned disciples, even champions. One was a Swiss anatomist and physiologist named Albert von Kolliker, who edited a respected journal in Germany. After leaving Berlin, Santiago received a letter from this kind, older gentleman who gushed with praise: "You deserve a great deal of credit for having used the quick chrome-silver method on young animals and embryos. I shall not fail to make your admirable work widely known. I am glad that the first histologist Spain has produced is a man as distinguished as you, a man worthy of the nobility of science." Kolliker published Santiago's articles next to articles from reputable anatomists who confirmed his work. It was an auspicious moment—a real break.

In all his reminisces of 1888, Santiago would remember Kolliker as a close friend, "the glorious master," he would call him, and know that without his unselfish support, recognition might not have come; for just then, the world woke up to what Santiago had done.

SANTIAGO'S DISCOVERIES SPREAD QUICKLY. An early admirer, van Gehuchten, popularized his findings in Belgium, Switzerland, and France; Waldeyer and His throughout Germany; Retzius in Sweden; Lenhossek in Hungary; and Azoulay in France, who also became Santiago's French translator for later works. In his Paris classroom, Professor Mathias Duval set up wall charts of Santiago's drawings. He said during the lecture, "This time light comes to us from the south, from Spain the country of the sun."[8] This broad appeal steered science away from the network theory to the neuron doctrine. Recognition flowed in, but his indefatigable work ethic kept him from enjoying it.

By the next year, he put forward a new theory called dynamic polarization. It had puzzled him how an impulse traveled from nerve cell to nerve cell. Was it, as put by the network theory, traveling in all directions all the time, or was there orderliness? He believed the latter. By studying the embryo, he mapped the orderly development of a nerve cell. It first grew its axon, then produced its dendrites. Impulses moved in one direction from dendrites to the cell and then to the axon which carried the impulses to dendrites of other cells. The process was orderly and confirmable. He compiled findings into a book, translated it to French and German, and sold out two editions in two months.

For five years, he had done his best work at Barcelona, so much so that in April 1892 the educational fathers of Madrid offered him a full professorship of histology and pathology. With six children now and a long outline of expensive experiments, he accepted the generous offer and moved his family to the nation's capital. On the way, he visited his ailing parents in Zaragosa, his father especially, whose approval he had long sought. As proud as his father was, Santiago still felt, by a warped chemistry peculiar to fathers and sons, a desperate need to achieve more.

So at age 40, his work continued at fevered pace in Madrid. Much appealed to him. He moved from the cerebellum to the retina to the cerebrum to the hippocampus, the last most of all because the density of fibers formed an artistic beauty that appealed to his eye and coloring pens. He confirmed that the perception and memory of odors resided in the hippocampus. By the density of fibers, he concluded that smell was our most powerful sensory input, triggering our most vivid memories. His work revealed too that practicing a skill— smelling, playing violin, strategizing in chess—dug a kind of cerebral trench from repeated use of the same neural pathways. It explained how practice made perfect, muscles gained memory, and a smell triggered a powerful memory.

Finally, in 1892, he asked an important question: What force compelled fibers to grow relentlessly in pursuit of other nerve tissue? Charting cells from the embryo to adulthood, he showed that they secreted chemicals with an affinity for nerve tissue. The chemicals were activated at birth or in response to a damaged cell. He called it his neurotropic theory. In future years, it became the basis for understanding and repairing damaged nerves, degenerative brain injuries, and neurological disorders.

These and other findings sprang from his sanctuary, the laboratory, but the world now demanded his time. In 1894, he received an invitation to give the prestigious Croonian Lecture before the Royal Society of London whose past members included Isaac Newton, Charles Darwin, and Benjamin Franklin. Santiago wanted to turn down the honor, believing himself unworthy to be counted among the scientific greats. It was his wife who convinced him to go. Unable to speak English, he prepared a lecture in French.

Sir Charles Sherrington, a member of the Society, invited him to stay in his London home. On the first night of dinner, white bait was served, a small fish eaten whole. With knife and fork, Santiago dissected the specimen, removing spinal column and bones with surgical precision and explaining each tiny segment. The next morning when he left his room, he locked the door behind him. Using her own key, the maid entered to change his linens and found a full laboratory of beakers, slides, and microscope. His work never ceased. Over two weeks, Sherrington got to know him. He wrote, "His science was first and foremost an offering to Spain, a spiritual motive which added to the privilege of knowing the man."

After his lecture on March 8, 1894, draped in velvet cloth and marching in to Beethoven, Santiago received an honorary doctorate from Cambridge. It embarrassed him. Later that evening, at the Spanish embassy, the ambassador raised a glass in toast. "In all my travels about the world," said the ambassador, "there have been three occasions when I have been deeply impressed: on viewing Niagara, on visiting the Coliseum at Rome, and on listening to Cajal's speech before the Royal Society." By all accounts, Santiago should have been thrilled by the glowing honors, but melancholy enveloped him. Before he left Sherrington, he said, "The grey matter grows well under grey skies," a reference to all the wonder he had seen in London among scientific men, and how little existed in Spain.

More honors came soon after. He was elected to the royal academies of Vienna, Rome, and Lisbon; gave a lecture at the International Medical Congress in Rome; and finally, in 1897, joined the Royal Academy of Medicine in Madrid. Ironically, his own country recognized his scientific achievements last. Still he harbored great hope that his work had not been in vain, that perhaps he, a humble man of stubborn will, had shifted public perception about the need for more scientific inquiry in Spain.

The hope was short-lived. In 1898, his beloved country embroiled itself in the Spanish-American War. What he said of it could have applied to science: "A country's misfortune lies not so much in its weakness as in the ignorance of its weakness on the part of those whose duty it is to know." After a few lopsided battles, the United States routed Spain. A treaty was drafted and signed in Paris in which Spain granted Cuban independence and turned over Guam, Puerto Rico, and the Philippines to the United States for $20 million. The Spanish empire, once spanning multiple continents, had been relegated to narrow borders not seen since the 15th century. Santiago felt humiliated for his country.

As DISRUPTIVE as the war had been, Santiago's fame abroad had not subsided. Not a year after the peace treaty, he received an invitation from Clark University in Massachusetts to give three lectures. The letter included a check for $600, a remarkable sum for a man earning $800 annually. Initially, he had resisted, despite the money, but the minister of education encouraged him, and his wife pushed him to accept.

He went with her to New York City where the temperatures hit 113 degrees. Santiago recalled little from the three lectures, though much from the United

States where reporters hounded him on matters far beyond his field. On war with Cuba: "It was like talking of the halter in the house of the hanged!" On women's suffrage: "In Spain, we are so backward that our women are still content to be feminine and not feminist." If nothing else, he had a careful diplomatic flare. Husband and wife toured the Statue of Liberty, Brooklyn Bridge, Fifth Avenue, St. Patrick's Cathedral, and Central Park. So much wealth, so much opportunity, he commented.

Following his trip, more awards flooded in. He received the Moscow Prize in Paris (1900), the Helmholtz Medal in Berlin (1905), and finally the Nobel Prize in Stockholm (1906). His father had died in 1904, never seeing his son in Sweden, but he had seen the publication of Santiago's magnum opus, *El sistema nervioso del hombre y de los vertibrados* ("The Nervous System of Man and of the Other Vertebrates"), a work of three volumes, 1,800 pages of text, and 887 original illustrations. It became an instant classic, still used today. "But before and beyond everything else," said Santiago, "I desired my book to be—pardon the presumption—the trophy laid at the feet of the languishing science of Spain and the offering of fervent love rendered by a Spaniard to his despised country." In that aspiration, one sensed that he still coveted the esteem of his father.

Among his awards—66 honorary degrees, 20 prizes from abroad, and 26 distinctions in Spain—it was still hard to feel Santiago's joy. He was so much a part of Spain that no matter his achievements, he suffered when Spain suffered. Nothing seemed to get better either. After the tragedy in Cuba, Alfonso XIII assumed the throne in 1902 on his 16th birthday and then married Princess Victoria-Eugenie of England in 1906. Then Spain launched another war with Morocco, sparking chaotic revolts and strikes between liberals and conservatives, clerics and non-clerics, northern industrialists and southern farmers. Multiple prime ministers passed in and out of office by resignation or assassination. Greatly saddened, Santiago built a cottage away from the political raucous of Madrid in the quiet community of Amanial. It was lined with flowers, gardens, grapevines, and orchards, much like Ayerbe or Zaragosa from his boyhood.

With the move to the country, a noticeable change came over him, as if finally he had emerged from the cave of his youth. "Boldness tries its strength and conquers or is conquered," he wrote, "but excessive modesty avoids the battle and condemns itself to shameful inaction." He wanted to fight for the soul of Spain. He formed the Junta para Ampliación de Estudios ("Committee for Widening the Scope of Education") to advance an agenda that he had long believed in, but only now had courage to support. It advocated for engaging foreign professors, sending students to conferences to interact with colleagues, establishing an industrial college for people with skills in commerce, building the health and character of students as in England and America, and creating an institute with equipment and facilities second to none.

The committee was a full-time job, but he still kept pace with research and teaching. Between the Nobel Prize and 1914, he maintained a second journal devoted to his own work and the work of students, and he wrote most of his lengthy, detailed autobiography. He also completed a landmark study on the degeneration and regeneration of neurons, deciphering why nerves failed and how they might be reborn. Most of all, however, he settled into being *el maestro*, the man whom all students revered or whose class they clambered to attend. He wore a flowing black cape, tied at the neck like a superhero. To be near him was to be in the presence of greatness in a country where greatness was in short supply.

Yet for each step forward, his country or world events pushed him back. In World War I, Spain remained neutral, but the great conflagration cut Santiago off from scientists in Germany, France, England, Italy, and the United States. He felt alone. The cost of equipment and chemicals tripled, hampering his work, and the anxieties of war took a toll on his health. He suffered a bout of flu that activated his tuberculosis, severe arthritis, and heart palpitations. He was forced to write from bed. When the war ended, most of his friends and colleagues in Germany and France had died.

At age 70, after 30 years at the University of Madrid, he retired in 1922 to fanfare and sadness. The Spanish Parliament appropriated funds for a biological research center in his name that would be dedicated within 10 years.

From his quiet cottage in Amaniel, he worried that his contributions to Spain might unravel. Dark forces were brewing across Europe: Mussolini in Italy, Primo in Spain, Hitler in Germany. Depression struck in 1929 leading to national revolts first among the Basque, then the Catalonians, until finally Spain's Second Republic emerged in 1931. Santiago watched Spain splinter and the world inch ever closer to another war worse than the last. Little progress emerged from students or universities, and his biological center was put on hold. The world seemed to collapse around him. His beloved wife of over 50 years died, leaving him still more isolated.

To avoid depression, he visited Café Suizo, an old haunt from university days. He met students who held him in the highest esteem, Santiago the Wise, they called him, thinner now with white beard and sadder eyes. He discussed their work, offering guidance and encouragement, and translated their papers to French. Being a teacher was one of his highest goods, second only to work, saving him from even deeper loneliness. In a book to young researchers, he said, "The teacher must not spend his declining years in a sad solitude, but must approach his end surrounded by a throng of young pupils capable of understanding what he has done and of making it fruitful and lasting."⁹

He did exactly that for as long as his small, weakened body would let him. Then at 11:00 in the morning on October 17, 1934, at his quiet cottage in Amaniel, surrounded by manuscripts and a microscope, Santiago Ramón y Cajal died in his bed. He had been in full command of his intellect, writing into the night only hours earlier. His imminent death had not scared him. He viewed it as a rational byproduct of nature, as he had all his scientific work. In his last book, *El mundo visto a los ochenta años* ("The World as Seen at Eighty"), published posthumously, he wrote, "When facts are faced squarely, we must admit that it is not so much the thought of our own death that grieves us as the realization that by it we are snatched from the bosom of humanity and thus robbed forever of the hope of seeing the unfolding of the heroic struggle constantly being waged between the mind of man and the blind energy of natural forces."

The sentiment was touching. It conjured the heroic struggle of a thoughtful man who imparted wisdom and hope to his students. Sitting among them, he had once said, "I am convinced that in those fields of study that require ingenuity, patience, and perseverance, the Spaniards will show themselves to be the equal of the men of the North." But he was an artist and a realist, a man who saw beauty in the world, but clarity and truth too in the small things under the microscope. In that same talk with students, he had said, "Let us love our country even if it is only for her misfortunes."

That, he sadly did. It was the only thing he could do.

Notes

1. In Spain, a person often takes the surname of his father and mother. The first, "Ramon," comes from the father; the second, "Cajal," from the mother. Both are of equal importance. Rather than decide which to use, the subject's first name, Santiago, is used throughout.

2. Spaniards faced the greatest army—mosquitoes—which killed with stealth, attacked en masse, and refortified daily. Not until August 1897, 25 years after Santiago's experience in Cuba, would a doctor named Sir Ronald Ross discover the malaria parasite inside a mosquito that four days before had fed on the blood of a malaria patient in India. It was a landmark moment in tropical medicine that would forevermore change our understanding of the transmission of disease and expand our methods for treating and fighting parasitic illnesses.

3. Histology is the study of the minute structures and functions of tissues and organs.

4. A German anatomist named Rudolf Virchow discovered the myelin sheath in 1854. Santiago studied the work of Louis-Antoine Ranvier who discovered the nodes

or gaps in the myelin sheath that became critical for his staining technique and his advances in neurology. Santiago also studied the works of Charles Darwin, especially his seminal work *Origin of Species*, as a basis for natural selection. Then he turned to Ernest Heinrich Philipp August Haeckel, a German biologist, naturalist, and physician who described and named thousands of new species and championed Darwin's theories. Haeckel's work often included drawings, which might explain why the work so appealed to him, especially the sketches of species in embryo. Not surprising, Santiago's great breakthroughs in neurology would be influenced significantly by the work of these scientists.

5. His experiments confirmed, moreover, that dead *comma bacillus* induced the production of antibodies in humans. Two American scientists—D. E. Salmon and Theobald Smith—are widely credited with making this finding in 1886, but Santiago Ramón y Cajal made the discovery a year earlier. Alas, no one at the time read Spanish reports, and no German or French journal ever received the discovery in a finished paper. Still, Santiago deserves some credit for his findings.

6. The term *neuron* was coined by the German scientist, Wilhelm Waldeyer, to describe Santiago's full blueprint of a nerve cell including dendrites, axon, nucleus, and component parts. It is used here to relate Santiago's neuron doctrine, which is how the world refers to it.

7. Since Santiago's discoveries in 1888, other scientists have added significantly to our understanding of the human nervous system. This description does not include those findings or detail, rather the findings of Santiago at the time. Still, his findings have served as the framework and building blocks for the work of later scientists.

8. Arthur van Gehucheten (1861–1915), professor of anatomy at Louvain. Wilhelm von Waldeyer (1836–1921), German anatomist. Magnus Gustav Retzius (1842–1919), Swedish histologist. Michael Lenhossek (1867–1937), Hungarian anatomist. Leon Azoulay (1862–1932), French anatomist and translator. Mathias Duval (1844–1915), French anatomist.

9. *Reglas y consejos sobre la investigación biológica* ("Rules and Counsels on Biological Research").

Cristóbal Balenciaga

The King of Haute Couture

IVE KINGS, four queens, 46 princes and princesses, hundreds of aristocracy—not since Elizabeth II's coronation had so many royals congregated.

And now they waited.

It was December 15, 1960, in chilly Brussels. All of Belgium, and much of the world, had waited a year for this most highly anticipated and celebrated wedding.

Outside the royal palace, a procession of long black cars, one with a glass hood, waited with motors running for the new bride and groom. Rows of white horses four abreast in splendid finery waited to lead the cars to the Catholic Church of St. Gudule. Bundled in coats and scarves, waving and smiling and cheering, multitudes of happy people waited 30 deep on both sides of the street in frigid winter air. None wanted to lose his coveted spot as a witness to history. Over 150 million around the world waited at home for their first glimpse of the royal couple on black-and-white televisions.

Inside the throne room, crystal chandeliers twinkled off the marble, bronze, and gold. Kings and princes and imperial old men waited at stiff attention. They darted their haughty eyes from man to man, measuring each brilliant baldric and chest of medals. Hooked on their husbands' arms, queens and princesses and majestic ladies—all champions of grandeur—waited in regal gowns and gloves. All had been trained in the best finishing schools of Europe. Legal officials of Belgium's highest courts waited to register the royal couple as husband and wife. A few clergy in pontifical garb waited to escort the legally wed to the church where God Himself waited to bond them in eternal bliss.

From one of his first collections, an editor described this satin dress as a "thick Spanish black, almost velvety, a night without stars, which makes the ordinary black seem almost gray." Photo courtesy of the Balenciaga Museum in Getaria, Spain.

Yes, everyone waited in this swirl of pomp and radiance—both inside and out—kings, queens, judges, clergy, commoners, and horses—all equally steeped in great anticipation.

Then the waiting ended.

King Baudouin entered the throne room first. He was a plain man with short black hair and thin-rimmed glasses. He wore a brown suit crossed with a red sash, yellow epaulettes, and military insignia at the collar. Around his neck was the Order of Isabella the Catholic, a large cross on an elaborate chain that hung to his chest. It had been conferred nine days earlier by Spain to honor this newly adopted son of Belgium. He had a noble bearing with head high, chest out, shoulders back. He was a king, stood like a king, walked like a king, and all royal and aristocratic eyes were fixed on him.

Then suddenly all eyes shifted. For once a king in his own land failed to be the most exalted in the room. In came the bride. She did not step, she floated—Fabiola de Mora y Aragón. She was a nurse by profession who hailed from one of Spain's most prominent families. Her hair, cut in a bob and curled at the ends, her long neck, alabaster face, red lips, and broad smile beamed with good health and vivacity. But the eyes in the room did not fixate on her face no matter how composed and pleasant. It was the dress—all about the dress!

Under the crystal chandeliers, the dress glowed in ivory satin. It dropped at the waist to outline her petite figure with a belt of white ermine fur and a slight pouf to the skirt. Around the neckline more ermine draped gently off the back of her shoulders along the edges of a 22-foot train carried by four attendants. The dress had no embroidered pearls or jewels or antique lace customary for royal brides. It was at once plain, modern, elegant, and timeless. Her veil was silk tulle held in place by an Art Deco diamond tiara that had been a gift from the Belgian people to the king's mother on her wedding day in 1926. The ensemble was finished with drop pearl earrings, opera length silk gloves, and a spray of white flowers.

As she glided up the aisle with the king on her arm, himself now a mere accessory, all the men in baldrics and medals and all the finely finished ladies in gowns and gloves dissolved into a nondescript, inconsequential mass of gray. Had it been night, she would have shamed the moon. The dress was, oh so Fabiola!—a stunning vision—a Balenciaga—simply the best of haute couture.

A BOY HOPPED BETWEEN gray doorways to spy on a woman. She sashayed with grace and bearing from her home on the hill, across Getaria's cobblestone through shadowed alleys near the Gothic church of San Salvador. She passed the wharf where fishermen brought in a catch, the breeze sprayed the

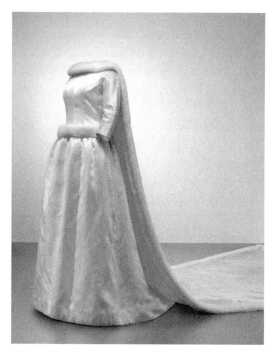

The wedding dress made by Balenciaga and worn by Fabiola de Mora y Aragón on December 15, 1960, during her marriage to King Baudouin I of Belgium. The dress is of ivory satin with a belt and neckline of ermine fur that drapes gently off the back of the shoulders and along the edges of a 22-foot train that four attendants carried during the ceremony. Photo courtesy of the Balenciaga Museum in Getaria, Spain.

sea, and the sun cut the dark of the village. She was a middle-aged woman, fully in command, every step purposeful. Her suit, touching the ankle, was silk and tasteful, a Drécoll or Redfern or Paul Poiret, colored robin-chest or darker rouge or playful purple, not at all like the town's stony gloom.

The boy with dark hair and dark eyes and wily smile did not miss any of her steps, how she moved or turned, how she bent or swayed her arms, or how the wet breeze stuck the silk to her old skin, bunching or creasing along the contours of her body. He was about 12, and watched from the comfort of shadows until courageously he came forward one day to speak with her.

"I want to make you a suit," he said.

"Why do you say this?" asked the old woman.

"Because I think I can," he replied.

The boy was Cristóbal Balenciaga, the woman the Marquesa de Casa Tor-res, a high-born matron with taste and fashion sense and the largest collection of dresses in Getaria, perhaps all of Northern Spain. The Marquesa sent fabric to the boy, and a week later, he returned a dress comparable to any in her closet. She wore it proudly. From then on, she took an interest in this quiet boy from the shadows.

The boy's mother, Martina Eizaguierre, had dressed the Marquesa since 1894, a year before Balenciaga's birth. From a modest home near the San Salva-dor church, she trudged up the hill to the Marquesa's stately summer home to kneel at a hem, narrow a waist, pouf a sleeve, or cut a collar, all to preserve the well-heeled lady as the showpiece and grand dame of haute couture in this small fishing village.

In the Marquesa's regal salon, the boy watched and learned. He thumbed fashion magazines or admired Goya and Velásquez on the walls, felt the texture of swatches, or ran fingers over elegant London furniture and Parisian drapes. For his mother, he held the fabric, needles, and thread, learning good cuts from bad, the fresh from the so-last-season, and what to hide or highlight. His play-ground dripped with Spanish style and aristocratic snootiness.

Whether natural or acquired, he had a knack for the trade. Early on he dressed the cat in a necklace and the dog in a coat that hugged its four legs, an early sign perhaps of his great love of sleeves. He cut and stitched costumes for his older siblings, a sister María Augustina and a brother Juan Martín,[1] who became business associates later in his career.

His father had little direct influence, at least none recorded. As a seafaring man, he skippered royalty into San Sebastián for summer holidays, reinforc-ing Cristóbal's world of high society, and even served a short stint as mayor of Getaria. But mostly as a fisherman, he spent considerable time at sea until his death of a heart attack in 1906. Cristóbal was 11 years old.

With the family needing money, Cristóbal left grammar school to appren-tice a year later with a tailor in San Sebastián. The Marquesa had arranged it. He then worked in a tonier shop called New England and finally in a branch of the Grand Magasins du Louvre department store. It was there that the Mar-quesa refreshed her wardrobe every year in spring and winter. Others did too, María Cristina, the dowager queen, in particular.

The boy's interaction with royalty might have gained him patronage, but he shyly honed his craft, his *métier* as he called it, using his hands, cutting the fabric, draping the silk, bunching or folding it, seeing how aristocratic ladies lit up or cringed after contorting before a mirror and admiring waist, breasts, and buttocks. Here at age 17, he cut and sewed his first public outfit, a black suit of silk with ivory lace jabot, a wedding gift for his cousin. His aptitude drew more from instinct than experience. No formal education could have developed this *métier* of turning cloth into a second skin. The work summoned his gifts and awakened his genius.

He was sent by the Marquesa to Bordeaux to study French, the language of fashion, though his guttural Basque and lazy Spanish thwarted any hope of commanding the soft beauty and allure of the Parisian tongue. He learned enough to remind everyone later that a true Frenchman he was not, only an import. Armed with a few mangled French phrases, he went to Paris at age 18 as a *vendeur*[2] for the Grand Magasins du Louvre, to buy the latest gowns. He had an eye for all things original, elegant, and fresh.

These public trips heightened an internal struggle. Into early adulthood his renown for deep privacy, even reclusiveness, had begun. He avoided restaurants, drinking clubs, the press, or repartee with other *vendeurs* at shows, absorbing with his eyes, making the sale, and returning to Spain. Yet he knew the value of being at the heart of fashion, seeing Poiret's flowing pantaloons, Doucet's pastels, Fortuny's pleating and dyeing, Vionnet's bias cut. During these trips, he would witness the birth of Art Deco and feel the subtle rise of the skirt from ankle to mid-calf to knee as women went to work in factories to supply an imminent world war. Fashion was the world's pulse, Paris the main artery, and French couture the blood of culture.

Yet for all his reclusive tendencies, he had a quiet arrogance that said he could exceed all of these designers whom he witnessed in France. In the war throes of 1918, he opened a salon in San Sebastián, calling it C. Balenciaga, with his older brother and sister financing much of the deal. With Spain neutral during World War I, his boutique shop flourished as commerce flooded industrial Bilbao and fashion houses from Paris showcased spring and winter collections in a few safe hotels in San Sebastián. He opened branches in Madrid and Barcelona with his sister María Augustina, niece Tina, and nephew José operating them.

He drew the high born as clients. First on the list was his old aristocratic friend the Marquesa who, quite feeble now, stooped in chic chiffon with a polished cane. Still at her age, she attracted others—the Queen Ena, Infanta Isabel Alfonsa, and Queen Marie Christina. Of all his patrons, royal and near-royal, Balenciaga owed most to the Marquesa who treated him very much like her own son. Long after she had died, he would return the generosity in 1960 by designing, cutting, and sewing a stunning ivory satin and ermine wedding dress for her great granddaughter. It was none other than Fabiola de Mora y Aragón.

Balenciaga met a special love at this time too: Vladio Zawrorowski d'Attainville, a Polish-French architect and decorator who hailed from a wealthy family in Paris. His hair shined like obsidian and his clothes were styled for public attention. Where Balenciaga was private, Vladio was gregarious with contacts across Spain and France, and where Balenciaga cocooned himself in the serious, Vladio preferred the playful. He designed hats to accompany Balenciaga's creations, the two working and living together for over 20 years, gaining reputations for well-heeled style, simple yet chic.

As much as royalty was the most prestigious and sought-after clientele with insatiable desires and bottomless purses, it cut both ways. In April 1931, Spain declared a second republic, deposing the royal family of King Alfonso XIII, which eroded much of Balenciaga's customer base and led to his bankruptcy.

With Vladio's help, he reopened under the company name Eisa, a rework of his mother's maiden name,[3] rekindling fashion lines for evening entertainment and offering a new wardrobe for sun-loving beachgoers. He retained a few noble ladies too, one especially who wore his black faille gown with a bias-cut. Her name was Carmen Polo, and she was the wife of Francisco Franco.

None of the dresses of the time showed his best work. Not that they were clumsy, but they lacked the exquisite creativity of collections that he would produce in the 1950s and 1960s. With practice the novice would disappear, though practice proved difficult. Fearing dark forces on the horizon, the well-to-do hoarded their assets with only pittance allowed for high fashion.

Things took a turn for the worse when, in July 1936, Spain plunged into civil war. When Franco bombed Madrid and Barcelona, Balenciaga kept his shops open, albeit with little business to show for it. Then as retribution against a recalcitrant Basque province, Franco bombed San Sebastián from air and sea, burning buildings, killing innocents, setting Nationalists against Republicans in the streets where blood flowed and the stench of death wafted into hotels and shops. Tourism plummeted, and so too the visits of *vendeurs* from London and Paris who no longer stopped in Balenciaga's shops for his spring and winter collections.

Gripped with fear, thousands fled the chaos by September 1936. With his neighbors, Nicolás and Virgilia Bizcarrondo, who had relatives in France, and his wealthy lover Vladio, who had contacts everywhere, Balenciaga packed his bags for Paris where the *crème de la crème* of haute couture scraped and clawed with finesse and elegance to dress the high born of the world.

"A GREAT LIGHT BURST ON THE FASHION WORLD," said Carmel Snow, the prominent editor of *Harper's Bazaar.* "His very individual style was too new, too different, to be widely appreciated on its first appearance, but I knew that this designer would revolutionize fashion." It was Balenciaga's debut collection out of Paris in winter 1937, a line of little black dresses, austere yet elegant, a "thick Spanish black, almost velvety, a night without stars, which makes the ordinary black seem almost gray."

The creations paralleled the times. That same year Franco had firebombed Gernika and fortified positions in Madrid, Barcelona, and San Sebastián. The Germans were mobilizing and the Italians too. The League of Nations had failed. War lay ready to pounce like a demonic lion, and all in Europe felt the menace in their bones as the old order gasped for breath. The world yearned for something, anything fresh and new.

After his first show, Balenciaga gained admirers. His dresses appeared in *Vogue, Harper's Bazaar,* and *L'officiel* in photos and articles of equal size and frequency as more established fashion houses such as Dior and Chanel. His clientele expanded to include the Duchess of Windsor, Mrs. Rodman de Heeren, Helena Rubinstein, Clare Booth Luce, and the Honorable Daisy Fellowes.[4] If designers made the wardrobe, these women made the designers. By simply wearing the dresses, they set the trends, screaming this-is-in, serving as living, breathing, aristocratic marketers of Balenciaga's high fashion. To be seen in less was *déclassé*. His gowns at once reflected the times and the fresh and new that everyone craved. By 1940, *Harper's Bazaar* declared that "almost every woman, directly or indirectly, has worn a Balenciaga."

Everything felt different about this man, including his new salon. With 100,000 francs from Vladio and the Bizcarrondos, he opened a shop on the fourth floor of an 1887 apartment building at 10 Avenue Georges V next to the Chicago-born couturier, Main Bocher, and down the street from Madeleine Vionnet, the queen of style, who invented the bias cut, fashion's equivalent of fire from Olympus. Where other shops bustled with models and ateliers, his stayed quiet as a cathedral with austere white walls, baroque scrolled moldings, and open spaces clear of rabble. Any visitors instinctively whispered. His street-facing windows showcased gloves, the best in Paris, and scarves designed by Sache. Inside fanned the sweet fragrances of Le Dix and Quadrille.

The spartan salon reinforced his reclusive nature and drew a cult following. Vladio interacted with the public, spoke of the dresses, and only alluded to the master, Balenciaga, as a monk in a cave, who cut and sewed the fresh and new with his own hands. It added mystery and secrecy. He literally became the man behind the curtain. He hung a drape in the salon with a peephole so he could spy on visitors, ateliers, and models without ever being in their company. If he wanted someone, he summoned her behind the curtain as all others gasped at the lucky soul who ventured into the usually forbidden inner sanctum. If the salon was a cathedral, Balenciaga was the high priest, secluded and off limits. Enamored by the intrigue, women were irresistibly drawn to the allure of his gowns like the devout to a cross.

He hired a brilliant woman, Florette Chalot, as his *vendeuse*, a 25-year-old, chestnut-haired wonder who brought her own book of clients. "I was recommended by a friend in the fabric business," she said. "I arrive, I find a very handsome and charming man who speaks French rather badly. He is in a big bare space which later became two workrooms, seated on a stool in front of a trestle table filled with swatches of fabric. He said, 'I am sorry I cannot offer you a chair because this stool and table is all there is.' He didn't even have any ateliers then." He assigned Florette two black dresses from the previous season and gave her 10 percent commission on all sales, though he reduced it to 5 percent after the first collection. She was so good, she made more than him. Her earnings accounted for half of Balenciaga's house.

Through Vladio's relations and Florette's salesmanship, Balenciaga stood at the top of the heap with Dior, Chanel, and Vionnet when the Germans marched into Paris on June 14, 1940. "Hitler wanted to transfer the French couture to Berlin," said Balenciaga. "He sent six enormous Germans to see me—much taller than I—to talk about it. I said that he might just as well take all the bulls to Berlin and try and train the bullfighters there." It was a fool's errand tantamount to relocating the Alps to Bonn, for haute couture was organically French and nontransferable.

Yet the Germans still imposed their will. The number of houses was limited to 30, and fabric consumption was cut by 50 percent. Each show was limited to 100 models, one fully clothed in lace and at least 10 percent clothed in elaborate embroidery. These last two mandates kept 97 percent of the couture workforce employed. To buy a dress, a woman needed a couture card that cost 200 francs and two kilos of fabric. "So many houses were closed and Balenciaga was much in demand," said Florette.

Indeed, if fashion suffered during the war, he suffered less than most. He had what all other couturiers lacked—Spanish citizenship. He could travel to neutral Spain, visit his couture houses in Barcelona, Madrid, and San Sebastian, and return to Paris with yards of fabric. It was not as good as prewar material, but better than anything in Paris at the time. He also gained publicity from an international press desperate for fashion news. *Vogue* had closed in Paris, but opened in Madrid where he often became the centerpiece of wartime coverage. In *Harper's Bazaar*, a massive spread on his creations ran in 1944 under the banner title, "Extravagance in Madrid." These gray years let him develop his craft, experiment, weave wartime austerity into elegance, give purpose to every shred of fabric like single words in poetry, and use embroidery and trim to augment not overpower style.

When the Allies marched down the Champs-Élysées to the Arc de Triomphe, liberating France on August 25, 1944, Balenciaga dined at his apartment on Avenue Marceau with Vladio, the Bizcarrondos, and the couturier Pierre Balmain.[5] Amid regal 16th-century furniture under white marble ceilings, they drank wine and listened to bells chiming in the city as the *Marsellaise* was sung from every quarter. It was the first time that that enchanting national anthem had been played in nearly five years.

A few months later, Balenciaga was the first to launch a new show. A giddy editor at *Vogue* said there was "a desire to applaud after each dress. One can imagine the joy of a Manet or a Whistler before such elegance." By the close of this disastrous war, the high priest behind the curtain was now a fashion god.

B liss it was to be alive, but to be young was very heaven. Wordsworth had best described optimism a century earlier. All the austerity and privation—all the limits on fabric and models and couture houses, all the hate and fear and angst, all of it!—had faded just as enthusiasm and energy, hope and new possibilities had become ascendant. Though Balenciaga had been first out of the gate with a collection of new designs, he was not alone in capturing the public imagination.

Under German occupation, the pendulum had swung so far to efficiency and minimalism that Christian Dior was determined to swing it the other way. On February 12, 1947, he introduced his Carolle line, named for petals on a flower. Wide at the base, the skirts used twenty meters of fabric instead of three, the waist pinched, and the bust perked. The taffeta crinkled and rattled with every step. The ball gown weighed 60 pounds with fasteners and apparatus to squeeze the waist. The line was elegant, big, and full, the excess serving as counterpoint to the strictures imposed by the former German overlords.

The fashion magazines gave Dior's collection a name worthy of its impact—the New Look. Many exalted it as a kind of declaration of freedom, while others denounced it as wasteful, excessive, even immoral in the face of so many in postwar Europe still languishing in stark poverty, homelessness, and starvation. But Dior thought only of happiness, and why not? His country had outlasted the Germans. Old and young rejoiced as a new world order took form under a United Nations, the Marshall Plan, NATO, and economic opportunity. The New Look was a New Life. Dior defended it when he said, "The prime need of fashion is to please and attract," and this New Look certainly did both.

Balenciaga said little about Dior's line, though by a subtle headshake or a crumpled brow, he had cataloged it in his mind's eye under a heading of vulgarity. He saw Dior as a great decorator, not inventor; not the automobile designer, but the one who adds the spinning rims, leather seats, and sunroof. While Balenciaga was quiet and private, inhabiting a cubbyhole behind a curtain, never giving an interview, Dior courted the press and sought the limelight. He commercialized his works, once putting his name to a tie that he had not seen, for example, while Balenciaga cut and puffed a sleeve repeatedly to arrive finally, painfully, at the right look. Years earlier, he had conceived Dior's collection of narrow waists, rounded shoulders, and broader skirts, but he hadn't promoted a circus around it or reveled in self-aggrandizement. If Balenciaga paralleled the simple elegance and artistry of an Emily Dickinson, Dior offered the barbaric yawp of a Walt Whitman.

Yet Dior knew his place in the fashion pecking order. He once commented, "If only I were Balenciaga." Among the great couturiers of the day, there was a sense that each played in an orchestra, each made beautiful music, all memorable if not appealing to everyone, but Balenciaga rose above the rest as the conductor—the original, the architect, the unique—who fused artistry with functional elegance. Indeed, Dior would call him "The Master of us all." If Dior's style insulted his sensibilities, it nonetheless helped Balenciaga realize that the constraints of the past had been lifted, that daring would be rewarded by a public that thirsted to break with the old and usher in the new.

He focused on the dress making the woman, not the other way round. He selected every model—no one stunning, no one ugly—though he preferred ugly over pretty in a pinch. His favorite model, Colette, was a slender creature with a low waist, long neck, and curved back. She was Balenciaga's perfect canvas, his designs curving and bending around her shapely torso—the padded hips, the set back neckline, a semi-fitted front, and the bloused back. Colette modeled a look that aging women would embrace for decades. He taught Colette to attack the catwalk with long strides, pelvic thrusts, and perky breasts. It was the swagger of the aristocrat, and she mastered it with the first step. Models thereafter aped the method.

And that was how it always was. Balenciaga never copied. To do so would have been crude and offensive. That doesn't mean, however, that he went out of his way to do the opposite, which in itself imparted too much influence on the original. What he did do was introduce a new concept to fashion with his first barrel line. Rather than hug the body like a sausage skin, his new silhouette encased the body like an hourglass, removing the waist, broadening the shoulders, and narrowing the hem. Colette modeled the barrel silhouette, Vladio hyped it with fashion magazines, and Florette sold it to wealthy women and department stores. It was a thoroughly modern shape that he and other couturiers would continue to work with and modify over the next two decades.

Sadly, the silhouette was hardly a few months old when Vladio died during a trip to Spain. He was 49 years old. The news devastated Balenciaga: his longtime lover, best friend, and business partner was gone. He receded into a shell of darkness and depression. Vladio had been the light and hope in the relationship, which left only gray wool over the whole house, the staff, the models, the work itself. "If Vladio had lived, the house wouldn't have been so serious, it wouldn't have had that weight," said Florette. "There was no one to lighten it up. Monsieur Bizcarrondo wasn't capable of chatting to clients, I told him he should show himself more, but he wouldn't. Nor would his wife."

So much of the business had depended on Vladio's interactions with clients and models that the whole enterprise felt rudderless. In spring 1949, Balenciaga unveiled a new line that did not build on the silhouette concept. It was hideous by most accounts. "It was a collection of mourning, all black, sad beyond belief," said Florette. "We thought if that's the way it's going to be there's no point in going on." He fell so deeply into despair that he considered entering a monastery in Sully-sur-Loire. "It would have been a catastrophe," said Florette. She saw the impact already in slow sales.

It fell to the Bizcarrondos, Balenciaga's business partners, to salvage the operation. They chose the only course at their disposal: finding him a new boyfriend. The one they found was Ramón Esparza, a 23-year-old Spaniard with a cleft chin and dark features who spoke English, French, and Spanish. He worked in the fashion house, had social flair, chatted with clients, and even designed and cut hats—not nearly as well as Vladio, but acceptable enough to complement Balenciaga's evening wear.

The loss of Vladio would stay with him, feeding a deeper vision, as a writer feels the gulag. In the quiet of the salon behind the curtain, this private man studied and perfected his craft, stitching the loss of Vladio into the seams and hems and ruffles of his dresses. From his misery and pain came a newfound artistry. "When he revealed his 1950 collection," said *Harper's Bazaar*, "there was a five minute ovation, but the 'monk of the couture' still refused to appear." Even in absentia, however, he had secured his place at the top of the fashion world.

B ALENCIAGA LIVED IN PARIS but was influenced by Basque and Spanish culture. His inspiration came in part from paintings of Goya and Velásquez that had hung on the Marquesa's wall during his boyhood and later the cubism of Picasso or the surrealism of Dali. From his hometown church of San Salvador, he mimicked rich reds and golds and browns, and he embroidered vests, lapels, or hems in matador swirls. He even reproduced the cut and texture of the rags of Basque shepherds. To classify some of Balenciaga's dresses as having a Spanish motif is an accurate yet incomplete temptation. It misses a larger point. His creations defied labels or classification. He established the barrel line to frame the silhouette of a woman and then carved new looks over several years. In any collection, he might have included a dress heavily influenced by Basque and Spanish art, religion, or culture, but it was not the sole determinant of his genius.

An example from 1939 showed the Spanish influence early in his career. It was a full-length gown of ivory silk satin with a broad base. Thick black silk velvet snaked like a candelabra from the waist to neck and along the edges of the elbow cuffs. The fashion industry gave it a name, even if Balenciaga had not— *Infanta*.[6] It resembled Velázquez's painting of 1653 titled *Infanta Margarita*. The painting shows a woman in white with black lace stripes embroidered around the neck, down each arm, a V at the chest, and wishbones from waist to hemline. What Balenciaga had done was transform a masterpiece of oil and latex into three dimensions of silk and satin. Rendered well, women became canvas and dresses like brush strokes.

Another example was from the winter of 1948. It was a form-fitting cocktail dress of rose *peau de soie* and black lace with a second layer over the upper bodice and the hem dropping to mid-calf. It was simple and light, airy, sleeveless, nothing like Dior's New Look or even the barrel line from a year earlier. The cocktail dress bore striking similarities to Goya's *Doña Isabel de Parcel* from 1805. The painting depicted her dressed in black lace with pink bleeding through. If not an exact match, it's not difficult to see the common features of both painting and dress.

Several other examples peppered his collections. In 1950, an evening dress of black wool with taupe silk and train resembled El Greco's famous *Crucifixion* with Christ's ribs protruding and a cloth covering and a sash trailing. A year later, Picasso's cubism birthed a dress of black and white triangles in *cloqué organza*. The black robes of a Spanish priest gave rise to Balenciaga's knee-length dress of black silk twill in 1952. A painting of Queen Victoria Eugenia in a regal robe dotted with furs inspired an evening gown in 1964 of black silk sprinkled with ermine tails. Even his mohair coat mimicked a Navarra shepherd covered in shaggy animal skins. Countless others mimicked the colors, dance, costume, and feeling of Basque and Spanish culture.

These dresses, while hinting at his origins, did not make or break Balenciaga. They distinguished him as an expert designer from Spain without being a Basque or Spanish designer. When buyers looked at these dresses, he would

Balenciaga made the Baby Doll dress in 1958. With short sleeves and ruffles at the hem, it represented an evolved silhouette that let a woman breathe and offered a welcome reprieve from a more formal evening gown. Photo courtesy of the Balenciaga Museum in Getaria, Spain.

tell them, "No, no, that is for show" and discourage them from plopping down good money. If nothing else, the works demonstrated his versatility and independence, a man unlike anyone else. He could match the very best of French designers, yet still offer something extra.

His genius echoed throughout these Basque and Spanish creations but reverberated most when he stepped outside the fashion world to introduce a new concept that moved the whole industry on to a new path. After he introduced the barrel line in 1947, he continued to rework the basic form year after year to move in concert with a woman's wish to retain tradition while seeking freshness. His barrel line of 1947 morphed into a loosely fit suit by 1951. It was form-fitting in the front and loose-fitting in the back. Within a few years, other variations emerged: a classic tunic and then the Balenciaga sheath in about 1956, a basic design in women's fashion still popular today. The sack dress in 1957 clothed women like an eggplant cinching one end around the neck and the other around the knees. A year later, the remarkable baby doll dress appeared to great fanfare.

It had short sleeves, a loose front and six or eight inches of bunched ruffles around the hemline. Finally, the envelope dress put women in thick black chiffon with four corners around the neck.

Throughout the 1950s, Balenciaga succeeded in tearing down the notion that a woman's petite waist defined attractive womanhood. The era of Victorian femininity had come to a close, and he had put a nail in the velvet coffin. He dissolved the waist, broadening a woman's ability to breathe so to speak, and replaced it with a smoother silhouette. There was freedom in the idea of a woman unconstrained, an outgrowth perhaps of Rosie the Riveter and all the new postwar ideas about how women could contribute more, be more, be free, and express that freedom in how she acted and by what she wore.

Balenciaga had unleashed this sentiment, perhaps unknowingly. But how he would survive the product of his genius, if at all, was the greatest challenge of his career.

HAUTE COUTURE was one of France's most distinguished exports. Hitler could not transplant it, nor has any other country copied it with any great success. But times were changing. The earliest hints of hyper-trade had crept into world markets. To safeguard its industry, the French offered subsidies to the Parisian fashion houses if less than 10 percent of their fabric came from outside the country. Most took the subsidies; Balenciaga did not.

He moved in the opposite direction. Reaching out to foreign companies, he imported fabrics best suited to the dresses of his imagination. He used textural woolens from Britain and new incarnations of silk and satin from Scotland, Lancashire, and Italy. In cooperation with Gustave Zumsteg in Zurich, he developed a new fabric called gazar, a stiff yet loosely woven silk gauze that let him cut and tailor crisp, shiny evening gowns that had something like the statuesque polish of a man's business suit.

The imports gave him yet another edge over the other couturiers of Paris. Stunning examples, one after another, strutted out of Balenciaga's salon on to a catwalk: a dress of ivory silk gazar and black lace (1962); a wrap of yellow silk with black silk satin bows (1965); an ensemble of black ziberline and bolero of pink silk gazar (1966); an evening dress of black silk crepe with a "chou" wrap of black silk gazar (1967); and an evening ensemble with a bodice of black silk leaves and skirt of black silk gazar. In attendance at many of these Balenciaga spectacles was *Vogue* editor-in-chief Diana Vreeland, who once said, "One fainted. It was possible to blow up and die. I remember at one show in the early 1960s, Audrey Hepburn turned to me and asked why I wasn't frothing at the mouth at what I was seeing. I told her I was trying to act calm and detached because, after all, I was a member of the press. Across the way Gloria Guinness was sliding out of her chair on to the floor. Everyone was going up in foam and thunder."

Balenciaga employed nearly 400 ateliers whom he guided—or more aptly, directed—to do his bidding. Even approaching 70 years old, he never let up, producing dress after spectacular dress. The 400 ateliers were needed to keep up and to cope with his severe focus on detail that grew ever more persnickety as Balenciaga aged.

One of his most aggravating hang-ups was the sleeve. If it wasn't right, he had to do it over—and it was never right. Nothing substandard could come out of his house. "In those days the buyers came by ship," said Florette, "and their orders had to be ready to leave with them, not on the next ship. Once I had a huge delivery and I saw he was taking apart the sleeves of a dress I had to ship that night. I said, 'Monsieur Balenciaga, you can't do this, they have to be there at six pm.' He said, 'They can't leave like this,' and kept on working. I finally started to cry and he said I was bad-tempered—*'et en plus elle a un mauvais caractére'*—and kept on pinning."

If he studied the work of others, he looked at the sleeve. It said something, he thought, about the rest of the ensemble. Dior's sleeves were ostentatiously puffed for the sake of flamboyance, an excess that Balenciaga considered vulgar. Chanel's sleeves, though simple, were tasteful, even underdone at times. He would tell her the same, their friendship lasting for years: the two designers most commonly mentioned in fashion magazines, the two most widely copied by amateurs, the two with the most broadly shared backgrounds. Unlike most couturiers born into families with fashion pedigrees, Chanel was the daughter of a laundry woman and a father who sold work clothes on the street. She and Balenciaga bonded over humble roots and the singular influence of a parent in each of their lives. She revered the man, calling him "a *couturier* in the truest sense of the word. The others are simply fashion designers."

One day in discussion with *Women's Wear Daily*, Chanel promised the editors a picture of her side by side with Balenciaga.

"Cristobal," she said, "I'd like to have my picture taken with you."

"Coco, with pleasure," he said, "but it's just for the two of us?"

"No, it's for a newspaper."

"Which one?"

"*Women's Wear.*"

"Not on your life!" he snorted.

Balenciaga considered *Women's Wear* the rag of fashion reporting and would not grace its pages and raise its stature with a rare photo of him in public, much less of him with Chanel in public. It would have been one of the few of the two together, a real coup for the magazine.

His refusal left Chanel angered. Instead of bowing out or offering only herself for an interview, she went on the offensive and wrote about Balenciaga in the pages of *Women's Wear*. She skewered Balenciaga in the puff piece, vilifying his homosexuality and claiming he knew nothing about women's bodies, which explained why he dressed them so shabbily. The article appeared in English, which Balenciaga could not read, but his boyfriend Esparza translated it for him.

"So I go to lunch and I find Cristóbal in tears," said Esparza.

"How can that have happened?" asked Balenciaga. "The gifts we exchanged, the things I did for her." The betrayal made him cry and cry. "I am leaving for Spain. I cannot bear such things."

For such a private man, the public disparagement cut deep. He stayed in Spain to lick his wounds, boxing up everything Chanel had given him and shipping it back to her. The two would never speak again, though in 1971, he attended her funeral even when others would not, the anger still alive and fresh in many who were loyal to Balenciaga. But he said at the time, "You know, in life there are things one must forget, the ills that people have done to you. May she rest in peace, *paix à son âme.*"

The long brooding over the photo incident fueled an anguished reflection about the fashion industry and his role in it. He saw one changing and the other not, and he wondered if he could keep pace or if he wanted to keep pace. He had driven trends; they had not driven him. He had unveiled the next illustrious dress and set the standard for all other couturiers, who then came up short. He never copied or followed. That was not his way.

When a person reaches the pinnacle of his profession in business or sport or politics or law or fashion, he often wants to stay there forever. The view is good. Yet he finds staying on top harder than reaching the top. If he resigns the mountain, he does so on his own terms, as king of the hill with no equal, and history reveres his unconquered stature. If he stays too long, the mountain resigns him, knocking him from the perch, and history records the fall. As a reclusive man, Balenciaga never spoke of this reality. His actions, however, suggested that at least instinctively, he knew the world was nipping at his toes and shaking the ground beneath his feet.

The fashion world respected him and his designs, but by the mid-sixties, the respect often felt like veneration or reverence rather than exuberance or high spirits about his newest dresses shown on the catwalks of Paris. When the magazines reported on him, the word "still" crept into the prose as in "still great" or "still one of a kind" or "still the best." But haute couture was passing him by, or, more accurately, passing out of style, and he knew it.

He dressed women of a certain age and type: a sophisticated woman, Catholic, well-heeled of regal or near regal pedigree through nobility or wealth, a woman who, though strong, fit into a traditional role and knew her place in a world largely dominated by men in business and government. Their age had inched them closer to retirement by now. When these women were seen in person or on new television screens, the same words perched on every set of lips to describe them—words like classy, sophisticated, proper—and many would owe the compliment to Balenciaga's well-cut and crafted attire.

But a new woman had come on to the scene, fresh from the street. She was the daughter, strong in her own right, eager to carve a path with or without a husband, with or without male permission, and with or without wealth. She sought independence, legal and social freedoms, equal opportunities, and casual love. The evening gown of ivory silk did not suit her, nor the cape of black satin, nor the dress with ruffles and puffed sleeves, nor the baby doll or sack or envelope. This new woman wanted to cast off these fashion chains and find freedom in dress as she would in society. In 1965, *Women's Wear* conceded of Balenciaga, "Why should he bother dressing the world at this point? Vicariously, he does dress a lot of the world when you see how his ideas filter down." It was praise, but hardly the praise he was used to.

Every morning, he would still go to work wearing a silk black hat tilted to the side, an overcoat with a single button, and a black tie with a white shirt. If not to the salon, he could have attended a funeral. His Basque secretary would announce him with "Monsieur is here." Ensconced behind his curtain, he would peek through the little hole to see the world closing in on him. His zest had gone.

Never wanting to be a man in decline, he decided in 1968 to retire while still on the mountaintop. He closed his salons in Paris, Madrid, Barcelona, and San Sebastián. It surprised the world. The *London Daily Express* headlined, Balenciaga decides to quit—and fashion will never be the same again. Across the pond, the *New York Times* proclaimed, Nothing left to achieve, Balenciaga calls it a day. Equally surprised were his 400 employees who received pink slips within a month. After 31 years of service as chief *vendeuse*, Florette received a severance only large enough to paint her one-room apartment.

The quiet, private man of 10 Avenue George V retreated to Spain where he'd live out the rest of his days with Esparza.

IN AUGUST 1971, Balenciaga at age 76 gave his first official interview to the
London Times. "Nobody knows what a hard métier it is, how killing is the
work under all this luxury and glamour," he said. Three years had passed since
closing his salons and his sense about haute couture's doom had come to pass.
"This age is marked by the lack of elegance in women," he said. "The life which
supported *couture* is finished. Real *couture* is a luxury which is just impossible to
do anymore." The British magazine *Queen* took another step when it reported,
"*Haute Couture* is dead and so is Balenciaga."

He did not return to fashion as a career. Occasionally, while dining with a
friend, he would comment on his suit or her dress. The fabric is fine, he'd say,
but the sleeve—dear Lord—the sleeve! Then he'd go to his apartment with the
offending friend in tow, stand on a stool with scissors, and dismantle and reas-
semble the sleeve. He was a perfectionist, an artisan who believed that creation
was divine, and to fit divinely was godliness.

On only one other occasion would he pick up his scissors again. In March
1972, General Franco's granddaughter, María del Carmen Martínez-Boriú y
Franco, married Alfonso de Bourbon y Dampierre, the grandson of Alfonso
XIII. The wedding gown was regal, fit for a queen, reminiscent of Isabelle's
Catholic glories. It would be one of his finest creations, and it had to be perfect.
"Two days before the wedding," said the bride, "he pulled the dress completely
apart because he didn't like the way it fit. I thought I'd never get married." But
her dress felt different from Fabiola's dress in 1960. The fanfare had gone. If
Fabiola's dress had been a bold statement, María del Carmen's felt more like a
soft echo.

The dress would be Balenciaga's last. Two weeks later, on a trip with
Esparza to Javea, Spain, a coastal town on the Mediterranean Sea, a sudden
heart attack ended his life on March 23, 1972. Within 24 hours, in accordance
with Spanish law, he was buried in Getaria's town cemetery. Father Pieplu, his
priest from Paris where he had attended mass, delivered the eulogy, wearing a
brilliant black-buttoned cassock that Balenciaga had made for him. *Women's
Wear Daily* headlined, *The King is Dead,* and all the fashion industry and the
women whom he had dressed mourned the death of a legend and the passing
of an era.

Esparza suffered thereafter since Balenciaga had not left a will. Having
spent every moment of the past 20 years with him, Esparza sued the family for
at least part of the Balenciaga's estate. He failed and went on to live a modest life
until his death in 1997.

After Balenciaga closed his salons in 1968, Florette worked for Givenchy
and then Courréges, her black book of clients worth a fortune in the fashion

Balenciaga at the end of his life, circa 1970–1971. He died of a heart attack about a year later on March 23, 1972, during a vacation in Javea, Spain. Photo courtesy of the Balenciaga Museum in Getaria, Spain.

world. She never tired of representing the last gasps of haute couture. At 90 years old, she sold a few of her Balenciaga originals to go on a birthday cruise, though she kept her favorite: a taupe evening gown, frilled with lace, covering a tan base and pink chiffon dotted in black. "In the back, there was a tiny velvet bow, really tiny," she said. "What was fascinating about it was just that little black velvet bow, so small among all that chiffon—that was what made it amusing." She enjoys the dress still today as she reminisces on the man whose hands cut the fabric and stitched the seams and hem, and then tore it apart and put it back together. The little black velvet bow had made it just right.

Although he wanted his name to die with him, Balenciaga went on without Balenciaga. His family continued the operations in Spain under his niece Manuela, adding accessories, perfumes, and ready-to-wear garb, all products that the master or king of haute couture would have labeled as vulgar. His name was bought by Gucci and then by the French tycoon Francois Pinault. The designer had become expendable.

Now Balenciaga is merely a brand, a good brand to be sure, quite public and ubiquitous, everything the man was not.

Notes

1. Balenciaga had four brothers and sisters, but two died in infancy. He did not know them. He was the youngest of the five.

2. Sales assistant or salesperson.

3. Under Spanish law, a bankrupt company that reorganizes and returns to business could not use its original name, which is what prompted the change to Eisa.

4. Each of these women had worldly prominence in their own right for different reasons. Wallis Simpson, the Duchess of Windsor, was actually an American socialite born in Pennsylvania who married Prince Edward, the Duke of Windsor. He had been King Edward VIII but abdicated his throne to marry her. Aimee de Heereen, born in Brazil, married Rodman de Heeren, heir to the Wanamaker department store fortune. She maintained homes in Biarritz, Palm Beach, and New York, spoke six languages, and, as her daughter said, "moved around society in a spectacular manner." Helena Rubinstein, born in Krakow, Poland, became an American business magnate. She founded a cosmetics company, Helena Rubinstein Incorporated, which made her one of the world's wealthiest women. Clare Booth Luce was an author of screenplays and a politician. Married to Henry Luce, publisher of *Time, Life, Fortune,* and *Sports Illustrated,* she campaigned in her own right for every Republican presidential candidate from Wendell Willkie to Ronald Reagan, becoming the first American woman appointed to a major ambassadorial post overseas. The Honorable Daisy Fellowes was a Parisian socialite, novelist, and poet, a beautiful woman in any age or by any standard, and the Paris editor of American *Harper's Bazaar.* She was a fashion icon herself and heiress to the Singer sewing machine fortune. With customers like these, Balenciaga had only to make them dresses and then let them walk in the world to be his living, breathing, aristocratic marketers of haute couture.

5. Not long after this dinner, Pierre Balmain opened a Paris fashion house called Balmain. His dresses were known best for their "architecture of movement." His clientele only rarely overlapped with Balenciaga's. He designed the wardrobe of Queen Sirikit of Thailand for her trip around the United States in 1960. Otherwise, he tended more to the commercial, designing outfits for flight attendants on TWA, Malaysia-Singapore Airlines, and Air France. Later, he designed dresses for Broadway and Hollywood stars, even receiving a nomination for a Tony Award in 1980 for Best Costume Design. Still today wearing his designs are Angelina Jolie, Penelope Cruz, Alexandra Kerry, Tatiana Sorokko, Kate Moss, Kristin Davis, and others.

6. Balenciaga did not name any of his dresses. Any names of dresses came from the editors and *vendeuses* who attended shows, wrote about the gowns, and bought them for clients or stores around the world. While Balenciaga never said why he refused to name his gowns, the speculation was that a name was too confining, that a dress was more than a word. Instead, each dress received a number.

José María Arizmendiarrieta

The First Social Entrepreneur

T ERRIBLE HEADLINES SCREAMED across newspapers and televisions in the United States, Europe, Asia, and Latin America. During 2008 and 2009, the words most often quoted were *downturn, collapse, crash, unemployed, foreclosure, setback, crunch, poor*, and *misery*. No part of the globe seemed immune, and no one had a solution for the financial freefall or the sudden and deep layoffs. Millions lost jobs and homes, credit dried up for consumers and businesses, portfolios and retirement accounts shrank. In the chaos and panic, misery reached levels not seen since the Great Depression, as whole lifetimes of work and savings vanished. Middle-income families joined the growing ranks of the poor, and seniors' golden years turned to lead. Suicides and murder-suicides surged. So many asked: where is the bottom, how deep will it go, and how can we prevent this in the future?

In Mondragón, Spain, in the heart of Basque country, the employees of Eroski grocery stores stayed calm and rose above the chaos. The workers, who are also the owners, came up with a different kind of plan. After three days of discussion, they decided that 20 percent of workers, chosen by lottery, would leave their jobs for a year while receiving 80 percent of their salary and additional training to expand their skills. After a year, if the economy had not recovered, this first group would return to work and another group would take a year off. The math came out right, the grocery stores still made a profit, and no one lost a job. There was shared pain to be sure, but not misery, not poverty or despair. The plan was voted on and implemented.

José María Arizmendiarrieta at age 28. He rode his bicycle around Mondragón and often into the lush green hills surrounding the town as a way to find privacy and to think. There he'd come up with ideas. When a heart condition made pedaling difficult, his students bought him a motor scooter. Photo courtesy of the Mondragón Cooperative Corporation.

Eroski is part of the Mondragón Cooperative Corporation (MCC), a consortium of over 250 cooperatives worldwide with nearly 100,000 workers and $24 billion in annual revenue. During the great recession of 2008–2009, the worker-owners of each cooperative, much like Eroski, discussed and adopted their own solution to the downturn, sometimes requiring no adjustments, moving people from one cooperative to another under the MCC umbrella, or approving a plan of shared pain. But in all cases, the worker-owners, answerable to themselves and each other, not to shareholders, suffered no layoffs and weathered the crisis.

This experiment started as the brain-child of Father Don José María Arizmendiarrieta ("Don José María" or "Arizmendi"), a Basque Catholic priest, who launched the cooperative idea in 1956 with five of his student disciples.[1] Having only one eye, wearing dark glasses and a long black cassock, Don José María looked thin and frail as if he might meet his Maker at any moment. He had a constant churn of ideas, an indefatigable work ethic, the heart of a social entrepreneur, and a belief in the dignity of work and the power of the human spirit. Such strength of character was critical for surviving the Spain of his time while helping his Basque congregants overcome unemployment, poverty, and misery.

Don José María at 26 years old arrived in Mondragón in February 1941, nearly two years after Spain's civil war had ended, and the Second World War had begun. The people of Mondragón called it the "hunger period," a time of poverty and starvation, high unemployment, dilapidated and crowded housing, little education, and outbreaks of tuberculosis. A privileged few dictated the destiny of Mondragón's 8,645 residents. People spoke of a spirit of hopelessness. "This was an active and restless town even before the war," said Don José María, "and there was a considerable socialistic orientation. There had also been serious social tensions."

Those tensions had only worsened after the civil war. Franco consolidated power and punished ethnic groups, especially the Basque, for their determined opposition. Don José María's predecessor had been shot along with fourteen other priests. Hundreds more had been shipped to concentration camps. The parishioners of Mondragón had lost their confessors, their guiding stars, who every Sunday had delivered sermons of oratorical brilliance about the meek inheriting the earth, the low smiting the high, and the virtuous reaching heaven and eternal bliss.

When the one-eyed priest with dark glasses took to the lectern, his poor congregants were woefully underwhelmed. His reading lacked fluidity, and even when he spoke without the Good Book, his voice stuttered and stammered. No one tingled or felt warm inside. Their communal voice had morphed from a ferocious lion into a wobbly lamb.

If the delivery was wanting, his message was even worse. He rarely invoked eternal salvation, concentrating instead on the pangs of daily survival: feeding the hungry, clothing the naked, sheltering the cold, tending the sick—all the things that many wanted to forget by coming to the safe harbor of a Catholic mass. From the outset his message included more economic theory and cooperative philosophy than Christ's parables. "It is a social monstrosity," he said from the pulpit, "that a system of social organization is tolerated in which some can take advantage of the work of others for their exclusive personal profit. The cooperativist distinguishes himself from the capitalist, simply in that the latter utilizes capital in order to make people serve him, while the former uses it to make more gratifying and uplifting the working life of the people." His flock started calling him the "red priest."

Lacking influence en masse, he made up for it by subtle persuasion in small groups and through a relentless work ethic. He had no choice really. His parishioners had asked the monsignor to replace him. To save his job, he talked to as many people as possible, sharing his thoughts and endearing himself to them. Once he started talking, the townspeople could not shut him up. It was an irony that his flood of ideas came with a poor facility to express them. He considered it a penance from God. But from these intimate conversations, he gained a deeper understanding of the community's needs.

He revived two defunct church organizations. For families, he established a medical clinic, and for blue-collar youth, a soccer field and sports league. He told the parents and children, "Sports unite us. Give us a field, and we will become champions."[2] All endeavors needed only work, he said.

That was his favorite topic—work. He spoke of it often on the soccer field, from the pulpit, and even in the confessional. He emphasized that work was not a punishment but a means for self-realization and dignity, a chance to gain education and technical skills, and an invitation for solidarity with other like-minded men and women who wanted to cooperate for mutual benefit.

He charted a careful path between capitalism and socialism. He saw merit in both: capitalism's devotion to hard work and individual achievement, and socialism's measure of all work as equal. But both systems, he felt, had faults. "It is the third way," he said, "distinct from egoist capitalism and from the mastodon of depersonalizing socialism. We want corporations that constitute a new social potential and, thus, are built by those who are not impelled by a myopic and limited egotism or by a simple gregarious instinct."

These teachings ran afoul of the chief employer in Mondragón, Unión

Cerrajera, a large foundry and metalworking company. Unión Cerrajera was owned by a small group of family members and friends. Twenty-five years earlier, workers had gone on strike, which had ended in favor of the company. Owners had refused to rehire 33 people considered ringleaders, and they blacklisted them from working at any one of 40 companies in the region with which the owners transacted business. Ever since, no one dared strike or fall out of line or challenge the status quo. The son of a worker resigned himself to being a worker too, never rising higher than a first line supervisor. That was the way of things. Fathers and sons had little hope of economic opportunity or political freedom, and mothers and daughters had no hope at all.

Unión Cerrajera had started a small apprenticeship program reserved for the sons of employees. The program offered little advanced technical training since no employee (and no son of an employee) needed skills beyond rudimentary assembly work. The owners sent their own sons elsewhere for higher education. One day the company invited Don José María to give religious instruction during an apprenticeship session. He gladly accepted but took the opportunity to urge the owners to admit boys who were unrelated to employees. The company flatly refused and then rescinded Don José María's invitation.

As a good man and a good priest, he forgave the slight, but during his short bike ride from Unión Cerrajera to the Catholic rectory, he conceived a school of his own. It would teach technical and industrial skills to boys ages 14 to 16. He quickly penned what would become his common slogan: "Socializing knowledge truly democratizes power." In the weeks that followed, he promoted the school in slow, staggering language from the pulpit and held one-on-one meetings over coffee and bread with local business owners. He formed a parents association to generate enthusiasm, and he raised funds at soccer games. Cleverest of all, he put boxes on street corners inviting all people of Mondragón to write on a slip of paper how each would support the new school by a cash donation or an in-kind contribution such as books and pencils, desks and chairs, food for the boys and teachers, or cleaning services after hours.

About 600 residents, or 15 percent of all Mondragón, pledged support including many of the town's small- and medium-sized businesses. Each contributor gained a single vote to shape policy and the ongoing direction of the school. Neither Unión Cerrajera nor the local government pledged support. The mayor in fact warned Don José María that his actions constituted acts of flagrant democracy that would not be tolerated indefinitely. Basque nationalists, on the other hand, criticized him for capitulating to local authorities. His monsignor advised him to tone down his sermons and avoid unorthodox behavior.

José María Arizmendiarrieta started a school in Mondragon in 1943 with 20 students. The school would teach technical and industrial skills to boys ages 14 to 16. By 1945, it was renamed Escuela Politécnica Profesional and today stands as Mondragón University, still a feeder institution for the Mondragón Cooperative Corporation and other businesses in Spain and elsewhere. Photo courtesy of the Mondragón Cooperative Corporation.

Despite pressure from all sides, Don José María opened the school in 1943 with 20 students.

Over five years, the new school thrived with an expanding student body and parents association. Aside from its status as a church program, however, it lacked legal recognition, which deprived it of national financial support that other schools received. Under Franco, most organizations had become illegal unless they vowed subservience to his dominant party structure. Don José María combed the statutes looking for a path to legal legitimacy and, after considerable effort, found an old 19th-century law that let him charter the parents association into a League for Education and Culture.

He formed the League with four levels of membership: (1) people who simply wanted to join but paid nothing; (2) people who paid dues or, in lieu of dues, taught in the school; (3) people who paid 1,000 pesetas annually (about $89 at 1948 exchange rates), which consisted mainly of small- and medium-sized companies; and (4) honorary members from local authorities. Each group elected 10 representatives to a school assembly, and then the assembly elected a 14-member school board. Six of the 14 seats on the board were set aside for contributing companies and one for the mayor of Mondragón, who by this point had joined the growing number of his constituents who supported Don José María.

As each class of students graduated, the school board added new educational levels. The basic level equaled grammar school (*oficialía*), the next a high school diploma (*maestría*), and the final level three years of an undergraduate degree (*peritaje industrial*). For the first time, young people of Mondragón had prospects for education that exceeded the rudimentary skills taught by the apprenticeship program at Unión Cerrajera. The school board renamed the League the Escuela Politécnica Profesional—the Professional Polytechnic School. By 1971, the Unión Cerrajera would shut down its own training program and join Don José María's school. It was a successful milestone, though not an end, for the one-eyed priest had a greater vision still.

THE FIRST GRADUATES of the Escuela Politécnica Profesional worked at Unión Cerrajera while they continued meeting with Don José María before or after hours. Unhappy in their jobs, their discussions started as venting sessions and ended with thoughtful dialogue about labor and capital, reform of private enterprise, self-management and worker ownership. The father turned daily unhappiness into prospects for change. One of his students commented, "In the calculations we were making in 1956, we counted more than 2,000 circles of study that he conducted: some for religious and humanistic orientation; others for social orientation." He also arranged with the University of Zaragoza to teach classes in Mondragón to confer advanced degrees. Through this agreement, 11 of his original 20 students earned a bachelor degree in technical engineering.

When Unión Cerrajera expanded the company's capital base with a round of fresh stock, it was Don José María's students who proposed that the workers be allowed to buy-in. The owners refused outright. The students petitioned Madrid to force an open sale of stock, but Madrid denied the request as well. Here at last was the split. Unwilling to indulge the futility of reforming private enterprise, five of Don José María's disciples—Luis Usatorre, Jesús Larrañaga, Alfonso Gorroñogoitia, José María Ormaechea, and Javier Ortubay—formed a new company called Ulgor derived from the first letter of their surnames.

Their immediate challenge was raising capital. What little savings each had they deposited in individual accounts, but they knew it would not be enough. Having watched Don José María all these many years, they knew the solution depended on Mondragón's residents. Taking advantage of an old custom called the *chiquiteo*[3] during which Basques gather after work, roam from bar to bar, buying drinks and socializing, the five disciples shared their vision with anyone who would listen. Most in town knew of these blue-collar graduates, the first of their kind from Mondragón, and respected the one-eyed priest who guided them. Through donations, small individual loans, and buy-in from other worker-owners, they raised 11 million pesetas (about $361,604 in 1955 dollars), an enormous sum.

Not one to frequent Basque pubs, the father focused on securing a foundry license to manufacture metal castings. He worked countless hours well into many nights, often by candles in the rectory, to assemble applications, but his every petition to Bilbao or Madrid resulted in a request for new information, a referral to a new agency, a correction of names, another fee for processing, or an outright rejection. One student remarked, "In 1955, authorizations for permits to establish a factory were subject to rigorous control, and those who had the authorizations looked upon them as if they were made of gold." Don José María prayed for the patience of Job, though not even Job could have found a successful end to this labyrinthine bureaucracy. It was not designed to stimulate growth or create jobs but rather to preserve a status quo that kept people immobile, controlled, and destitute.

Into the surrounding hills he rode his bicycle to think, pedaling along the Deba River, his lanky legs straining from the climb out of the valley where Mondragón is situated. The fresh air, the thick trees, the quiet peace—all gave Don José María clarity and vision, enough that after many miles, he resolved simply to bypass altogether the cumbersome licensing law.

In Vitoria, he located a private firm that had gone bankrupt a few years earlier. It had no money and few assets or equipment. Those it had were of dubious quality and long obsolescence. But it had a license—a broad license, in fact—to manufacture electrical and mechanical products. Hearing the father's idea, the five disciples used some of their capital to buy the business and move its headquarters to Mondragón. A year later Ulgor launched on November 12, 1956, with 23 worker-owners, the five original founders and 18 others, who set to work manufacturing kerosene lamps, heaters, and stoves.

Ulgor was not to be a replica of Unión Cerrajera, nothing close in fact. It was new and different. Every worker was an owner and a member of a general assembly where one-person-one-vote replaced one-peseta-one-vote. The manager had the same vote as the janitor. From this general assembly, members elected a governing council that selected the manager and division heads who made up a separate management council that ran daily operations. The governing council also appointed an independent audit committee that reviewed finances and ensured compliance with the cooperative's policies and procedures. Members of the governing council served four-year terms, as did the manager who acted like a chief executive officer subject to annual performance reviews.

No one in the cooperative owned or bought stock as one might expect in a private company; rather each made a contribution and paid entry fees that the governing council set and the assembly approved. Every person then received a capital account. After tallying profits at the end of the year, 10 percent went to educational, cultural, or charitable contributions; another 50 percent went to a reserve fund to weather downturns; and the remainder went to the capital accounts of each member in proportion to his pay rate and hours worked. When a member retired, he received the full value of his capital account. Every cooperative from Ulgor's creation in 1956 to the present followed this same structure, though new features were folded in over time.

About a year after Ulgor's inception, Don José María encouraged the addition of a social council. He wrote the modification himself into the constitution. For every 10 rank-and-file workers of a division, a representative would be elected. Although its role was ambiguous, the social council assumed several duties at different times such as enhancing communication, increasing decision making for more worker-owners, serving as a focal point for collective bargaining, advising the governing council, and setting forth grievances.

Other structural changes surfaced as Ulgor grew. Although women were hired on an equal footing with men, they were forced to leave the cooperative once married. This policy reflected the traditional function of women as homemakers and mothers, and men as primary breadwinners. By the mid-1960s, however, Ulgor abandoned this policy and granted women full equality with their male counterparts. For all workers regardless of gender, the governing council set salaries equal to private sector wages of similar skills, including bonus potential for high performance. The cooperative also published all salaries without exception and set a maximum ratio of 4.5-to-1 (now 8-to-1) between the highest- and lowest-paid worker-owners in the company.[4]

In a town where a single employer had dictated the lives of residents, Ulgor proved to be a breath of fresh air. It gave people a say in their own destinies, an outlet for pent-up creativity, and a chance to work hard, contribute, and reap the rewards of high performance. It felt fair. The cooperative expanded as worker-owners opened new markets in Mondragón and in surrounding Basque towns. A rare optimism grew from hopelessness and spawned new cooperatives to feed growing community demands.

Don José María helped pattern these new enterprises on the Ulgor model, but something still troubled him. From the vantage point of Madrid, Ulgor on paper appeared to be owned and operated by a single person. The new structure and policies that he had midwifed into being had no official blessing from Franco's government. Fearing reprisal, he studied the law once again to find a hook on which to hang Ulgor's legal legitimacy and then traveled alone to Madrid to argue his case. He met there an attorney named José Luis del Arco, who represented Obra de Cooperación, the agency that oversaw, regulated, and approved cooperatives in Franco's Spain.

What happened here remains a debatable point. One of Ulgor's founders said many years later that Arco "yielded to the tenacious defense by Don José María." But Arco himself, who became a great defender of the priest and was aligned personally with his philosophy, maintained that "Padre Arizmendi came to consult me on problems for which his reading of the text of the law did not provide any solution. I gave him the answers, because the letter of the law is one thing and the spirit of the law is that which can bring the letter of the law to life. In short, I did not surrender to Father Arizmendi, but I provided him with the solutions that he had not been able to find."

Regardless of which version proved accurate, Don José María returned from Madrid with the legal legitimacy that Ulgor needed by appealing, as he often did, to the spirit of the law. Now over this hurdle, Ulgor and its cooperative offspring flourished. As the number of worker-owners expanded, it created ever more sophisticated layers of finances, prompting the priest to mount his bicycle and ride up into the green hills of Mondragón. There along the peaceful wooded banks of the Deba River, another thought blossomed in his fertile mind.

WHEN THE SPANISH CIVIL WAR erupted in July 1936, Don José María was 21 years old. He joined the military of Vizcaya and Gipuzkoa against Franco whose forces had just taken Vitoria. With only one eye, he could not shoulder a rifle, so he took up the pen, starting a Basque newspaper that described Franco's advances and the fervent Basque opposition. From varied sources—military and civilian, factual and anecdotal—information flowed his way that offered a broad understanding of the war's overall progress. In June 1937, the city of Bilbao fell and he knew it was only a matter of time before Franco would declare final victory.

In a calculated gamble, he turned himself in rather than die at his typewriter. He languished in prison for a month with 28 others and then was dragged in chains before one of Franco's tribunals.

"How have you been supporting yourself?" he was asked.

Never impulsive, he paused a long time to think, which aggravated his inquisitor who demanded an answer. He replied finally, "I've been a soldier in the Basque army." The tribunal classified him as a prisoner of war.[5]

When posed with the same question, other prisoners said they had served as journalists. The tribunal rewarded their honesty with a bullet to the back of the head. In reviewing his life, some called his achievements mere luck, but it was no such thing. It was a combination of cleverness, shrewdness, hard work and thought—never luck. He would sometimes comment that the harder he worked, the more luck fell with grace upon him.

Not long after his bike ride through the Mondragón countryside, he popped his head in uninvited at one of Ulgor's governing council meetings. All discussion stopped; it was the *padre* after all who deserved patience, if not reverence. He told his former students that Ulgor needed to form a bank and then described the reasons why: capital, private accounts for worker-owners, profit-sharing, retirement security, and investments toward other cooperatives. The words came out slow, stuttered and thoughtful, yet by the end of what seemed like a long sermon, no matter how well meaning, the members were unconvinced. "Our initial reaction was one of annoyance," said one of the founders, "and we literally sent Don José María packing. It seemed to us just a fantasy and a bad one because of our total lack of knowledge of the field."

But the good priest did not pedal away from the meeting with any hint of disappointment, only energetic resolve. He had often told his students that to be a good idea, it had to be translated into a word, and to be a good word, it had to be translated into action. Short of action, an idea was never good. Following his own advice, he studied the law in search of another hook and found an old rule called *ahorro obrero* (literally "labor savings") that allowed banks to pay interest of 0.5% more on accounts of blue-collar workers than on other accounts. It was perfect. It would give the bank a legitimate way of attracting depositors and strengthening the cooperative's finances without resorting to private banks for capital, credit, or savings.

On his own, Don José María drafted a new constitution. He enlisted José Luis del Arco in Madrid to help craft the legal language and complete an application for approval. One document Arco needed was a copy of the minutes from a pre-organization meeting of the bank. The father happily produced the document. It was dated March 15, 1959, and among other components, approved the constitution and by-laws, appointed a temporary governing council and audit committee, and included signatures from Alfonso Gorroñogoitia and José María Ormaechea, two Ulgor founders. It was everything that Arco could have wanted—of course it was! The document was fabricated, and the signatures forged.

Why his dancing within the spirit of the law turned to a blatant step outside the law was never revealed. Perhaps he remembered Christ's advice to be gentle as a dove yet wise as a serpent. Or maybe he looked at rosters of deception, and seeing so many hash marks under Franco's column, he justified this single hash mark for the Basque people. Or perhaps he thought that to do a big right he

Five of José María Arizmendiarrieta's students—Luis Usatore, Jesús Larrañaga, Alfonso Gorroñogoitia, José María Ormaechea, and Javier Ortubay—formed the first Mondragón cooperative called Ulgor on November 12, 1956. The name derives from the surname of these founders. Not shown is Javier Ortubay. This first cooperative grew into the Mondragón Cooperative Corporation of today with 257 cooperatives on five continents employing nearly 100,000 worker-owners. Photo courtesy of the Mondragón Cooperative Corporation.

had to do a little wrong. Whatever his reasoning, the bank gained approval on September 24, 1959, as the Caja Laboral Popular—the Popular Labor Bank.

Don José María turned to José Ayala to head up the new organization. Ayala had worked with the father as president of the Youth Sports Club during the 1940s, helping to build the soccer field and organize competitions with surrounding towns. He was hard-working and honest, and he dressed remarkably well, as a banker should. But most important, Ayala's wife hailed from a well-to-do family in Mondragón, which would add to the bank's prestige and attract the trust of the community. Many years later, after Ayala had died, his wife would comment, "What is clear is that we were among those committed to the apostolic work and we cast our lot in this way more for the man, Don José María, than for his ideas." The same might have been said for Ormaechea whom the father convinced 18 months later to be the bank's chief executive officer, and for Gorroñogoitia who accepted the chairmanship of the governing council; soon after, Usatorre and Larrañaga joined as well. By the close of 1961, four of the

five founders of Ulgor worked directly with the Caja Laboral Popular. Within a
few years, it became one of the leading banking institutions of Spain, just as Don
José María had envisioned from the start. Tenacity led to victory.

In addition to savings, the bank offered social security to worker-owners
who, not considered employees by law, did not qualify for national retirement
benefits. The governing council deposited a small portion of each paycheck into
each member's capital account where it grew alongside annual profit-sharing
and semi-annual interest payments. The bank also sponsored a health clinic for
members and dependents that dramatically lowered out-of-pocket expenses.[6] By
1967, the social security division of the Caja Laboral Popular had grown so much
that Don José María proposed it become its own cooperative. Having learned
not to question him, the governing council abided by the request and established
Lagun-Aro, with its own governing council, audit group, social committee, and
assembly.

The spin-off demonstrated a vital point. Cooperatives often suffer from an
excess of democracy, a need to question every decision and to send every action
to assembly for approval, producing a kind of paralysis that dooms them in the
face of a highly competitive, fast-paced, first-to-market world. Don José María
believed, on the contrary, that when a division became efficient and profitable, it
should become its own cooperative. This rule instilled innovation and reinven-
tion, favored small, nimble organizations, promoted competition, and encouraged new cooperatives as a way of casting wider nets for customers in other
communities or even countries. Woven into Ulgor's cultural DNA, this rule
helped the cooperative diversify products and, as time marched on, proliferate
beyond Mondragón.

Before Don José María entered theological study at age 12, he grew up on a
farm in the village of Markina about 30 miles from Mondragón. It was there
as a baby that he lost his eye in a farming accident, and there too where he learned
to milk lambs and goats and to harvest timber from the thick pines that lay like
plush carpet over the rolling hills of northern Spain. He had a younger sister and
two younger brothers, but as the eldest son, he was destined to inherit the farm.
The livestock, the milking, the cutting of trees, the exceptionally hard work—he
knew the life well, even at a young age, yet it was not for him. Encouraged by
his mother, he left home, turning over the farm to his brothers and joining the
seminary.

His father and now his brothers were part of a farmer cooperative that
bought raw goods from stores and delivered finished products such as milk
and lumber for sale. The farmers were owners; the storekeepers were workers.

The model yielded little profit yet frequent disputes. Don José María was well versed in this relationship, recalling from boyhood the nights when his father and mother had counted their meager pesetas at the dinner table at the end of a season. Having heard of the Mondragón miracle, his brothers reached out to Don José María hoping he might help improve their plight.

The good father was more than happy to oblige. In a few weeks, the priest reorganized the farmers and the storekeepers into equal owners of a new cooperative called Lana. Under the arrangement, the two sides no longer competed for separate profits at the expense of one another. From raw materials to production to market, both sides cooperated to maximize revenues and minimize costs, which resulted in greater profits for all. From 25 farmers and one storekeeper in 1961, Lana grew to include over 400 in a few years.

Other residents of Mondragón saw the Ulgor experience as an opportunity to chart their own course. Over coffee and bread, Don José María educated eager parishioners about workers' rights, ownership, the value and dignity of work, and responsible finances. His small group discussions rapidly bore fruit, and a plethora of new cooperatives emerged: Arrasate, which manufactured machine tools for Ulgor production; Copreci, which provided spare parts for Ulgor's stoves and heaters; Ederlan, which took over a bankrupt foundry; and Fagor Electrotécnica, which formed out of Ulgor, Arrasate, and Copreci to create electronic components.

There were principles at the bedrock of cooperation, he told each new wave of disciples. At first, listeners felt bored by his slow, monotonous voice, but then drawing energy from his soft passion, they learned the new philosophy, absorbed it, and passed it on. "One is not born a cooperator," he told them, "because to be a cooperator requires a social maturity, a training in social living. For one to be an authentic cooperator, capable of cooperating, it is necessary to have learned to tame one's individualistic or egoistic instincts and to adapt to the laws of cooperation . . . one becomes a cooperator through education and the practice of virtue."

Guided by his teachings, Mondragón boomed. The "hunger period" had ended. People found jobs and earned money, but most of all, they felt a sense of purpose and a renewed drive. From other Basque towns—Murgia, Vitoria-Gasteiz, Besain, Lekeitio, Gernika—and from as far away as Bilbao and San Sebastián—people poured in looking for work. Between 1940 and 1970, the population tripled. It caused a housing shortage that local authorities struggled to address. Don José María organized new cooperatives, 17 in all, to build residential high rises and commercial buildings, many still there today, to accommodate the influx and relieve the overcrowding. Mom-and-pop shops sprouted to feed, clothe, and offer entertainment. A new Mondragón rose from the ashes of the civil war and the austerity of the Second World War.

Parents clamored to enroll their children in the Escuela Politécnica Profesional, which served as a feeder program into this burgeoning job market. When some students reached the bachelors program, however, the father discovered that they had to drop out for lack of funding. The program's fees were very low, but for some students whose family had no tradition of education, college or otherwise, any fee was prohibitive. He wanted to remedy this. Gathering students who could and could not pay, and reaching out to various cooperatives now in vogue across Mondragón, he established the Alecop cooperative to match student skills with job opportunities. It became the first work-study program, defraying the cost of education while reserving a job for each student after graduation.

By the mid-1960s, programs such as Alecop and the construction co-ops cemented Don José María as the most authoritative figure in Mondragón. As if they had spotted a celebrity, people on the street would often stop and point when he pedaled by wearing his brown ankle-length cassock. He acknowledged everyone with a wave and attracted no shortage of disciples. His greater challenge was finding time to help as many as he could, and for the right reasons. Some wanted to get rich; others wanted merely to find purpose or to climb out of destitution. He loved the eager, energetic, hard-working poor most of all.

He took a special liking, for example, to a sewing circle of women who had spent their formative years as housewives, tending to husbands and raising children. Now they wanted to do something more, something meaningful for themselves. None of them had educations beyond high school, and most had dropped out long before earning a diploma. Several were semi-literate and lacked basic skills in math. Yet all were hard-working and determined. "Let women decide their fate for themselves," he said of them. "Half of adult people do not have any right to rule the destinies of the other half."

He asked them, "What skills do you have?"

"We can cook. We can clean," they said.

He set them up preparing meals and cleaning offices after hours. The 12 eager women formed Auzo-Lagun and, within a year, opened a small restaurant. Their services expanded until the sewing circle grew to include 360 women serving 1,500 meals daily and providing custodial services for at least 10 buildings. All were owners, enjoyed annual profits, and became self-sufficient with capital accounts and healthy retirements. Not one had ever dreamed of such security.

As Auzo-Lagun got underway, another cooperative called Eroski fell on hard financial times. It was a chain of grocery stores across the Basque region that seemed well positioned as the economy expanded to sell more food and supplies to families with better wages. One of its challenges, however, stemmed from a law that forbade consumer cooperatives from selling products to non-members.

Don José María did not know at first how to help them. To think on the matter, he did what he always did. He pedaled his rickety bicycle into the Mondragón countryside to breathe the fresh air and smell the sweet pine. Until then, Eroski had focused on encouraging members to buy more or used marketing gimmicks to attract new members. Nothing seemed to work. When the father returned to the rectory, he knew the solution lay not with gimmicks but with the words *member* and *non-member*, which the law used to distinguish who could shop at an Eroski store and who could not. What he proposed was that every consumer, whether he walked in as a member of Eroski or not, would walk out as one by paying a small fee at the cash register with his groceries. The fee was nominal, hardly noticeable, but it would grant all people the right to shop and benefit from Eroski's lower prices. The bank helped with the modifications in exchange for Eroski aligning its constitution, governing council, audit committee, and social council with the Ulgor model. The deal was struck, and in no time Eroski flourished, becoming one of Spain's biggest consumer names.[7]

What the Caja Laboral Popular demonstrated with Eroski was that it could provide more than savings accounts and social security. It could be a superstructure and a hub around which cooperatives could form as spokes, offering a model constitution and consistent policies. Without the father's early vision on the bank, cooperatives might have proliferated with wildly different policies, procedures, and constitutions, some succeeding, others failing, some collaborating, others not. The bank served as a covalent bond between like-minded organizations.

The bank's stabilizing force was critical. Within a decade after Ulgor's formation, the Mondragón experience (as many had begun to call it) had evolved from a simple worker-owner cooperative of 23 people into a labor phenomena employing thousands in manufacturing, finance, retail, food services, and construction. The movement had gained a life of its own with new cooperatives cropping up every month.

Don José María called it a wall of solidarity, writing, "the company is the first economic-social cell, a society made up of individuals within a community." To add another brick, he proposed a kind of cooperative of cooperatives, a federation built around principles of work, democracy, human needs, and responsible capital. He pulled together the original five—Ulgor, Arrasate, Copreci, Ederlan, and Fagor Electrotécnica—to form ULARCO whose name derived from the initial letters of the first three. The priest wrote a new constitution for the community of companies, worked out the details of a common governing council, audit committee, and social council, and convinced the participating members to share 100 percent of profits. Then he shepherd other cooperatives, most of which he had had a hand in creating, to join the federation. Through this collaborative structure, ULARCO became one of the top 100 industrial firms in Spain. Most of all, it positioned the worker-owners for what loomed on the horizon—either an awakening or a civil war—no one could be certain. Franco was dying.

F RANCISCO FRANCO had ruled Spain as a dictator since the end of the Spanish Civil War in 1939, a conflagration that left half a million dead, an economy in tatters, and a legacy of concentration camps that killed 200,000 to 400,000 Basque and Spanish citizens who opposed his regime. Those who could—doctors, nurses, teachers, lawyers, judges, professors, and businessmen—fled the country. Left behind were the unskilled hordes.

From the early sports league to the technical school to Ulgor to the bank to the ULARCO federation, Don José María had transformed these unskilled hordes—or as he might have contended, they had transformed themselves—into hard-working, contributing, and responsible citizens. But as a handful of worker-owners turned into thousands across multiple industries, he could no longer command the same intimate influence, especially with those who had come from distant places to join the Mondragón experience. Worse, the ailing Franco had turned the country into a pressure cooker in which each group— private businesses, worker cooperatives, the church, the military—jockeyed for political position before the death bells finally rang out across the land. In this politically charged milieu, the worker-owners grew restless.

The first hint that all was not well arose in March 1971. At one of two Ulgor facilities, a few workers tried to rally strikers over job evaluations: how jobs were defined, how workers' performance was evaluated, and how wages were set. The attempt fizzled before it got underway, but when the three ringleaders ended their apprenticeships, the governing council cut them loose and enacted a new policy. The policy distinguished between strikes brought about from internal struggles, and strikes due to external circumstances such as unjust government pressure, a poor economy, or solidarity with other cooperatives. The first would be tolerated, even endorsed by the governing council, but the second would be viewed as a direct assault on the cooperative itself and would be met with resistance, fines, even termination.

During the next three years, no one dared challenge this edict. But the sentiments that had led to the failed strike had not dissipated, only gone underground. What had caused nerves to rub raw? Part of the answer stemmed from the charged political environment, from every Basque and Spaniard watching Franco teeter between life and death and not knowing what the future held. More practically, however, decisions that had been made six year earlier in 1965 now haunted them. Back then, the governing council had crafted different evaluations for blue-collar, white-collar, and managerial worker-owners, each with different compensation and benefit structures. For many, the separation insulted the egalitarian nature of the Mondragón experience.

Hoping to remedy this inequality, the governing council of ULARCO embarked on a federation-wide effort to standardize job descriptions, evaluations, and wages for the nearly 3,000 jobs across the five cooperatives. That meant, of course, that some would get a wage bump, and others would not; some would improve their evaluation criteria, and others would not; and some would gain a more favorable title, and others would not. Bottom line, not everyone would be happy.

When the study concluded, nearly 80 percent had an upgrade or no change in their position. In Ulgor, however, 22 percent saw a downgrade. Over 1,000 grievances were soon filed, the majority from Ulgor personnel. Circulars popped up calling for a strike. The chair of the governing council warned would-be strikers of punishment and fines, as he and other members worked to address the grievances. The warning backfired.

On June 27, 1974, about 400 worker-owners walked out of the Ulgor plant. They marched to Arrasate to recruit others, but workers there barred the doors. Across the street the marchers entered Fagor Electrotécnica and gained followers; others resisted, nearly to the point of fisticuffs.

The governing council expelled 17 of the main rabble-rousers and fined 397 who had followed their lead. To counter, the marchers issued a list of demands, which the governing council refused. The strike was broken. Over the next week, all but the 17 expelled worker-owners returned to their jobs.

The incident rumbled across Mondragón like an earthquake. The militant arm of the Basque nationalists, Euskadi Ta Askatasuna (ETA), issued a cloud of words, all in general disagreement with Ulgor's actions: "To break with capitalism, we must place ourselves in the land of reality (the class struggle) and not that of wishful thinking. . . . We must not forget the role of the state as supervisor and driving force of capitalism and that of the working class as the only agent capable of destroying it." But the more pointed denunciation came from the Catholic Church whose social secretariat penned an edict titled *Conflicts in the Cooperative Movement*, which was read from every pulpit in the Basque country.

It stated, "As always, the workers have suffered under the elitist behavior of the cooperative leaders and the virulence and crudeness of the cooperative leaders greatly surpasses that of the firms that they disrespectfully call capitalist."

The governing council responded forcefully against ETA and the church. But the one voice that everyone wanted to hear, the one voice that often stammered and stuttered from the pulpit, was the one voice that remained silent throughout this episode.

Don José María's silence might have been forgiven due to poor health. In 1974, he had undergone bypass surgery to correct a weak heart. For anyone else, that alone might have excused the silence during such a critical event. But after leaving the hospital, hardly a week had gone by before he was back working, talking to students, and sharing ideas.

Why he uttered not a peep about the strike and took no side was never explained. It might be that he could not bring himself to criticize "the crudeness of the cooperative leaders" whom he loved like his own children. Or maybe the church hierarchy had warned against countermanding his ecclesiastic elders, knowing he had done so in the past. Perhaps he had viewed the struggle as a natural evolution of the Mondragón experience where once starving people now had strength to stand and march. What seemed more likely was that this adopted son of Mondragón who had conceived the first sports league, the first technical school, the first cooperative, and the first bank tended to hover above the daily operations and disputes of individual human interactions. Living in a world of thought, as he so often did, relegated a strike to the realm of his disciples, not to him. It was little surprise, therefore, that as he recuperated from heart surgery, and as protesters walked off Ulgor's factory floor, Don José María was focusing his thoughts and attention on a new project, something for the future. He wrote, "Our people require of our men the development of the means to scale the heights of scientific knowledge, which are the bases of progress."

Indeed, around the world private companies and national governments had begun investing heavily in new technologies to gain efficiencies in the workplace. He wanted to keep pace. Working with Manuel Quevedo who ran shop operations at the Escuela Politécnica Profesional, he developed a plan for an industrial research program. He sprang the new idea on ULARCO's governing council just as it debated the strike and labor negotiations. For the time, it was an extraordinary proposal: 112 million pesetas ($2 million) for new buildings, laboratories, and an automated quality control structure. "We opposed this idea as we did other ideas when Don José María first presented them to us," said one of the Ularco founders, "but he always succeeded in convincing us." Even the bank leadership, whom he had invited to the meeting, approved the plan.

José María Arizmendiarrieta circa 1976, the year of his death. Photo courtesy of the Mondragón Cooperative Corporation.

During that single afternoon, he breathed life into Ikerlan ("Research"), a new enterprise that would go on to guide research and development for a generation. It would be his last brick of solidarity.

In November 1975, Franco died, his reign of 36 years ending with one final irregular heartbeat, releasing the Spanish people once and for all to their own destinies. A year after Franco's death, nearly to the day, surrounded at his bedside by the men whom he had first taught and guided on the cooperative path, Don José María spoke his final words. He said, "Looking back is an offense to God, you must always look forward." Then he closed his eyes and breathed no more.

The church bells rang out across Mondragón for this little one-eyed man, this father who had seen further than most. On December 1, 1976, his disciples hoisted the coffin to their shoulders and walked a cobblestone path slowly with only the clop-clop of their footfalls to break the crisp cold air. Men and women and children, all somber and weeping with bowed heads, all dressed in their finest suits or dresses, lined the streets in thick masses to get one last glimpse of this important man. He died with no money or title besides *Padre*, but anyone there would have said that he had left each of them so very much, a legacy of coopera-tion, work, solidarity, dignity, and hope. What more could there be in the world?

A CCORDING TO LEGEND, Mondragón derived its name from a ferocious dragon that roamed the countryside, burning homes and farms and livestock, fanning the flames with its mighty wings, dining on the ashes of bodies and buildings, and pushing each generation to the brink of extinction. And so it went year after year until a wily man, a stranger to the town, banded the villagers into an opposing force. They were stronger and smarter than the dragon, he told them, and the villagers believed him, and together they vanquished the beast, never again to feel the searing pain of burned homes, lost livelihoods, or starving children.

Don José María would have liked this story, though he would have declined any recognition as the wily stranger who galvanized the people. As his thin legs had grown thinner with age and he had suffered his first angina attack in 1968, his students had replaced his popular bicycle with a motor-scooter. They had wanted to buy him a car, but he had refused, as he had refused nearly all conveniences or public displays of praise. The credit for Mondragón's success, he had maintained, belonged to the people who had found courage in themselves and solidarity with each other.

After his death, recognition came anyhow. A street was named after him. His portrait or bronze bust popped up on walls or in lobbies of various buildings in Mondragón and elsewhere, and quotations from his prolific writings highlighted key points in the cooperatives' annual reports. When the Escuela Politécnica Profesional became Mondragón University, he was hailed as the city's Renaissance man and as a guardian angel who had swooped down in Mondragón's darkest hour to guide people into the light. In 50 years, the school that had started with idea-boxes on street corners had grown to more than 3,500 students, nearly all engaged in work study or exchanges with universities around the world. To this day, it has an aggressive placement program that on average finds a job for every graduate within three months.

The bank retained its prominence as a superstructure and hub for the cooperative federation. With over $24 billion in assets and branches throughout Spain, it became a key stabilizing force not only for Mondragón and the Basque region but for much of the country. As Spain and the world faced lean years in the 1980s, after September 11 in New York City, during the Great Recession of 2008–2009, and still today, the cooperative struggled as nearly all businesses struggled. But the difference between it and a privately owned company was how each responded to the economic challenges. Many private firms laid-off workers as a kneejerk response, but with the bank's assistance, laying-off workers at the cooperative was a last resort. That doesn't mean that layoffs didn't happen, only that they happened far less often.[8] Instead, the cooperatives in the federation shared resources, the strong lending support to the weak, knowing at a future date, their roles might be reversed. Through a shared pain, the whole survived.

Adopting the slogan Humanity at Work, the ULARCO federation became the Mondragón Cooperative Corporation (MCC) during the 1980s when Spain prepared for entry into the European Union. Today, the MCC has grown to 257 cooperatives on five continents, employing nearly 100,000 worker-owners. About 40 percent reside in the Basque country, another 40 percent in the rest of Spain, and the remainder in other countries. When King Juan Carlos visited the headquarters, he praised Don José María so many years after his death. "MCC is good for Euskadi, for Spain and for workers," he said. "It would be very good if there were a lot more MCCs." Following this pronouncement, the United Nations declared 2012 the International Year of Cooperatives and cited Don José María's words: "The cooperative movement is the affirmation of faith in people, in work, in honesty, in living together."[9] Then in late December 2015, Pope Francis signed a decree recognizing the father for his "heroic virtues," the first step in a long process toward beatification and canonization.

The good father would have been embarrassed by this extraordinary recognition. Bowing his blushing thin face, high cheekbones, and sunken eyes, he would have passed the credit to the men and women who had born the daily struggle. Then pausing to think, he would have climbed on his bicycle or motor-scooter for a ride through the lush green of the Mondragón countryside. Along the upper Deba River as a breeze rustled the pines, he might have whispered something that he had so often told his parishioners in the confessional or his students over bread and coffee at a local café. Maybe too it applies still today: "Only together do we build the road as we travel."

Notes

1. The first record of a cooperative is from Rochdale, England, in 1844. A group of workers in the cotton mills suffered miserable conditions and low wages. No matter how hard they worked, they could not afford food and basic household goods. They decided to pool their meager resources and formed the Rochdale Equitable Pioneers Society. In the beginning, they sold flour, oatmeal, sugar, and butter and stayed open only two nights per week. They then made a collective decision to include their customers as owners, arguing that a share of profits would encourage repeat customers. Within three months, the Rochdale Cooperative had grown so much, it had to open its doors five nights per week. The foundation of honesty, openness, and respect that these pioneers established still serves as the basis for all cooperatives, including the ones championed by José María Arizmendiarrieta.

2. In 1944, three years after Don José María built the soccer field and established the

sports league, the kids of Mondragón defeated the kids of Tolosa, a much larger city, to win the soccer championship of Guipuzcoa.

3. No reliable evidence exists on this point, but it is possible that Basques invented the pub crawl, a well-known tradition in Western civilization especially during spring breaks, weddings, divorces, and nights of general carousing with friends. Basques spend countless hours each year perfecting this part of their ancient heritage.

4. A not inconsequential comparison might be made with income disparities in the United States. According to the U.S. Bureau of Labor Statistics, the average American worker received $24.57 per hour in December 2014, an amount equal to about $49,140 annually. In the 2012 Fortune survey, *Forbes* magazine reported that average compensation for Fortune 500 CEOs was $10.5 million, consisting of $3.5 million in salary and bonus, $3.8 million in personal perk packages, and $3.2 million in stock options and awards. The ratio, therefore, in the United States is 213-to-1. Though these salary figures come from different years, the disparity between high and low wage earners in the United States has only widened since 2012 when *Forbes* conducted this survey.

5. Although Don José María was released from prison following Franco's ultimate victory, a document from the library of Ikasbide shows that he was listed for execution by Franco's forces. How or why he was saved remains a mystery.

6. The health clinic became a highly successful model for health care delivery to senior citizens, cooperative members, and their dependents. During the 1980s, the Spanish government took over the health clinic, expanding access to other Spanish citizens and using it as a model for other clinics around the country.

7. To say that Eroski flourished is an understatement. After gaining the assistance of Don José María and reorganizing to comport with the demands of the Caja Laboral Popular, Eroski grew to include nearly 50 hypermarkets, 800 supermarkets, 600 self-service shops, 2,800 associated franchise self-service stores, 30 cash-and-carries, 25 gas stations, and over 100 travel agencies. These numbers increase frequently as Eroski expands through acquisition or by organic growth. Eroski was included in the introduction as one of the cooperatives that proposed a unique solution for weathering the 2008–2009 recession around the world.

8. A conspicuous example of failure came in 2013 when Fagor Electrodomésticos declared bankruptcy. The bank and other cooperative members of the federation had tried to save it by lending money, absorbing labor or administrative costs, helping with restructuring, and focusing on new product lines. But in the end, the cooperative failed because of product obsolescence more than anything else. Of the workers who lost their jobs, many were absorbed into other parts of the cooperative federation immediately or over the next two years. In the end, there was pain, but the pain was mitigated by the cooperatives' structure and philosophy.

9. According to the International Cooperative Alliance, cooperative enterprises worldwide employ 250 million people and generate $2.2 trillion USD in turnover while providing the services and infrastructure society needs to thrive. In Spain, 15 percent of the workforce now operates in a cooperative of one form or another, many of them within the Mondragón Cooperative Corporation.

Paul Dominique Laxalt

The First Friend

"**D**o I have to call you Mr. President now?" asked Laxalt.

"Only in the presence of others," said Reagan.

Otherwise it was *Ron*, and his friend called him *Paul*, and that's how it had been for 16 years. Then the friends hung up the phone.

In Nevada, Senator Paul Laxalt had won reelection handily with 59 percent. Earlier in the day, he had visited his campaign workers in Reno. "I don't usually predict how a race will come out," he said, "but this time I'm going to make an exception. Before the day is out, Ron Reagan will win in a landslide." Everyone cheered.

That evening at a private home in Reno, Paul stared at a small television screen like so many other Americans around the nation. He watched President-elect Ronald Reagan walk to the stage, a place of comfort for much of his life, to deliver his 1980 victory speech before a throng of well-wishers at the Century Plaza Hotel in Los Angeles.

Paul felt exultant for this man he knew so well. He was the only senator who had supported Reagan's bid in 1976 against Gerald Ford. Now in 1980, he chaired his national election committee, even put his name into nomination at the convention, all to bring victory over a sitting president and lift the spirits of a nation. Few had worked harder. Three weeks earlier, over two-thirds of Americans had said the country was doing *pretty bad* or *very bad*. When so many called the race a nail-biter, even in the final days, Paul believed it wouldn't be close at all.

Nevada governor Paul Laxalt with California governor Ronald Reagan and his wife Nancy Reagan at Lake Tahoe in April 1967 for the Federation International de Ski World Cup. Photo courtesy of the Ronald Reagan Foundation.

All night long, Paul watched newsmen call state after state for Ron: the rust bowl of Ohio, Michigan, and Indiana with its blue collars; the Deep South devotees of the military, motherhood, and the Maker; the wealthy educated elite of the Northeast; and the rural, rustic, freedom-loving libertarians of the West. By the night's end, Ronald Reagan would win 44 states, flip Senate control to Republicans with 12 gains, and add 34 new Congresspersons, four new governors, and several state legislatures. Rarely in American politics had a landslide deserved the name more.

But governing was different than campaigning. Paul knew that from his days as governor of Nevada and as a US senator now with one term under his belt. Watching his friend on that television, he saw the moment as a profound mandate from the American people for a dramatic change in direction. He had helped Reagan come this far and now aimed to push his agenda of lower taxes, stronger defense, and less government—the three planks of the campaign—from a comfortable perch inside the United States Senate where he could do his friend the most good.

What a distance he had come from Carson City, the smallest capital in America he liked to boast, to this pinnacle of power on the world stage. His daddy had been an old Basque sheepherder from the French Pyrenees, a man of "leather and bronze" as Paul's brother Robert had described him, who knew the foothills and craggy caves of the Sierras better than any house with four walls. Paul had often spent time on the family ranch near Marlette Lake about 1,000 feet above Lake Tahoe, his "slice of heaven on earth," to herd sheep, check up on dad, or get his head straight after the war.

His momma, the more business savvy of the couple, had kept the white frame home in Carson City, run the French Hotel, and tended six kids: Paul the eldest, three brothers (Robert, John, and Mick), and two sisters (Suzanne and Marie). Several times a week, Paul would sup at the French Hotel near politicians with big bellies and big stogies who would point to him and say, "That boy will be governor someday," and his momma would wave it off along with the smoke as a lot of hot air.

Paul would get a taste for politics then. After attending Santa Clara, a Jesuit college in California, he signed up for the army, and saw combat at the Battle of Leyte in the Philippines. He graduated with a law degree from the University of Denver after the war and returned to Carson City to run for district attorney, his first victory. A few years later in 1962, he won election as lieutenant governor and immediately launched a bid for the US Senate in 1964 when Barry Goldwater stood for the Republican Party against President Lyndon Baines Johnson.

Goldwater had been sinking dramatically in the polls with no hope of winning, and he wanted to visit Las Vegas. Paul was advised to avoid the man like kryptonite. "Listen, Barry Goldwater is my friend," he said, "If I snubbed him now, I could never look him in the face again. I would rather lose." Meeting on the tarmac, the two shook hands and the next morning, the photo flashed on the front page of every Nevada newspaper. Paul lost his race by 48 votes but came away with two great assets: first, a steely clarity about the kind of man he was, and the value he placed on friendship; and, second, a growing bond with another fellow, Ronald Reagan, who had spoken of Goldwater's virtue and trumpeted the principles of conservatism in a riveting speech called "A Time for Choosing."

When Paul and Ron met again, each had been elected governor in 1966, Paul in Nevada and Ron in California, two conservative titans of Goldwater's legacy. Paul invited Ron and Nancy several times to his family getaway, the sheep camp near Marlette Lake, where the two friends bonded over the outdoors. During one of their first visits, Paul shared a great irony. "Ron, I've come to a real bad conclusion here," he said, "but I don't think I can avoid it. I think we're going to have to go for a tax increase." Then Ron, with that soft face and warm grin, said, "You know, Paul, we've come to the same conclusion." When he recalled the story many years later, Paul smiled then laughed and said, "So we both went for a tax increase, and we used to joke about it because the tax increase rejuvenated our respective economies, and the people who succeeded us as governor had all the money in the world for years. But we bit that bullet."

The family getaway hosted a discussion of Lake Tahoe too, the bright green-blue wonder swaddled in pines that straddled their two states. Paul and Ron met there in April 1967 for the Federation International de Ski World Cup, the two becoming an overnight sensation, tromping through the snow, posing for pictures with children and dogs and well-wishers, and throwing or getting hit by snowballs. It was the first time that Reagan and Nancy had visited Lake Tahoe, and they fell in love with the crisp clean air and the natural beauty.

When developers set their sights on this emerald of the west, it took hardly a nudge for Ron and Paul to carve out a plan to preserve it. Developers wanted to expand the Tahoe Basin from 12,000 residents to over 200,000 by 1984 and build a high-speed freeway around the lake and a bridge across Emerald Bay. "Tahoe was a ticking time bomb," said Paul. "Unless we did something, it stood a real chance of turning gray on our watch." Their meetings near Marlette Lake culminated in the Bi-State Compact, a rare agreement to halt runaway growth, oversee planning, and preserve this azure majesty of the Sierras. It was signed by Paul and Ron, passed by both state legislatures, ratified by Congress, and signed into law by President Nixon in 1969. At the sheep camp still, there's

a wooden table where Ron and Paul sat and talked and looked at the meadows and sunsets, where Paul's dad took his meals, and where the ranch hands
grubbed during lambing. But the table's real charm comes from a carving on the
top. It shows a heart encircling the initials *R.R.* and *N.R.*

Watching the television now and hearing Ron's victory speech, these memories rushed in, so good and wholesome and thick that Paul couldn't brush them
away even if he had wanted to. But the moment conjured bad memories too.
Paul had spent four years in the governor's chair at great cost to his wife and six
children. "My marriage was deteriorating and my family disintegrating," he said.
"When my little ones called me 'Governor,' I decided I wanted out." He opted
against reelection, saying he had had a "gut-full" of politics. Over the next four
years, he spoke to Ron only rarely, who was then in his second term as governor,
and focused his energies instead on a new business venture. He and brother
Mick, recalling their hard-working momma at the French Hotel, opened the
Ormsby House, a hotel and casino in Carson City. It didn't go well and the
brothers were forced to sell not long after. Paul's marriage didn't survive either,
although his six children went on to successful careers and families of their own.

In 1974, US Senator Alan Bible, a 20-year incumbent, decided not to seek
reelection. Finding his gut not so full after all, Paul decided to throw his hat
in the ring. It was a hard fight. In the middle of the campaign, President Ford
announced a pardon of former president Richard Nixon for his involvement in
the Watergate scandal. It became "a hundred pound weight around my neck,"
said Paul, but he went on to defeat Harry Reid, Nevada's lieutenant governor. It
ended up being the only Republican gain in the country that year.

The friendship that had cooled over the past few years was rekindled. Just
as Paul became the junior senator from Nevada, Ron ended his second term as
California's governor in 1975 and asked Paul to head his presidential campaign
organization. "I didn't find anyone in town who could communicate as well
as Ron," said Paul. He worked tirelessly, traveling to 41 states, giving stump
speeches, raising money, extolling the conservative virtues of his friend. Paul
was the only US senator to endorse Reagan; all others had stayed with President
Ford who bested Reagan in New Hampshire, Florida, and Illinois.

Then North Carolina came up. Paul urged Ron to oppose President Ford's
plan to give up control of the Panama Canal, building the campaign around
this issue. By Election Day, the gamble paid off. Reagan took North Carolina,
cracking Ford's armor, and went on to win Texas and California too, pushing
the nomination to the Republican convention in Kansas City. Though down to
the wire, Reagan lost in the final tally—1,187 delegates for Ford, 1,070 for Reagan.
Then Ford lost in the general election to Jimmy Carter.

In the morning after, Paul sat with Ron and Nancy at their home in the Pacific Palisades in California. "We all assumed Carter would have eight years," he said, "but I suggested that Ron never close the door. Things were politically volatile." Within two years, Paul sensed "a smell of death about the Carter Presidency." He wanted his friend to have another run, so he readied for the fight, preparing like John the Baptist.

Running against an incumbent president who retains all the trappings of power—Air Force One, a loyal cabinet, entrenched money interests, the bully pulpit, and so many other advantages—has never been an easy undertaking in American politics. No inch of ground was gained without considerable strain, and up to October 1980, it was neck-and-neck. There needed to be a breakthrough, and one finally came. "The presidential debate in Cleveland between Ron and President Carter seemed to satisfy millions of Americans," said Paul, "that Ron was a responsible, decent man who, contrary to his critics' suggestions, wouldn't blow up the world."

As Ron finished his victory speech in Los Angeles on election night, November 4, 1980, Paul sat on the couch still watching that television and then stood and sat and stood again with nervous energy. Yet he felt excitement too for all that was to come. He knew his friend had been cast in the role of a lifetime.

"I ONLY WANT DIBS on one appointment," said Paul.

"I know what it is," said Ron.

Shortly thereafter the two drove together from the tarmac on Reagan's first official visit to Washington DC as president-elect in 1980. Speculation swirled about who would be in the cabinet. Early talk included Laxalt as secretary of state before Alexander Haig gained the slot by the urging of Nixon and Kissinger. Paul had no interest. "I made it clear to him and everybody else in the process that I just wanted to stay where I was," he said. "I'd just been reelected to the Senate, and I had a contract with my people."

But the "dibs" were a different matter. He wanted to handpick the secretary of the interior, an overlooked position in the East, though vitally important among Westerners whose livelihood often depended on federal public lands, water rights, mining, ranching, and timbering. "Because of the November election, it's a whole new ballgame," said state assemblyman Dean Rhoads of Nevada, who had organized ranchers, miners, hunters, and Western-elected officials into the so-called Sagebrush Rebellion against federal encroachment of states' rights. Paul agreed.

He wanted Cliff Hansen at the Department of the Interior, a former governor and senator from Wyoming, but Cliff's health wasn't good. So he talked with Western conservatives who collectively put forward one name: James Watt. "I arranged a meeting," said Paul, "and he and the president got along just famously, but he just tended to talk too much." Although Watt's confirmation quelled the Sagebrush Rebels, Paul's concern of "talk-too-much" led to Watt's downfall nearly three years later.[1]

Paul weighed in on other appointments, serving as a conservative litmus test. His brand of conservatism mixed well with the more libertarian, anti-government sentiments that were ascendant in the Republican Party. As the eldest son of a sheepherding father who had spent more time in the hills than in Carson City, Paul had acted as a bridge between Momma and his brothers and sisters, and he played the role of peacemaker later in life too. He had been a conduit of information and a trusted, reliable settler of disputes. These skills served him in Washington, DC, reassuring conservatives that the president would not forsake them. He also carried messages from the US Senate to the White House and back again.

After the transition, Reagan's presidency throttled forward. During the campaign, he had promised to increase defense spending; cut waste, fraud, and abuse; and reduce tax rates to bolster economic growth. To do all of it required the cooperation of Congress. Although Paul had no special title besides senator and held no chairmanship of any committee, he was asked by Senate Majority Leader Howard Baker Jr. of Tennessee to be an "unelected member of the Senate leadership." The role often put him next to the president behind the French doors of the cabinet room or with Senator Baker and House Minority Leader Robert Michel of Illinois at budget talks in the Oval Office. If asked by the press why he was there, he said, "I went along because I was asked to go by the president." His was an unprecedented role.

He enjoyed enormous influence. He joked that the White House staff planned to set up a cot for him in the West Wing. An example of his clout came in 1981 when he met with America's mayors, who said the president's proposed cuts of $13 billion to cities and states would cripple them. Hearing their arguments and finding them sound, Paul spoke to reporters outside. The next morning, the president told an aide, "Hey, I see that even Paul is critical of us. We've got to look at this again." The trim went down to $4 billion. By 1982, Paul had helped pass $39 billion in budget cuts, reduce taxes by 25 percent over three years, and accelerate write-offs for investment in business, all while increasing outlays for defense.

The economic policies worked only partly as intended, however. Inflation had dropped from 13.5 percent in 1980 to 5.1 percent in 1982, but the country had plunged into a severe recession, driving unemployment to over 10 percent and causing the deficit to explode. The policies needed adjustment, and someone had to deliver the bad news. Who would it be? The go-to guy was Paul.

In one meeting, the president had invited 25 Republican Congresspersons to the White House. He urged them to reverse previous cuts by $98 billion to avoid ballooning deficits. There were no takers. A deathly silence settled over the room. Then Paul told the young bucks that cuts from the previous summer had been too deep, the effects too severe, that a correction was needed, and it all depended on them. "If there had been a secret ballot in the Senate last year," he said, "there wouldn't have been more than 12 votes for the tax cuts." But no one wanted to appear to be doing nothing. Worse, no one wanted to disappoint a leader who had carried 44 states in most demographics coast to coast. Out of these discussions grew select tax increases and additional budget cuts to stave off higher deficits. Paul called the measures "running room" to let the economic policies reach full effect.

Paul and Ron were not all about business. They gabbed on the phone for no reason at all or hosted the wives at a private dinner in the residence. These were men of the West hailing from small towns where handshakes mattered more than signed papers. A man's word was his bond. There was loyalty, devotion, and kindred spirit between them. They had known each other before either was anyone important. In his office on Capitol Hill, a picture sat on Paul's desk showing him and Ron, with a note scrawled at the bottom: "A favorite picture of my two favorite fellas. Fondly, Nancy."

In good times, friendships can be misleading and seem strong only because of circumstances. It is only in bad times that the true depths of a friendship are revealed. The true colors of Paul's friendship shined through in a moment of tragedy—Monday, March 30, 1981.

Paul was eating lunch with Elizabeth Drew, a reporter from the *New Yorker Magazine*, when he got a call. It was Ed Hickey, the head of security at the White House.

"Christ, Paul, some son of a bitch just shot the president."

Ed swung by to pick him up and the two made their way to George Washington University Hospital. There they met Mike Deaver, the deputy chief of staff.

"Where's Nancy?" asked Paul. Mike pointed to a small room set aside for her.

He went there, and Nancy fell into his arms. "I held her as I would one of my children. She trembled," he said.

Prepped for surgery, Ron was wheeled by on a gurney. He looked at Nancy with scared eyes to quip, now famously, "Honey, I forgot to duck." Paul teared up.

The bullet had come within an inch of Reagan's heart. Some who didn't know Reagan speculated later that he wasn't the same after the bullet. Paul thought it was nonsense, though he acknowledged "there was a certain sadness. You could see it in his eyes. It wasn't just the physical pain. I think that he was deeply hurt, emotionally, that this could happen to him."

During Ron's recovery, Paul worked with Senate leadership to keep the economic and tax reforms on path. He shuttled between the Capitol and the hospital to check on Ron and share legislative updates. Secret Service agents had encircled the president, but all recognized Paul with each visit and let him pass.

During one of those hospital visits, Paul told Ron of a burr under his saddle, one particular to Nevada, which had begun to rub harder and deeper. Ron listened attentively, as he always listened to his friend. It was a new defense system, explained Paul, called the MX missile program. Ron knew of it from the campaign. It had sprung from a deep concern in military circles that if the Soviet Union launched a first strike, America would lose about 90 percent of its land-based force, rendering the United States defenseless. A solution had emerged for a mobile missile system, namely the MX, which called for 200 new missiles, each with 10 warheads, to be moved along a racetrack of sorts with 4,600 shelters. A missile could be launched from any shelter at a moment's notice. The US Air Force had calculated that the Soviets, not knowing its secret launch point along the track, would have only a 1-in-23 chance of hitting a missile.

Proposed first by President Carter, the MX quickly gained broad support. Support came from the Joint Chiefs of Staff, the secretary of defense, the National Security Council, both houses of Congress, and then President-elect Ronald Reagan, who had embraced the concept during the 1980 campaign. The racetrack would cover parts of Western Utah and Southern Nevada.

That's when Paul had entered the fray. Not wanting Nevada to be a target of attack, he called the scheme a "Rube Goldberg invention."[2] His steady drumbeat against the MX swelled the opposition, a rare mixture of environmentalists and ranchers, antiwar liberals and evangelicals, who all spoke of ecological catastrophe; budget hawks who raised alarms about cost; and diplomatic elites who doubted that the MX would deter the Soviets or enhance America's survivability.[3] By mid-1982, a full year after Reagan's release from the hospital, nearly three-quarters of Nevadans (and an equal portion of Utahans[4]) opposed the MX due in large measure to Paul's public pronouncements, his pressure at the White House, and his cooperation with Senator Jake Garn of Utah.

The effort paid off. Within a year, the president issued a formal statement killing the MX program in Nevada and Utah. Majority Leader Howard Baker said that Reagan's decision had "nothing to do with politics and nothing to do with geography and certainly nothing to do with friendship." One is

Paul comforted Nancy on the day President Reagan was shot. Here he visits with his friend Ron in the hospital a few days after the assassination attempt on March 30, 1981. During Reagan's recovery, Paul served as a conduit to the US Senate for assorted policies under consideration. Photo courtesy of the Ronald Reagan Library.

left wondering. Conspicuous in Reagan's announcement was a kind, though tongue-in-cheek acknowledgement: "We plan to produce the MX missile, now named Peacekeeper, and deploy it in super hard silos at Francis E. Warren Air Force Base, near Cheyenne, Wyoming," he said. "That seems to be the most cost-effective location, but I appreciate the enthusiastic offers by the citizens of Nevada to base the missile in their state." No mention of Utah was made.

Next to the President's MX announcement was wall-to-wall coverage of the upcoming midterms. Republicans feared that they'd be blamed for high unemployment and budget deficits. Their fears were not misplaced. After election night, the US Senate lost only one Republican seat, letting Howard Baker retain his post as Senate majority leader. However, in the House, Republicans lost 26 seats, giving Speaker Tip O'Neill greater leverage over domestic and budget policy. Among some in the press, the outcome portended badly for 1984, forcing a natural question: Will Reagan run again?

There were ambiguous signs. The White House made no definitive announcement one way or another. A month before in the White House residence, Ron had asked Paul if he'd serve as chairman of the Republican Party.

Paul declined, not wanting to give up his Senate seat for the full-time role. Then the request came again. Paul said publicly, "I told them it was not my preference and that's what I meant. They know how I feel, now they are making another run at me." As a close friend and confidante of Reagan, his resistance signaled to media and others that Reagan may indeed not run in 1984 or that the prospects for victory appeared so dim that even the president's closest allies were distancing themselves from the ticket. It left the politics of both parties frozen with uncertainty.

In late November, a new post was created: general chairman of the Republican Party. "I just don't want to be worried about that political situation. You've just got to go in there and handle this for me," said Ron, and Paul accepted. That's what friends do when asked. In this new position, Paul oversaw the national party, congressional campaigns, and the White House political office. The role, like his unelected leadership position in the US Senate, was unprecedented. By February 1983, Paul installed one of his protégés, Frank J. Fahrenkopf Jr. from Nevada, as the new national chairman, replacing Richard Richards. With Paul at his side, Ron signed a letter in October 1983 launching his campaign. It was game-on for a second term.

T HE NATIONAL ECONOMY was on the upswing, the "running room" that Paul had described paying dividends with lower inflation, lower unemployment, lower interest rates, and higher economic growth. For a voting public that valued pocketbook issues, this was manna from heaven, and for Paul and Ed Rollins, the new campaign manager, it afforded an easy campaign theme: "America is back" and "Morning in America." Paul hoped that the worst was behind them, that the economy had turned finally in their favor, and that his friend would enjoy smooth sailing. But there were whispers, and whispers in Washington DC can be deadly things. Those whispers grew into a full-throated dialogue about Reagan: Was the man too old?

Few in the public gave the idea much thought really, perhaps a comparison of Reagan with an uncle or grandfather who had reached the ripe age of 73 years old. "He's doing fine," they'd say, or "my grandpa just finished the Boston Marathon and he's older than 73." In the same breath, they might acknowledge that the old uncle or grandpa might be a bit forgetful or slow, but few believed these maladies, if true, warranted the president stepping aside. The public afforded him the benefit of the doubt. Democrats feared a backlash if they claimed old age as a disqualifier, though they stoked the rumors and the media ran stories almost daily on the question. None of it stuck.

Then came the first debate against Walter Mondale, the Democratic nominee, on October 7, 1984, in Louisville, Kentucky. Over 90 million Americans tuned in, one of the largest television audiences up to that point. The president stammered and stuttered, spewed statistics, lost trains of thought, mangled facts, and mixed metaphors. Tired, discombobulated, out of sorts, lost—these were the words that people used to describe him immediately after. "He didn't know where the hell he was. He was punchy, and it showed," said Paul. "He looked and sounded like an old man." Gallup declared Mondale the victor with a 54 percent tally to Reagan's 35 percent. Headlines screamed the next morning: "It's a brand new race," "Mondale Buoyed by His Success in First Debate," "Mondale Wins Credibility in Debate," and "Mondale Wins Newsweek Post-Debate Audience Poll."

Flying to Washington that evening, Paul joined Nancy to talk through what had gone wrong. He wanted to safeguard Ron and avoid the creeping perception that he might indeed be too old for the job. Nancy was angry. "Find out who did this," she told Paul. She wanted a head to roll. Paul talked with Ed Rollins and several others in the White House who had led the briefs before the debate. The culprit was not the candidate, concluded Paul, but the debate preparation. The preparers would never know his friend like he did. Paul believed that Ron had a thematic style, one that didn't do well when loaded down with too many facts and figures. "Unless you've got an accountant's framework, that type of mind—and very few people have—stay away from that," said Paul. "That will kill a candidate."

In a press conference the next morning, he confronted the issue head on. "Our candidate had not done well, but it wasn't his fault," Paul said. "He'd been brutalized by those who'd prepared him for the debate." The reporters loved *brutalized*, a wonderful, powerful word that deflected concern over Reagan's performance and begged the question: Who exactly "brutalized" the president? Who were these scoundrels? One name emerged—Richard Darman, from the Office of Management and Budget. He bore the brunt of the criticism. Thereafter Washington coined a new term for the political lexicon: *Darmanized*. To this day, it describes a state of being too prepared to one's own detriment.

As much as the first debate had blown wind into Mondale's sails, angered Nancy, and elevated age as a legitimate issue, Paul discovered that it had done something else too. It had changed the yard stick by which Ron would be measured in the second debate. His second debate performance would not be compared with the image of a glamorous, well-polished, elusive Hollywood performer but with his performance in the first debate, a low point to be sure in his public appearances. If ever there was a silver lining, this had to be one, and it gave rise to Paul's simple strategy: "Let Reagan be Reagan." People related to

Ron not because of a wonkish command of policy but because of his warmth, certitude, and unwavering belief in America.

Two weeks later in Kansas City, Missouri, a different man took the stage against Mondale, not Reagan the President, but simply Ron, Paul's friend, the underdog, and the man whom so many had grown to love and admire around the country. The debate focused on foreign affairs, heady topics of terrorism, the Nicaraguan Contras, and the Soviet Union—issues that the United States had been wrestling with during the 1970s and 1980s and to a large extent still does today. Beyond topics of foreign relations, the moderator finally asked Reagan the million-dollar question: "Is 73-years-old too old to be president?" Ron retorted with a line brilliantly delivered, and now part of presidential lore, "I will not make age an issue in this campaign. I am not going to exploit, for political purposes, my opponent's youth and inexperience." The audience howled and clapped and roared! Even Mondale turned and laughed, and so too did the moderator.[5] Any question about his age or unfitness for office, justified or not, vanished in those few seconds.

In the final week before Election Day, the campaign staff pondered visiting Minnesota, Mondale's home state. Reagan thought it would be disrespectful to campaign in the man's backyard. Paul said, "It isn't fair to the people of Minnesota not to make at least one visit." Ron relented. To avoid a spectacle, the drop-in would be discreet at a rural airport with little more than radio, television, and word-of-mouth announcing the arrival 24 hours before. "What happened next," said Paul, "was one of the most moving experiences I've ever had." Several dirt roads were clogged with pickups. Whole families climbed out of the backs, moms and dads, and old people and children. They streamed in from every direction, walked across meadows to find a place where they might glimpse this man who had come to their living rooms over the past four years, a man who had campaigned on America's restored place in the world. To see him on that day was to bear witness. "It was a fitting close to the campaign," said Paul.

On election night, Ron wrote in his diary, "Well 49 states, 59% of the vote and 525 electoral votes. The press is now trying to prove it wasn't a landslide . . . onto the ranch."[6]

EIGHT MONTHS after Reagan's second inaugural address, Paul called Ron to tell him he would not seek another term in the US Senate. It was August 18, 1985. "He was not exactly jumping up and down with joy," said Paul. "He was deeply disappointed but he understood, which is what friends are all about, I guess." With control of the US Senate hanging in the balance, many tried to convince him to stay. He had his reasons, maybe to spend time with family, make money in the private sector, or tend to a legal battle against the *Sacramento Bee*. Regardless, he planned to stay in Washington until Ron's term ended in 1988. "The Reagans want me to be there," he said. "I want to be there at their side. I will continue to be available for whatever they need me to do."

It was not long after, probably a couple months, that Senator Danny Inouye of Hawaii approached Paul on the Senate floor.

"We just had a very important meeting on the Philippines," he said.

"Where'd that take place?" asked Paul.

"In the White House," he said. "I don't know whether I should have done this, but I hope I didn't take your name in vain."

"What the hell did you do?"

"A guy like Marcos likes to be able to talk to the top, and he knows he can't talk to the president, so I threw your name in," he said.

"Thanks one hell of a lot," replied Paul.

Ferdinand Marcos had served as the Philippine president since 1965 and as prime minister since 1978.[7] When his terms of office bumped up against a constitutional limit in 1972, he declared martial law, claiming that an insurgency of Muslims and communists had threatened to dissolve the country's democracy. The state of emergency was not lifted until 1981, marking a decade of deep corruption, graft, land confiscation, and hoarding of wealth by him, his wife Imelda, and the Rolex-12.[8] The United States tolerated the Marcos regime to safeguard its two military installations in the archipelago—Clark Air Base and Subic Bay Naval Station. The Philippines' discontent mounted like steam in a pressure cooker.

In solidarity with these frustrated Philippines, Benigno Aquino Jr., the leader of the opposition, who had spent years in exile, returned to his country in August 1983. He stepped off the plane ready to embrace his homeland and was assassinated at the airport. The country exploded. Opposition groups coalesced around his wife, Corazon Aquino, a petite, mousy, pious woman with glasses not accustomed to the limelight, who called for democracy, human rights, and an end to corruption. People took to the streets, the economy declined, and reports of terrorism surfaced around America's military bases. In August 1985, Philippine officials drafted articles of impeachment against Marcos, listing as primary offenses the diversion of US aid, the confiscation of private property, and direct theft from the country's treasury. A longer list could have been presented, but these offered overwhelming (some would say undeniable) evidence against the Marcos family.

Paul went to the White House after talking with Inouye on the Senate floor. "I know this is a tough assignment, and you needn't go," said Ron. Paul had hoped for a quiet departure from the Senate, a few dinners with friends and staff, a quiet ride into the sunset like a cowboy in the Old West. When Ron told him he did not have to go, he knew in his heart that the opposite was true, that he had to go, that the bond between them made it a duty, not a request; so Paul accepted the assignment. Ron handed him a letter to deliver to Marcos. Both the letter and the trip were to be on the hush-hush.

"This was a complete graveyard trip," said Paul who left the United States quietly on October 12, 1985. "We were supposed to be treated that way, and we're on the plane, and one of the NSC [National Security Council] guys tipped off one of his buddies on the *Washington Times*. So, hell, by the time we go there, it was public. We had this whole crowd of Philippine reporters there."

Paul met Marcos at his opulent palace and handed Reagan's letter to him.[9] It encouraged Marcos to announce credible elections, reform the military, reduce corruption, and propose new legislation to halt the country's economic slide. It also called for Marcos to be neutral in the trial of the 26 men implicated in the assassination of Benigno Aquino.

Marcos seemed embarrassed, even resistant. His spokesman said, "Mr. Reagan has not been getting the whole picture of what is going on. Mr. Marcos knows what is going on better than all those kibitzers." The regime issued no formal press statement, denying at first that the meeting was taking place. Only three of six newspapers ran stories, one framing the article this way—"Another Meddler from U.S. Arrives." As Paul left the country after four days, newspapers screamed "Good Riddance" to the "Meddler" from America. Still, despite all the resistance, Paul assured Marcos that he was only a phone call away.

The Philippines continued to deteriorate politically and economically. Opposition groups grew in number and strength, their tactics bolder and more abrasive. In a call to Paul back in Washington, Marcos maintained that he was beloved by his people. To counter the unrest, he planned an appearance on David Brinkley's show, one of the Sunday morning broadcasts in the United States. Paul suggested that it would be a wonderful, dramatic moment to announce snap elections. If his support was as great as he believed, then surely he could withstand a verdict from a ballot box.

Marcos did as Paul recommended. He surprised everyone by announcing the elections on David Brinkley's show in November, and the election was held in late 1985. As expected Corazon Aquino ran in opposition. Widespread abuses were reported on both sides: box stuffing, ballot burning, intimidation, even killings. An independent oversight committee put Aquino ahead, but on February 7, 1986, Marcos was declared the winner. Unwilling to accept the outcome, the opposition inaugurated Aquino on the same day that Marcos accepted his next term. The country teetered on the precipice of civil war.

Paul received another call.

"How are the elections being treated out there?" asked Marcos.

"You're pretty suspect," said Paul.

"Why?" asked Marcos.

"Just one example: In one of your districts in your home area you got every vote," said Paul. "God damn, I couldn't carry my own family with every vote."

"Well, you Basques," said Marcos, "you're just too damn independent. We tend to be more clannish."

Days passed and the country started coming apart. The defense minister mutinied, joining Aquino and seizing two Manila military camps. Troops defected. To protect them, Filipinos surrounded the soldiers, kneeling in front of Marcos' tanks. Loyalties frayed, gunfire rang out. The people's movement was turning into a people's war.

President Reagan sent Marcos a note calling on him to quit. "Attempts to prolong the life of the present regime by violence are futile," he said. "A solution to this crisis can only be achieved through a peaceful transition to a new government."

Marcos read the note in the early morning and phoned Paul in a panic, his voice frail and tired. He offered to share power with Aquino and demanded to speak with President Reagan. Paul said he'd speak with the president and call him back.

In a 13-minute conversation, Paul and Ron concluded that a power-sharing deal was impractical, but that the United States could offer Marcos and his family refuge, a chance to leave the Philippines safely, and, most of all, a way to prevent bloodshed.

Paul called Marcos back at 5:00 a.m. Manila time to make the offer. Marcos listened and paused for nearly a minute.

Then he asked Paul, "Well, what would you do, Senator?"

"Respectfully, I think it is time that you cut and cut cleanly. I think the time has come," said Paul.

There was silence.

"Mr. President, are you there?" asked Paul.

"I'm here, Senator," said Marcos. "I am just so very, very disappointed."

On February 26, 1986, Ferdinand and Imelda stepped to their balcony one last time above a crowd of thousands. They sang together in a warm embrace "Because of You," before they and their entourage of 60 departed for Hawaii. Upon arrival, US Customs officials discovered 24 suitcases of gold bricks, diaper bags full of diamond jewelry, and certificates for gold bullion valued in the billions. When the Marcos' palace was raided, Imelda's closet contained over 2,700 pairs of shoes perched neatly on shelves.

This whole affair of covert meetings, secret letters, and snap elections that finally brought down a corrupt regime without civil war seemed like a worthy and honorable end to Paul's 12-year career in the US Senate. It relied so much on deep loyalty between a president and a senator, a leader of a country and his unassailable messenger, two friends who trusted each other implicitly.

Paul would leave his seat as planned in January 1987, Harry Reid having won it in November 1986. He expected a quiet two months of cocktail parties and warm farewells among colleagues and staff with whom he had worked for so many years. From the Senate floor, the late Senator Ted Kennedy of Massachusetts, the liberal lion, spoke for many when he said, "Paul Laxalt may be Ronald Reagan's best friend in the Senate, but it can also be said of Paul Laxalt that no senator has more friends on both sides of the aisle than he does." And from Senator Daniel Patrick Moynihan of New York, the reputed intellectual of the chamber: "My colleague, Paul Laxalt, the strong silent Gary Cooper of the US Senate, is, to a degree, enigmatic. This trace of mystery is perhaps in keeping with his Basque heritage, a people whose origins are unknown. The senator from Nevada keeps his distance, maintains perspective, and remains objective."

That's how Paul wanted it, a quiet end, a few kind words among friends, mannerly exchanges, backslaps and handshakes. But that was not all he got. He received a phone call in late November from his friend, a call of the gravest shock that upset the quiet, equally upset the American people, and risked bringing down a presidency.

"PAUL, I think we've got a bit of a problem," said Ron over the phone. "Some Beirut newspaper has just run an article indicating that we're exchanging arms for hostages in Iran."[10]

Paul was in Bermuda when he took the call, golfing with Senator Dan Quayle of Indiana, Senator Malcolm Wallop of Wyoming, and Tom Korologos, a Washington lobbyist. The foursome wanted to avoid the Capitol where a week before, the mid-terms had returned control of the US Senate to the Democrats, and a state of euphoria or death still lingered in several congressional offices.

The article from the Beirut newspaper had launched the media into a feeding frenzy. Everyone wanted to know if the allegations were true, and if so, did the president know about them. If he didn't know, why didn't he? Those who had endured Watergate sniffed scandal and cover-up, and they believed the offenses and the president's complicity, if proven, could lead to impeachment.

Attorney General Ed Meese led an investigation. He confirmed details about the story only a few days later. In 1985, Iran and Iraq were at war. Iranian officials asked the United States for weapons, a request that National Security Advisor Robert McFarlane honored. He thought it would improve relations with Iran, and by extension Lebanon, where seven American hostages had been held for months. He reasoned that the United States had a duty to bring those Americans home.

The deal was cut with an added feature. Israel, serving as an intermediary, paid the CIA for the arms and then sold them through a Saudi arms merchant to the Iranians for a much higher price. The difference, a sum of about $30 million, was deposited in a bogus account called the National Endowment for the Preservation of Liberty, and transferred to the Palmer National Bank of Washington, DC, where Adolfo Calers, a Nicaraguan Contra leader, accessed and withdrew the funds. This transaction violated the Boland Amendment, part of a congressional act that banned aid to the Nicaraguan rebels who had been fighting the Cuban-backed Sandinistas.

A swirl of activity erupted. The president denied that the United States had any role in these events but retracted the claim a week later. He maintained all along that the transaction was not an "arms-for-hostages" deal. Only 14 percent of Americans believed him. Paul knew that this lack of trust from the American people would sting his friend to the core, just as an assassin's bullet had hurt his feelings more than it had hurt flesh and bone.

Swift action was taken. By the end of November, the president replaced National Security Advisor John Poindexter, who had succeeded Robert McFarlane 11 months earlier; fired Lieutenant Colonel Oliver North, who had been at the heart of the controversy; and appointed a three-person commission to investigate the matter.[11] Attorney General Ed Meese appointed a special prosecutor on December 1, and both houses of Congress convened committees to investigate the scandal in January 1987.

This frenetic pace started a serious round of finger-pointing and scapegoating, everyone wanting to blame someone. "A lot of CYA going on," said Paul. "I didn't participate in any of the discussions. I just watched the aftershock. Both of them really, George [Schultz, secretary of state] and Cap [Weinberger, secretary of defense] to a certain degree, let it be known that they leaked, that their people leaked to the papers that they weren't all in favor of the policy."

With so many protecting themselves, few were left to protect the president. Sensing this vulnerability, Nancy emerged, at least in private, as her husband's greatest defender. White House Chief of Staff Don Regan, former CEO of Merrill Lynch, became her target. Paul said of Regan, "He just wouldn't be

Ron and Paul listen to updates regarding the Tower Commission that convened on November 26, 1987, to investigate the Iran-Contra affair. The results of the investigation led to the resignation of White House Chief of Staff Don Regan and eventually to Paul helping Ron to land Howard Baker as the new chief of staff to navigate the aftermath of the controversy. Others in the photo include (seated from right to left) *Vice President George Bush, David Abshire, Marlin Fitzwater, and Dennis Thomas. Photo courtesy of the Ronald Reagan Library.*

deferential. He was a CEO. No one was going to tell him what to do except the president, which is not good strategy. Then when he didn't take Nancy's phone calls a few times, that didn't go well either. It was a matter of time before it would be *hasta la vista* to Don."

Not all knew of Nancy's distaste for Don Regan or had read the tea leaves, but Paul had. He began fielding questions from eager reporters who speculated that he might be Reagan's next pick as chief of staff. At this point, Paul had moved on from the US Senate, wanting to gravitate away from politics, not climb deeper into its bowels. "I decided that I had better start helping to find a replacement, lest I get an 'I-need-you' call from Ron," he said. On a legal pad, he sketched out alternatives: someone compatible with Ron and Nancy, credible with the Congress, respected by the media, someone who knew his way around Washington, who wasn't an ideologue or had his own agenda or political ambitions. The list was short, very short. Paul settled on a single name and set up a meeting with Ron and Nancy in the White House residence.

"Senator Howard Baker," said Paul.

Nancy said nothing.

"I thought Howard was going to run for president," said Ron.

Paul explained that a run for Howard seemed unlikely, that he might prefer an elegant way to avoid it, and serving as chief of staff would give him that off-ramp.

"How can we get in touch with him?" asked Nancy.

"Howard is in Florida visiting his grandchildren," said Paul. "Call him there."

Then Paul left. Within a couple hours, Ron called to say that Howard Baker had agreed to the position.

"I suggest a quick meeting at the White House," said Paul. "I'll attend if you want."

"I do," said Ron.

A day later, Paul picked up Howard and the two drove to the White House where Ron and Nancy and Howard had a meeting of the minds. They all thanked Paul, and then Nancy hugged him. He was, after all, one of her favorite fellas.

The change couldn't have come soon enough. The Tower Commission investigating the affair planned to release its findings any day. Paul proposed announcing the new chief of staff the day after to show immediate action. He expected the report to be scathing, even damaging to the whole administration. He was not wrong. It held "Reagan accountable for a lax managerial style and aloofness from policy detail." It added further detail to earlier findings: "Using the Contras as a front, and against international law and US law, weapons were sold, using Israel as intermediaries, to Iran, during the brutal Iran-Iraq war. The US was also supplying weapons to Iraq, including ingredients for nerve gas, mustard gas and other chemical weapons."[12] The report implicated Oliver North, John Poindexter, and Caspar Weinberger, among others. An appendix to the report opened with the Latin phrase—*Quis custodiet ipsos custodes?*—from the Roman poet Juvenal. Translated, it means *Who will guard the guards themselves?*

With Paul's help, Ron had an answer. Howard Baker gave a press conference on February 27, 1987, at his law office and started as the new White House Chief of Staff on the same day.

Under Howard Baker's careful direction, the administration weathered the scandal, though the Iran-Contra affair tarnished Reagan's image temporarily. The independent counsel concluded his report after eight years, charging 14 people with operational or cover-up crimes. Oliver North's conviction was overturned on a technicality; John Poindexter, convicted on five counts, had the

ruling overturned; and six others later received pardons from President George
H.W. Bush. No one involved in the affair served jail time.[13] Reagan left office
in 1989 with a 63 percent approval rating, the highest of any president since
Franklin Delano Roosevelt, his boyhood hero and Paul's too.

E VERY YEAR, Paul hosted a Basque lamb-fry at the Georgetown Club. Ron
looked forward to the event annually, except for "the delicacy of the evening . . . Lamb gonads. They made for lots of humor but they're not my favorite
food," he wrote. Others from Senate and House, select journalists, and members
of the Cabinet joined the dinner too. The guests wore tuxedos and the waiters
donned traditional Basque garb of red beret, white shirt and pants, and red sash.
The event reflected those enigmatic and mysterious roots of Paul's that Senator
Moynihan had referred to in his parting comments.

In 1986, the lamb-fry had gotten underway, but Ron hadn't shown. Reagan's
diary explained the absence:

> "I can't go to Paul Laxalt's Basque B.B.Q. at 7PM our time, A.F. F111's
> from an Eng. base & planes from our 6th fleet carriers will hit mil. tar-
> gets in Libya. It wouldn't be seemly for me to be out socializing. Some
> time later I'll go on TV to tell the people the details."

No matter the event, one friend seemed always to have the other on his
mind. Through summits with Gorbachev, the Space Shuttle *Challenger*, a new
Supreme Court justice and chief justice, the 100th anniversary of the Statue of
Liberty, the speech at the Berlin Wall, and other events, Paul and Ron talked and
exchanged ideas, calling each other in times of need and drawing strength from
their closeness. Rarely in American political life has a friendship grown as strong
or lasted as long. Today, still, we would be hard pressed to find its equal.

Three months out of the Senate in April 1987, after helping Ron land Howard Baker as a new chief of staff, Paul formed an exploratory committee for the
1988 Republican presidential nomination. Declaring "there is much unfinished
work to do," he said "this hired hand is ready to take over as foreman." He set
a fundraising goal of $6 million, including $2 million by October 1.[14] When he
raised only $1.3 million, he withdrew, saying, "We are a family of very modest
means, and I wasn't about to embark on a campaign that would have led us into
a financial black hole." It was one of the shortest presidential bids on record.
He would not run again in his life, though a grandson would run and win the
election for Nevada attorney general in 2014.

Ron spoke every year at Paul's annual Basque Lamb-Fry Dinner at the Georgetown Club. The waiters dressed in red berets and sashes according to Basque tradition. As Ron described it, "The delicacy of the evening . . . Lamb gonads. They made for lots of humor but they're not my favorite food." Photo courtesy of the Ronald Reagan Library.

After Ron left office in January 1989, the two friends talked off and on, Paul attending the opening of the Reagan Library in Simi Valley, California, and Ron sending his regards to the annual lamb-fry for as long as it lasted. Paul launched a new business, the Paul Laxalt Group, that guides "CEOs through the dangerous Washington waters." The business thrived and continues today under the watchful eye of Paul's daughter.

Away from the bustle of the beltway, he often traveled west to the family ranch at Marlette Lake, finding quiet and peace there and remembering days gone by when he sat with Ron and Nancy at the old wooden table to talk of Lake Tahoe or the country or foreign intrigue. Then he would hike a mountain and watch a sunset like his daddy had done so long before, and the noise of the world would fade away.

Ron and Paul remained interested in politics. They took on the role of observer more than participant—that is, until the run-up to the 1994 Senate election in Virginia. They tag-teamed to oppose Oliver North, the very same lieutenant colonel, now retired, who had been involved in the Iran-Contra affair. Even though the Democrats lost eight seats and control of the Senate chamber in 1994, the Democratic incumbent in the Virginia race retained his seat for another six years due in no small measure to Ron and Paul's efforts.

For a moment, it must have felt like old times. Yet a scant few days later, Paul heard shocking news. It might have been the only thing he didn't know about his friend, a grave and sad secret. Ron wrote a letter in his own hand to the American people announcing he was "one of the millions of Americans who will be afflicted with Alzheimer's disease," he wrote. "I now begin the journey that will lead me into the sunset of my life. I know that for America there will always be a bright dawn ahead." Paul was teary eyed when he learned the news. He flew out to see his favorite couple. Nancy hugged him and Ron squeezed his hand for a long time. "Although he is physically strong," Paul said, "his memory has gradually faded away." The last face Ron recognized, Paul said, was Nancy's.

Ron died a decade later on June 5, 2004. With the nation mourning, Paul remembered the warm smile and genial nature, the battles on Capitol Hill and around the world, the epic struggle to advance big ideas and change a nation, and then he said quite simply, "I'm proud to be a friend of his."

Notes

1. In September 1983, during a speech to the US Chamber of Commerce, James Watt mocked affirmative action. Referring to a Coal Advisory Commission, he said, "I have a black, I have a woman, two Jews, and a cripple. And we have talent." Outrage ensued from Democrats and Republicans. President Reagan accepted Watt's resignation October 9, 1983, less than two weeks after the incident.

2. Rube Goldberg (1883–1970) was a Pulitzer Prize–winning cartoonist who drew complicated gadgets to perform simple tasks.

3. Estimates suggested that building the MX Program in Nevada would require 50,000 personnel, 250 square miles of land, and about 121 billion gallons of water, a rather rare commodity in the desert of southern Nevada.

4. On May 5, 1981, the Church of Jesus Christ of Latter-Day Saints issued a statement against the MX missile system, saying that church pioneers had chosen Utah as a "base from which to carry the gospel of peace to the peoples of the earth." This proclamation influenced public opinion in Utah.

5. In December 2000, Mondale gave an interview with Jim Lehrer as part of the *PBS Newshour*. Lehrer asked him about the second debate with Reagan and about the line Reagan delivered. Mondale replied, "If TV can tell the truth, as you say it can, you'll see that I was smiling. But I think if you come in close, you'll see some tears coming down because I knew he had gotten me there. That was really the end of my campaign that night, I think. [I told my wife] the campaign was over, and it was."

6. President Reagan lost one state, Minnesota, Mondale's home, but Paul observed, "If Ron had worked the state even for one full day, I believe he would have carried Minnesota too."

7. Spain first claimed the Philippines when the Magellan-Elcano expedition arrived in 1521. It remained a Spanish colony until 1898 when the Spanish-American War over Cuba resulted in Philippine independence, though it is still today a protectorate of the United States.

8. Ferdinand Marcos consulted with 12 people before signing Proclamation No. 1081 on September 21, 1972, which imposed martial law in the Philippines. Originally, they were called the 12 apostles. But a story emerged that each man received a Rolex watch directly from Marcos. The name switched to the Rolex-12. The story proved not true, but the name persists.

9. Marcos admired Reagan. When Reagan was governor of California in 1969, he and Nancy visited Manila, recalling often the lavish parties thrown by Imelda. Reagan remembered too Marcos's well-told stories of anti-Japanese guerilla combat during World War II. Reagan considered Marcos one of the world's "freedom fighters" in the ongoing battle against communism.

10. The name of the newspaper (or magazine) was *Ash-Shiraa* (or *Al-Shiraa*). It means *The Sail* in English. Founded in 1948, it's one of the oldest publications in Lebanon. The exposé about the arms-for-hostages deal was first reported on November 3, 1986.

11. The commission convened on November 26, 1987, consisting of former senator John Tower of Texas, former secretary of state Ed Muskie, and former national security advisor Brent Scowcroft. It became known as the Tower Commission.

12. The following arms were supplied to Iran: August 20, 1985, 96 tube-launched, optically tracked, wire-guided (TOW) antitank missiles; September 14, 1985, 408 more TOWs; November 24, 1985, 18 Hawk antiaircraft missiles; February 17, 1986, 500 TOWs; February 27, 1986, 500 TOWs; May 24, 1986, 500 TOWs and 240 Hawk spare parts; August 4, 1986, more Hawk spares; October 28, 1986, 500 TOWs.

13. In John Poindexter's hometown of Odon, Indiana, a street was renamed in his honor. A former minister, Bill Breeden, stole the street sign in protest, demanding $30 million in ransom, the amount received for the weapons plus the transfer to the Contras. Breeden was arrested and imprisoned. Some sardonically point out that Mr. Breeden was the only person to see jail time for the Iran-Contra affair.

14. Today, these sums seem laughable. In 2012, the presidential election exceeded $2 billion for both candidates, far more than the 2008 presidential campaign. For the 2016 race, at least one candidate has pledged to raise $100 million in a single quarter.

Edurne Pasaban

The First Woman to Summit 14 × 8,000m

"MR. HILLARY, it is a real honor to meet you," said the young Basque woman. She was a vision of health with dark eyes, a wide smile, thick black hair, and a square jaw. "My name is Edurne Pasaban and I'm on my way to summit Everest."

With Nepal's Himalayan peaks behind him, the man of 80 years looked like he belonged there. He had a weather-beaten face, strands of white and brown hair, bushy brows, and thin eyes. He raised a tremulous hand to the young woman, a third his age. "Pleased to meet you," he said. "I wish you all the luck in the world. Above all, be very careful. Mountains are there to be enjoyed, and life is a beautiful thing." Then he walked away. If she ever believed in omens or luck or the will of the mountain, then surely this counted as the greatest boost to her ambition.[1]

In 1999 and 2000, Edurne had tried to climb Everest, but the mountain had beaten her with waves of bitter cold, blizzards, and glacier shifts. In those years, climbers had disappeared into crevasses or plunged to their death off sheer ice walls.

Now on her third attempt, those early heartbreaking failures had infused her with confidence, given her valuable experience, and garnered her respect for the mountain. Most of all, they had given her a reliable companion. By Edurne's side was the man she loved, Silvio, an Italian whom she had met on Dhaulagiri in 1998 while attempting her first 8,000er.[2] She was 25 years old then, and her attraction for him was immediate. They flirted while trudging through

On May 23, 2001, Edurne Pasaban became the first Basque woman to summit Mt. Everest, the tallest peak in the world, at 8,848 meters (29,029 feet). She was 27 years old and would go on to be the first woman to climb the 14 tallest peaks in the world. Photo courtesy of Edurne Pasaban.

knee-deep snow, hung side by side from ropes, and crossed dangerous crevasses
together. They never made it to the top, but their trip ended with several days
of passion in Kathmandu. From then on, the pair would rendezvous on the
mountain, Edurne from Spain and Silvio from Italy. Their friends nicknamed
them the "Himalayan couple."

She had invited him to Tolosa, her home in the Basque country of Spain, to
meet her parents. They had taken a quiet liking to him, commenting only that
he was much older than her, and then had sent him off with an Iberian ham as
a peace offering. During every encounter, Edurne would lose herself in Silvio's
brooding eyes, his warm strong embrace, his rugged features. She would nearly
forget that he had a wife and child at home.

After leaving Edmund Hillary, Edurne and Silvio joined with their three
team mates to fly from Kathmandu to Lukla and then trek by foot with a
Sherpa and a hundred porters to the Everest base camp. The journey often
took seven days.

Climbing an 8,000m peak starts long before setting foot on the mountain.
Each day of hiking or resting acclimatizes the body to thinner air and colder
temperatures. With each step after 6,000m (19,685 feet), concentration becomes
harder, lethargy sets in, reflexes slow, and alertness dims. Even ordinary tasks
like tying boots, pulling on a sweater, or assembling a backpack become sluggish
and clumsy. It feels like a never-ending hangover.

Above 8,000m is the death zone, a section of land and sky where oxygen
falls below 33 percent of normal and temperatures drop to −40°F. Water boils
at a mere 165°F. Wind gusts can reach 200 mph. The human body is not built to
last long in such conditions. A climber can develop pulmonary edema, a buildup
of fluids in the lungs that can't be pumped out for lack of pressure and oxygen.
A person can literally drown on the tallest peaks. Climbers often carry oxygen
above 8,000m, though a daring few reach the summit of Everest without oxygen.
Others try and never return to tell the tale.[3]

Leaving base camp, Edurne's team crossed the Khumbu Icefall, a jagged
surface of broken and refrozen ice called a *serac*. For six hours, they hopped over
crevasses or crawled over aluminum ladders strapped end-to-end spanning the
gap and sagging in the middle. At one point, Edurne heard a terrible rumble as
the serac calved below her. Had she and the team been an hour later, they would
have been torn away. The glacier growled like a monster when it shifted. That's
how Edurne and others saw Everest, as a monster—colossal, unpredictable, wild.
Some tamed the beast; others became its prey.

Arriving at Camp 1 in the Valley of Silence, Edurne and her team rested
only an hour, then trudged to Camp 2 to overnight in spacious tents. They

reached Camp 3 the next morning to acclimate at 7,200m for two days. They were on schedule and felt good. It was quiet too, a deathly quiet.

On the radio, a scratchy voice broke the calm. It sounded urgent. A British climber was trapped on Lhotse, an 8,000m peak near Everest. Edurne huddled with her team and decided to help the recovery. It seemed like an obvious choice, but nothing on Everest or any 8,000m peak was obvious. Morality thins with oxygen. To attempt rescue might kill several to save one. All knew and accepted this risk of death. They switched gears and saved the Brit, but the rescue left them depleted. They descended to base camp and then to Lobuche, a local village.

The feeling upon reaching the village was amazing, thick oxygen filling their lungs, bestowing strength and energy; they felt as if they could lift a house or run a four-minute mile. After two days of engorging their cells on oxygen, they climbed with Mercury's wings back to Camp 3. On route, Edurne passed the body of Yasuko Namba, the Japanese climber who had died in a blizzard with seven others in 1996. She had been only a few feet from shelter in an Everest blizzard. She might as well have been a few miles.

At Camp 4, the wind roared, snow drifted, and temperatures dipped below zero. "It is hard to imagine," said Edurne, "a bleaker, more inhospitable landscape than Camp 4." Littered everywhere were oxygen tanks, shredded tents, food tins, and other human riff-raff. She knew she could not stay there long. Unable to sleep, her body nonetheless ached for sleep. It was twenty below.

She started her rituals before the summit, anything to stay alert. She put on a white shirt, a gift from Silvio and then tucked her grandmother's prayer cards into her down suit. She clutched a new pair of wool socks to her chest to get them snug and warm, and oh when she pulled them on, for just a moment, they felt so wonderful and good against her frozen feet.

She set off with her team at midnight. It was a frigid starless night in a great void. Knee-deep in snow, using supplemental oxygen, Edurne walked behind Silvio to the Hillary Step, a steep, narrow passage through which only one climber can pass at a time. It acted as a funnel, slowing traffic. If too many climbers bunched at the entrance, they often trapped themselves as hours ticked away and the weather turned bad. Many had died this way. She funneled through and slogged the last 45 minutes at a shallow angle to the peak.

Shortly after 11:00 a.m. on May 23, 2001, Edurne Pasaban became the first Basque woman to reach the peak of Mt. Everest. She embraced her love, Silvio, and snapped pictures with him and with Iván Vallejo and the Sherpa Dawa. She did not stay long—no one does. The mind pulls the body from these extremes, demanding reprieve and safety, an end to the madness. Edurne did not know at the time that Everest would be only a first conquest or that she'd have to conquer monsters of her own.

ABOUT 18 MILES SOUTH of San Sebastián sits the small town of Tolosa at the foot of the Pyrenees surrounded by dense foliage. The Oria River flows along its edge, reflecting on clear days the Gothic Santa Maria church, a spanning bridge, and residential apartments. Old and new feel balanced like a stalemate in tug-of-war, tension on both sides. There is respect for heritage and grudging acceptance of modernity.

Edurne Pasaban was born into this town of rich tradition on August 1, 1973. Her great-grandfather had started a company, Talleres Pasaban, before the Spanish Civil War to manufacture paper-cutting machines. After he died, the business passed to her grandfather and then to her father, who ran it when she came into the world. If tradition held, and no one expected it would not, she and her brother would follow these footsteps, eventually bequeathing the same to their children. "I was born at the factory," she said.

As the company thrived under her father's hard work and careful management, she wanted for nothing—food, clothes, a home, and education. But the family's success came at a price. Edurne rarely spent time with her father. He traveled often to visit customers around Spain and elsewhere in Europe, and even when he was home, he remained the quiet stoic, seemingly emotionless, a common refrain among Basque children with fathers from the old country.

Her greatest bond developed with her mother. Edurne described her as "over-protective" but also as "my best friend, my perfect companion, the one I can tell everything to . . . she is my confidante in every respect."

A fond memory formed later when Edurne, wanting to share a piece of her life, took her mother to the Everest base camp. Her mother suffered from altitude sickness and carried on as if she were drunk or delirious, crying and sputtering and arguing. "You don't love me, Edurne!" she said in tears. "How could you do this to me! Why did you have to bring me here?" Then in a two-handed steel grip, she grabbed a nearby Sherpa lamenting, "You do love me. You're not like her. You're going to help me, right?" The Sherpa didn't know what to make of it. To this day, mother and daughter laugh about the experience, though it leaves the impression that all 8,000m expeditions wreak havoc on a sane mind.

It was in adolescence that Edurne most needed her mother. "I felt dissatisfied," she said. "I thought I was ugly, and I had little self-confidence. Many of my girlfriends already had boyfriends or some dating experience, but I had a hard time relating to people." Her mother offered a shoulder for tears, the hushed whispers that everything would be alright. Edurne believed her and always

Edurne and cousin Asier during one of their climbs. Asier introduced Edurne to the world of climbing when she was 14 years old. The two have climbed together ever since. Photo courtesy of Edurne Pasaban.

would. Their bond had a warm soft quality, yet was unbreakable. Still, it could not wipe away all of Edurne's adolescent discomfort or feelings of isolation. She still wondered where she fit in.

One day a climbing club opened in Tolosa, and Edurne—now 14 years old—signed up. It was taught by Asier Izaguirre, who happened to be her second cousin, though until then she had had no idea of his existence. The two became fast friends and in later years would ascend some of Asia's mightiest peaks. Edurne called him "one of the most important people in my life." Under his guidance, she gained technique, knowledge of equipment, ropes, crampons, and most importantly a new direction and purpose in life, a chance to channel her energy into climbing. She had become stronger too, no longer a thin-armed, petite, weak creature. When her girlfriends dated and danced on weekends, she escaped to the Pyrenees to hone her craft, often with Asier, whose wife loathed climbing and happily shooed him from the house to a mountain. Within two years, Edurne would summit Mont Blanc (4,810m) and the Matterhorn (4,478m) in the Alps.

By age 19, she traveled to the Andes, those colossal craggily peaks that hug the west coast of South America. She conquered Chimborazo (6,268m) and Cotopaxi (5,897m), summiting both on her first try. A fellow countryman crossed her path there, an old man talking Euskera, who told her, "You do very well in high altitude. I bet you one of these days you'll climb an eight-thousander." It was perhaps a revelation. Hearing it had made the idea possible, not ludicrous, and she tucked it away for the future.

Back in Tolosa, studies and the family business kept her from the mountains. She preferred a degree in physical education to complement her love of climbing, but her father's wishes and the long chain of familial expectations from her great-grandfather on down coaxed her into the field of industrial engineering. To resist proved futile. The degree came in 1997, and right away, her father put her to work filing and sorting. If the mind-numbing tasks offered any consolation, it was that she could think of the next mountain without compromising her performance as an administrative assistant. She could also daydream of Silvio, her great love. It made the day pass sweetly and quickly, and she didn't have to think too hard about how ill-suited she was for the family business.

Her duties expanded over the next two years. The design team negotiated the specifications of whatever paper-cutting machine clients wanted, and by 2001 Edurne oversaw these conversations in Spain, South America, and part of Asia. With each new duty, she was dragged deeper into this business world.

A tug-of-war raged in her. Pulling on one side was mountaineering; on the other, tradition, family obligation, love of parents, the fear of disappointing her family, and the expectation of marriage and children. The battle was lopsided and unfair, and it kept her toiling in the company, her mind preoccupied with each monotonous task, yet her heart out on the mountain with Silvio.

The ascent of Everest in 2001 where she had met Sir Edmund Hillary had changed the calculus. "I wanted things to be different," she said. The success had convinced her that she was no longer the shy, awkward, weak child that her parents saw when they looked at her. Everest had been her declaration of independence. "My decision to leave the family business was an easy one," she said.

Edurne's father set her up to run another family business, Abeletxe, an inn and restaurant for travelers. It was located in the green country of Zizurkil a few miles from Tolosa. The arrangement seemed perfect: a business for travelers where she could plan expeditions of her own and get out from under her father's thumb. The work was hard, different, the guests expecting constant attention, but it was hers to make of it what she could. It also let her think about the next mountain and plan the details of the climb. Her heart ached for thin air.

THREE YEARS EARLIER in 1998, she and Silvio had kindled their love on Dhaulagiri (8,167m). She wanted to start there. Burning up phone lines all summer, she assembled a team to depart on September 1: Silvio Mondinelli,

Mario Merelli, Carlos Soria, and Pepe Garces. It took so much energy to organize the expedition while running Abeletxe that she landed in the hospital for two days with fatigue and low blood pressure.

Then two days from departure, a customer at Abeletxe complained about—of all things—the lack of cheese with his dessert. Angry, Edurne confronted the waitress in the kitchen who argued the point. It sent Edurne into a tirade and she put her fist through a glass door. The blood flowed, badly.

"Please, just stitch me up," she pled to the doctor. "I'm leaving on an expedition this Monday." After stitches and a graft, the doctor replied, "You have to stay, Edurne. The graft is still too fresh. You can't go."

"I'm going!" she exclaimed. "I'll remove the stitches at base camp."

So much went wrong from there. She and the team helicoptered into Pokhara high up in the Himalayas near base camp. It saved time but limited acclimation. Immediately, they hiked to Camp 3 overnight. At dawn, she and Silvio left for the summit, arriving at the snowy slope where she had stopped three years earlier. Out of breath and fatigued, she said, "Silvio, I'm not going," and his reply, "I'm going," and the two parted. On her way back, she passed Pepe and Mario who were on the way up, so she waited alone at Camp 3 in the bitter cold and slight air, her hand throbbing. Silvio returned and so did Mario, but not Pepe. The mountain had bitten. Pepe had slipped and plunged from the Dhaulagiri's rocky face. He was dead.

Edurne reminisces still about the *jotas* that Pepe would play on the mountain and how she'd call them noise to get a rise out of him. Then she'd laugh at the vein pulsating across his forehead. At high altitudes, thin oxygen thickens blood; not surprisingly, climbers find family on every path to a summit. Bonds are strong, and so are losses. "Pepe was like a big brother," she said.

As sad as Pepe's death was, Edurne felt more determined than ever to tackle another 8,000er. By then, hopefully, her hand would be healed, her confidence restored, and the tragedy of Pepe less sharp.

The opportunity came the next year, May 2002, on Makalu (8,485m). Edurne's team included Silvio and Mario again and three others. They flew to Tumlingstar in eastern Nepal, landing in a field with grazing cows, to trek 10 days through the Arun River valley to base camp.

With a hundred porters and Sherpas, they came to Sedwa on the fourth day. It was a small village along a disputed border between Nepal's Maoist rebels and the legitimate government. In the town center, a charred heap smoldered where Maoists had burned books and archives the night before. The mayor had been shot too. The rebels wouldn't return, assured the villagers who then offered Edurne the local school for her team.

Hardly an afternoon had passed when two young boys, wearing red head-bands, armed with rifles and grenades, stormed the classrooms, demanding money and equipment as a fee to pass in safety. To concede everything as the young boys had asked would have ended the expedition, so after a bit of negotia-tion, the team offered 3,000 Nepalese rupees (about $30). The boys accepted it.

"But how can we be sure we won't have to pay at every village?" asked Edurne.

Irritated by the question—a question from a woman no less—one boy scrawled a note: "These have already paid." The team relied on these four words to carry them all the way to the Makalu base camp.[4]

It was early in the season so Edurne's team had to fix the route, trudging first through the snow, plowing stakes, and slinking ropes. It was an exhaustive undertaking. "I had never before seen so much ice in one area," said Edurne. "The ground ice was so hard that we couldn't drive in our tent screws." A German-Japanese expedition joined the effort. Its members wanted to be first to summit Makalu that year. One German even set off alone—a foolish act.

The route was fixed to Camp 3, allowing a rest before the final push. They headed out at dawn. Along the path, they saw the lone German—dead, frozen. Edurne managed a glance, no more. It reminded her that climbing alone often meant dying alone. His comrades would retrieve the body later that day.

She reached the top at midmorning on May 16, 2002, Edurne's second 8,000m summit. She balanced on the peak as Silvio snapped her picture. On top of the world, their relationship thrived, reinforced by the danger of the climb, the singular goal, the shared plight of deadly cold and little oxygen, and the absence of other people above the clouds. With each descent, however, cracks formed in their bond. It started with a gruff voice, a note of impatience, or an abrupt disconnect on the telephone. Edurne sensed daylight between them. She wanted to move in together, even agreed to settle in Italy, but Silvio confessed in early spring the next year that his wife was pregnant again. The Himalayan couple was no more.

WHAT FILLED EDURNE with dread was the great unanswered ques-tion: Can I climb without Silvio? He had been with her during all her 8,000ers, through the successes and failures, the exaltation at the summit, the bright crisp days in heavenly light and the dark lonesome voids in the death zones. He had been the strong one, experienced and mature, exuding security and confidence. She no longer knew if she had climbed because of Silvio or simply with Silvio.

The question plagued her over the next months at Abeletxe where she poured herself into the restaurant and inn. "I decided that I had to go," she said.

She had to prove, if nothing else, that she was her own person, not dependent on Silvio. She had climbed before him in the Pyrenees, the Alps, and the Andes. She could climb without him again.

Later that year came the test. She assembled a team to tackle Cho Oyu (8,201m). She set off in late September, summiting on October 5, 2002 at 8:30 a.m. "The ascent was flawless," she crowed. "By 4:00 p.m., I was already taking a shower back at base camp. I had never performed so well."

The success empowered her, charged her batteries. At Cho Oyu base camp, she had met her friend Iván Vallejo and the great Basque mountaineer Juanito Oiarzabal, and they agreed even before reaching the top to meet at her restaurant to plan their next expedition together. She could hardly wait to get started. At Abeletxe, she welcomed Iván, Juanito, and another climber, Jon Goikoetxea, to hatch a plan to climb Lhotse (8,516m) in spring 2003.

The Lhotse ascent went off like an afternoon stroll. Edurne felt wonderful, experiencing a mixture of health and confidence that she had rarely enjoyed in her climbs. She trudged with the team across the Khumbu Glacier, hopping crevasses and traversing ladders tied end-to-end, sagging at the center over the gaps. After climbing at an astounding pace, she was snapping pictures at the peak by early morning. It was March 26, 2003, and it was her fourth 8,000er. "I don't know what you did," said Iván, "but I couldn't catch up to you." Edurne had energy to spare.

People took notice of her exuberance, Juanito Oiarzabal particularly, who had accompanied her to Lhotse and had climbed more 8,000ers than any other human. He also had a relationship with *Al filo de lo imposible* (The edge of the impossible), a Spanish-Basque television program that highlighted dangerous, death-defying feats largely in the Basque climbing culture. Juanito had been featured in several of its episodes on different continents, usually to commemorate an important event like the 50th anniversary of Hillary's Everest climb.

Juanito pitched an idea to *Al filo's* director, Sebastián Álvaro, to film a summit of Gasherbrum I (8,080m) and Gasherbrum II (8,034m). Until then, *Al filo* had never featured a woman on any expedition. Juanito wanted to correct that oversight. Immediately, Edurne came to mind, and without hesitation she accepted the challenge.

Gasherbrum I and Gasherbrum II (GI and GII) lie in the Karakoram Mountains of Pakistan, not the Himalayas of Nepal. Of the 14 tallest peaks, nine are in the Himalayas, of which Edurne had already climbed four, and the other five in the Karakorams. Though linked by geography, the weather determined when each could be climbed: monsoon season forces Himalayan climbs in the spring or fall and Karakoram climbs in the summer. The arrangement allows two (sometimes three) ascents per year if climbers plan carefully and have the physical prowess.

Through *Al filo's* sponsorship, Edurne found herself in Islamabad in the summer of 2003. "The city is noisy, dusty, and chaotic," she said. She compared it to Kathmandu, which she had grown to love as a second home. "In Islamabad, I don't feel like leaving my hotel," she said. In Kathmandu, she stayed for weeks as if on vacation. In Nepal, she received welcoming bows of *namaste*. In Pakistan, she was met with scolding eyes for walking in pants or short sleeves or without a headscarf.

Beyond the city, the experience was different too. Unlike Nepal, Pakistan had not developed a robust industry around mountain climbing, which limited access to experienced, well-trained guides and made travel to and from the mountains difficult. There were no Sherpas, only porters, who hiked only to base camp and did not own equipment. Edurne's team paid for a hundred pairs of socks, a hundred pairs of boots, a hundred packs, and more to equip the entourage. The porters brought a cow and a goat, slaughtering the cow on route, allotting slabs of meat to each man according to Muslim tradition. It turned Edurne's stomach. She named the goat and fed it each day.

To reach base camp, the team slept on the Baltoro Glacier. There was no firewood. "It is a bleak and desolate landscape, a cold and gray, sad place," said Edurne. It felt tedious too, slow paced, as the team stopped every few hours for the porters to stretch rugs, kneel, and pray toward Mecca. As supplies dwindled and with less to carry, porters began to peel off. At base camp, the few remaining butchered the goat for the trek home. They offered Edurne a bowl of goat soup, but she politely declined saying, "I know its name."

Climbers say that after Cho Oyu, GII is the easiest climb of the fourteen peaks. When Edurne reached base camp (shared by GI and GII), it was clear that a large number of expeditions had the same understanding and were planning GII ascents. To avoid the crowds, Edurne's team decided to tackle GI first, setting the route to Camp 1, adding provisions, and then climbing to the higher camps, pitching tents, and storing supplies. The work acclimatized them. All was going as planned.

Then came a rumble and a growl like a beast clawing from the bowels of the earth. Amplified by glacial ice, it crescendoed and boomeranged through the valley. The ground shook as ice and snow calved and flowed down the mountain, wiping clean all the weak elements of man and nature that dared stand in its path. If magic had not been countered by science, it would be easy to blame the fury of gods for the ferocity of sound and destructive might of the avalanche. Few forces of earth or heaven compare—maybe earthquakes, maybe volcanoes, yet little else. When the terrible thunder faded, Edurne knew that higher up, a large volume of snow still lay on the path, too much, in fact. To go forward would risk encountering more avalanches or hidden crevasses that might send any one of them plunging a few hundred feet into the belly of the mountain.

Edurne and the *Al filo* crew agreed for safety that tackling GII first made more sense, giving GI time to shake off its excess snow, harden, or reveal its hidden dangers. They fixed the GII route over a few days. By week's end, they left at midnight under a clear, brisk, night sky with twinkling stars and a cold breeze. As the sun rose, big and bright along the horizon, on July 19, 2003, Edurne reached GII's summit.

She descended GII and started up GI immediately. The climb was tough. After climbing two mountains back to back, her concentration was fading and her muscles were aching. Within sight of the top she thought about giving up. Her mind demanded it. The higher she climbed, the more instinct pressured her body to seek safety, to stop and go down. To climb higher defied instinct. It would be so easy to stop and sit down, she thought. Everything was so quiet, and she hurt all over. Iván's voice broke the silence. "Come on, sister! You're almost there!" he yelled. "The summit is right there!" To know she was not alone gave her strength. It kept her going. GI became her sixth 8,000er on July 26, 2003.

What had started with trepidation and self-doubt after her break-up with Silvio had turned out to be a magical 18 months. Edurne proved that she could climb without him and perhaps believed for the first time that she was a professional mountaineer after all. This realization enlarged her unresolved tug-of-war between climbing and living a *normal* life with a nine-to-five job, a husband, and children. If the tug-of-war were a voice, it had gone from a whisper to a yell.

K2 (8,611M) IS A DRAGON'S TOOTH of limestone and ice with all angles sloping at 45 degrees or more. It's called the Savage Mountain by climbers, requiring 2,500m of rope on the south side and over 5,000m on the north side, rope that the climbers themselves must string up and down the face without the Sherpas and porters who are accustomed to high altitudes. Unlike Everest where four-day windows of good weather open periodically, K2 affords no such hospitality. Climbers must climb in bad weather. The mountain rises higher than all others around it, and it disrupts the jet stream, like a rock poking from a river causes eddies. K2 turns these swirls into violent storms of ice, wind, and snow. Since Hillary and Norgay climbed Everest in 1953, more than 4,000 climbers have repeated that feat. During the same time, only 337 have summited K2. The dragon's tooth is a climber's mountain, the ultimate test of technical skill, physical

prowess, endurance, and heart. It distinguishes the one-time thrill-seeker from
the true mountaineer.

Ten years earlier, *Al filo* had sponsored a team to this dragon's tooth to
commemorate the 40th anniversary of its first ascent. By the end, one Basque
mountaineer had died and another had lost eight fingers. It was the worst tragedy in *Al filo's* history and Sebastián Álvaro, the director, had vowed never to set
foot again on K2—until now.

With the 50th anniversary approaching, he reached out to Edurne after
the successes at GI and GII and asked her to join the expedition. "I hadn't ever
foreseen I would be climbing K2," she said. But if she ever wanted to, it would
be unlikely that she'd find a more qualified and talented group—Juan Vallejo
(Iván's brother), Mikel Zabalza, Ferrán Latorre, and of course Juanito Oiarzabal. Together these men had more experience, skill, and knowledge than any
foursome from any country. If she had any hope of success, it would be side by
side with them.

No matter how much she trusted their skill and experience, she was scared
by K2. It demanded more courage than any other 8,000er. Climbers had a
27 percent chance of dying on K2, compared with a 9 percent chance on Everest.[5]
But courage was not advancing without fear, she reasoned; it was feeling fear and
still advancing. "That's what mountaineering truly is," she said, "a passion that
borders on irrationality." She was in.

Before leaving Spain, she gained her first taste of fame. Journalists pointed
out that no woman who had climbed K2 was still living. The last had been Julie
Tullis in 1986 who, after reaching the top, perished on the way down along with
12 others that season. K2 chewed people up and spit them out. The media ate
up the danger and the opportunity to track this lone woman, Edurne Pasaban,
as she tamed the Savage Mountain among a group of burly men. The attention
fueled her confidence, though it added pressure and raised expectations. She felt
thousands of eyes watching as the team left Spain for Pakistan.

The expedition passed through Islamabad in May 2004, crossing the Baltoro Glacier toward the K2 base camp. With each step, "I told myself, 'I don't
want to die here.'" She still had much to live for. Since Silvio's departure, she
had met someone else, a man whom she was "madly in love with, and thanks
to him, I had begun to feel there was more to life than the mountains." It was
a rare admission for someone who, up to that point, had climbed with singular
determination. To admit a crack in this iron veneer just as she embarked on the
most daring climb of her life highlighted the persistent and powerful tug-of-war
that framed so many of her key decisions. At one point amid the cold and quiet
desolation, she wondered, "What am I doing here? What do I care about K2? I

just want to go back and be with my boyfriend, have a normal life, start a family." The tug-of-war raged, but she trekked on.

At base camp, other teams had gathered—Polish, Japanese, Korean, German, Andalusian, Catalan, and most importantly Italian. The Italians climbed to honor their countryman, Ardito Desio, who had ascended K2 first in 1954. Among them was Silvio, still one of Italy's best.

Edurne and her team acclimatized and then climbed to set camps and leave supplies. They spent little time above 7,000m because the camps teetered on the edge of unstable ridges prone to avalanche or rockslide. Their only recourse was multiple trips up and down the mountain fixing and refixing rope, outlining the route, knowing of K2's vicious habit of shaking off humans like fleas from a dog. After a week of roping the route, they returned to Camp 1 to find their tents and supplies wiped clean by an overnight storm. K2 had reclaimed its territory. The fleas rebuilt.

The forecasters from each expedition huddled and predicted July 26 as the best contender for a clear sky over the peak. It meant that Edurne's team would need to leave three days earlier, spending a night at each camp and summiting K2 near noon on July 26, allowing a descent in daylight. Many more had died descending than ascending K2. Everyone knew that, everyone felt that.

Edurne's team split in two. Juan and Ferrán decided to go to Camp 2 on the 24th. Edurne, Juanito, and Mikel opted to use all three days. They set out on the 23rd in a blizzard with temperatures below zero. Ice flew, cold chilled the bone, snow blinded. It did not let up the first day or the second. No one would have blamed the trio for turning back. But they went on to Camp 2, their skin frigid and numb, bellies empty, muscles aching, breath short. They waited with the Italians for Juan and Ferrán.

Juan and Ferrán had left earlier that day in a blizzard. Ferrán took ill and turned back. Juan climbed alone. He rendezvoused eight hours later with his team at Camp 2. Sometimes K2 rewards audacity.

All night the wind howled, rattling the tents. It felt like K2 might bring the whole mountain down on them. Yet the next morning, it was almost magical. A spot of blue sky had torn a hole in the dark clouds and the sun had peeked through. Edurne and her team headed out with the Italians for Camp 3 and then Camp 4. "It was a grueling ascent," said Edurne. At an angle of at least 45 degrees, it "gives you the feeling of constantly looking up." They hit Camp 4 at 3:00 p.m., pitched tents, and rested.

In the distance was the K2 Bottleneck, a treacherous tower of ice overhung with delicate seracs and new-fallen snow that concealed countless crevasses. After 10 hours of rest, they made the final push at 1:00 a.m. It was a cold clear night, the moon casting a pale light. Four hours later huge gusts of icy wind wailed, knocking them off balance. Some of the Italians, including Silvio, were already ahead; others turned back. K2 had beaten them.

"They're turning around," yelled Juanito, the wind stealing his voice. "It's worse than we expected. The wind is too strong. I think the best thing is to go back."

"I'm already here," said Edurne. "Of course I'm cold, but I want to try to go up a little higher. What do you think, Juan?"

"I'm good," he said. "Let's go a little farther."

Through wind and ice and blizzard, Mikel belayed the path, fixing ropes up the Bottleneck. Onward they went across a 200m slab of new-fallen snow that sunk them to their knees and hips. Silvio came back to help. Edurne had wanted to summit by 1:00 p.m. for a daylight descent, but already it was mid-afternoon.

Back at base camp, *Al filo* radioed them to turn around immediately. "Having made such an incredible effort," said Edurne, "we simply couldn't give up. It was not an option." A little farther, she'd say, and the time ticked away. Just a little farther, she'd say again, and the sun drooped at the horizon. Finally at 6:00 p.m. with the shadows of dusk creeping across the land, Edurne summited K2, fully spent—"I was utterly exhausted!"

Staying only long enough to snap pictures, Silvio went down first, then Edurne, then Juanito and Juan. Juanito was coughing, his coordination off, his breathing shallow, his eyesight fading, all signs of pulmonary and cerebral edema. The foursome crossed the snow slab, hooked into their ropes, and slunk down the Bottleneck just as the last bit of sun cast the Karakorams in a hue of pink and yellow.

"Here is the fixed rope," said Silvio. He led Edurne's hand around it. "I'm freezing and totally exhausted. I'd rather go down fast. I'll send help when I reach Camp 4."

"I'll be alright," said Edurne. "I'll go down at my own pace. Juanito and Juan are right behind me anyway."

Silvio left her and went ahead.

There she was, alone. In the deep gray before the swallow of darkness, Edurne watched the twilight cast K2's shadow on the deep snow. "It was one of the most magical experiences I've ever had on a mountain," she said, "and one of the most wonderful moments of my life." In fact, for many of the others who had seen it, the sight had come at a price—death. Few descended K2 at this hour and lived to share the moment. The magic then disappeared, replaced by the impossible blackness of a K2 night.

A person has a 27 percent chance of dying on K2, which Edurne climbed on July 26, 2004. During the descent, she lost her head-lamp and glove, sat down, and fell asleep. A fellow climber heaved her to her feet and brought her back to camp. This near-death experience led to the loss of two toes from frostbite and a long recovery. Photo courtesy of Edurne Pasaban.

She clipped into her rope, trudging through snow up to her knees, the tem-perature falling.

Then she dropped her headlamp and lost a glove.

The dark enveloped her like a tomb. She rummaged for lamp and glove, poking fingers in the snow at her feet, her hand and forearm numbing instantly. It was useless, and she was so tired, so very tired. Waiting for Juan and Juanito, she sat down in the snow for a rest, just a little rest. In no time, she was asleep.

How long she stayed there, she could not say. What she thought, she could not say. What she dreamed, if she dreamed at all, she could not say. The next thing she knew Juan was pulling her up and wrapping her arm around his shoul-ders. "I can't go on," she told him. Her legs wouldn't work, her muscles had seized. As he dragged her down the mountain, headlamps were coming up. It was a new team that had left Camp 4 at 1:00 a.m.. Edurne had been climbing for 24 hours, and for 21 of those she had been above 8,000m, in the death zone. At Camp 4, exhausted, incoherent, hungry, short of breath, all she could say was "my feet are so cold."

HER TOES LOOKED LIKE purple grapes, her feet like footballs. Frostbite took the second toe on each foot. Juanito had fared worse, losing all ten toes. When the bandages were peeled away in a Zaragoza hospital, her mother cried, and her father stared quietly with a stone face.

Her boyfriend stayed by her side. After three weeks in the hospital, the two of them decided to move in together in his home in the Andorran mountains. "I found love, fulfillment, and complete connection with another person," said Edurne. She seemed so very happy, enjoying a life that was "serene and pleasant." It momentarily nudged the tug-of-war in favor of a normal life. But it did not last long.

Even before the stumps had healed on both feet, she left Spain under *Al filo*'s sponsorship to climb Nanga Parbat (8,126m) in the Karakorams. It was an all-woman team who met in Islamabad, trekked to base camp, and headed out. Silvio was there too, part of another team that merged with Edurne's. During the climb, her only concern was her feet and whether the pain would force her to forgo a summit. But the climb went off brilliantly, in good weather, putting her on the peak in the early hours of July 20, 2005. It was her eighth 8,000er.

Returning to Spain, she felt good and happy, still at the peak of health after the K2 injuries, still summiting the world's tallest mountains, and now going home to a loving boyfriend, a "life partner," she called him. The tug-of-war had balanced harmoniously, she thought, until suddenly, painfully, the relationship ended. It was late September. Edurne felt loneliness deeper than on any mountain, even in utter darkness without a headlamp in a perilously cold death zone. "I was thirty-two and hadn't achieved anything," she said. "I didn't have a steady partner and had not a penny to my name." She had quit managing Abeletxe, and her only activity, besides climbing, was an MBA program in Barcelona.

At her mother's request, she went home for Christmas. Family and friends saw her anxiety, the sadness of her eyes and the dark rings. They encouraged her to leave Barcelona to be closer to Tolosa. She refused, stubbornly. Not that she was happy in Barcelona, far from it. But she wouldn't be happy near her parents either. She didn't know where she could be happy. She confided to her mother, "I just want to take a pill and make all of this go away." After a week of unwanted advice, she broke down again, this time wailing, "I can't go on! I want to die! I want to die!"

Her parents admitted her to a hospital in Pamplona. Patients there crocheted or assembled puzzles or sewed. Some sat for hours staring blankly or muttering to themselves. Edurne refused the activities. After all, she was Edurne Pasaban, mountaineer, conqueror of Everest and K2 and six others. She would not be crocheting any time soon! The doctors described her condition as an extreme case of emotional dependence, a pathological need to please and gain praise, to find acceptance and avoid conflict. It entwined with her self-worth and self-confidence. She saw herself only through the eyes of others. Her value derived from how others valued her. Leaving the condition unchecked had driven her into a bottomless depression.

One week turned into two, then three. Edurne then crocheted a doll, attended group, and started a regimen of antidepressants. By the fourth week, her parents took her home to Tolosa. To keep up on her MBA, her mother went with her to Barcelona on Mondays and Tuesdays. Slowly, she improved, stabilized. Adjusting to a new routine had been difficult, but it took hold. She felt better, she insisted, well enough to go to Barcelona alone.

It was too soon.

Like an infinite darkness, the depression reared up again. "I felt so lonely, so miserable," she said. "I was in such depths of despair." She swallowed her bottle of antidepressants and slit the vein of her left wrist. Then she dialed emergency services.

Back in Pamplona, among crocheting patients, the doctors prescribed new meds and started more aggressive therapy that included her overprotective mother and her stoic father. To talk of feelings with a man of stone proved challenging for Edurne and her doctors, but her father made the effort, and naturally so did her mother. Both wanted only the very best for their daughter.

After three weeks, Edurne was discharged into their custody. She resumed school and by June earned the MBA. "I was starting from scratch," she said, "but taking off from a more solid foundation." Now from a sturdy base, she could climb from there.

Years before she had been forced to answer a difficult question: Can I climb without Silvio? She had discovered she could, and quite well in fact. Now she faced another question, much bigger than the last: Do I love climbing enough to choose it as my normal life? Day by day, the answer came to her. More smiles more often crept over her face. One side of her tug-of-war now showed a definite advantage. Perhaps for the first time, she knew where she fit.

EDURNE HAD NOT EVER thought of the 14 × 8,000m challenge. She had approached each peak as it had come without any grander ambition. But after a year of recovery, the challenge emerged as a possibility, though she found it hard to pinpoint the exact genesis of the goal. It might have been when she traveled with her cousin, Asier, to climb Shisha Pangma (8,013m) and met the famed Korean mountaineer Oh Eun-sun ("Miss Oh"). It might have been when good cousin Asier told her, "Edurne, your life is on the mountain. Any man who comes into your life will have to respect who you are and what you do. You are a mountaineer. Be loyal to who you are." Most likely, it was some combination of the two. Even though she and Asier had failed to summit Shisha Pangma that first time, she had returned to Spain with a new clarity and purpose.

In 2007, three women led the 14 × 8,000m challenge: Edurne, Nives Meroi of Italy, and Gerlinde Kaltenbrunner of Austria. Of the 14 tallest peaks, Edurne had completed eight, Kaltenbrunner seven, and Meroi nine. None of them would meet the challenge that year or the next, probably not until 2011 or 2012 by the look and pace of the field.

Feeling healthy and eager that summer, Edurne set off with Asier for Broad Peak (8,051m). On their final push at midnight, they were joined by Silvio to summit nine hours later under a beautiful blue sky. Few days had felt so right, said Edurne. Standing at the top on July 12, 2007, they laughed and cried and hugged in the thin air. It was Asier's first 8,000m and Silvio's 14th, making him the 13th man in history to meet the 14 × 8,000m challenge. Edurne notched her ninth. They locked the moment away as one of their fondest memories.

Edurne's delight was tempered by a new player entering the race. Miss Oh of Korea had scrambled up Cho Oyu in May and then K2 in July. A petite 5'1" with black cropped hair and a wide smile, she had climbed seven mountains with seven to go, well behind the leaders. But the Korean media, with its love of sport, had turned Miss Oh into a celebrity, helping her attract sponsors with deep pockets. With the eyes of her country watching, the next year, 2008, she moved at a frenetic pace, climbing four 8,000ers in one season: Makalu (May 13), Lhotse (May 26), Broad Peak (July 31), and Manaslu (October 12). It was a shocking display of brilliant mountaineering. It put Edurne, Meroi, and Kaltenbrunner on notice. Miss Oh was more than a gadfly. She was a true competitor who wanted the title of being first, and she had the means, skill, and endurance to fulfill her ambition.

The tempo quickened. Just as Miss Oh scaled Makalu, Edurne pivoted to Dhaulagiri with Asier and Kaltenbrunner. Ten years earlier, Dhaulagiri had been Edurne's first 8,000m attempt, and three years later, the place where Pepe had died. The mountain oozed memory and pain. Her summit on May 1, 2008, became a sweet personal victory. Asier yelled from the top, "Finally after so many years!" Edurne planted a flag. It was her 10th, Kaltenbrunner's 11th.

As Miss Oh capped her momentous season of four 8,000ers—now boasting nine ascents—Meroi trudged up Manaslu on October 4. The next day, Edurne followed. Each leader had three to go, Miss Oh still had five.

Edurne tried inching into the lead by climbing Shisha Pangma. So late in the season, however, the bitter cold and winds stopped her. The devilish Shisha Pangma had beaten her a third time. She and Asier went home.

With Edurne, Meroi, and Kaltenbrunner tied and Miss Oh coming on strong, climbers perked up to watch this old-fashioned race across the highest points on the planet. What they got was a bit of gravy.

One of Miss Oh's countrymen, Go Mi-sun ("Miss Go"), a kind, thin-faced woman of slight build, emerged as a dark horse. Through 2007, she had only topped four 8,000ers, though her bona fides included championships in Asian women's sports climbing, Asian women's ice climbing, and Korean women's mountaineering and skiing. In 2008, she topped Lhotse, K2, and Manaslu, all Himalayan peaks, in a single season. It was a new record that leapfrogged her to seven ascents. Her muscles and lungs had to scream. Most believed that Miss Go had exhausted herself and couldn't reproduce her 2008 performance. Few paid her much attention.

Edurne wanted to ascend her final three mountains in 2009 and 2010. She arrived at the first, Kangchenjunga (8,586m) in eastern Nepal,[6] in May 2009. Meroi was there, and so were the Koreans, Miss Oh and Miss Go. Miss Oh had brought her television cameras and planned to climb Kangchenjunga and then Dhaulagiri right after. She was already halfway up Kangchenjunga when Edurne arrived.

From base camp, Edurne tracked her with telescopic binoculars. Wind and sleet slowed Miss Oh's progress and then a bank of thick clouds, like cotton dipped in tar, rolled in to smother the whole death zone. "All I could think of was how glad I was it wasn't me up there," said Edurne. In the dense suffocation of clouds, everyone lost sight of Miss Oh.

The following day, Miss Oh came down. Her lips had been peeling and bleeding. She looked haggard. Her Sherpa suffered frostbite on their hands. People rushed to her, the medical staff offered treatment. She sat on a rock, her breathing heavy, her eyes sagging with fatigue.

"So you feel like going to Dhaulagiri now?" asked Edurne, jokingly.

"No, I'm going back to Seoul," she said in a stuttered exhaustion.

"So you're not going to Dhaulagiri?" pressed Miss Go.

"No, we're going home tomorrow," repeated Miss Oh.

The next day, a helicopter picked up Miss Oh and her television cameras. But it did not take her home. Within a week, she had summited Dhaulagiri. It brought her count to eleven, tying the field.

Edurne, Meroi, and Miss Go heard the news at Kangchenjunga's Camp 3. The deception did not surprise them, though they spent little time fixating on it. Just then, Meroi's husband, her longtime climbing partner, became short of breath, delirious, and uncoordinated. As a trained nurse, Meroi knew the symptoms well and descended with him to base camp. Later in Italy, doctors said he could no longer function at high altitudes, forcing Meroi to withdraw from the 14 × 8,000m challenge.

After Meroi's departure, Edurne and Asier started their final push for Kangchenjunga's peak at 2:00 a.m. on May 18. Toeless Juanito joined them. Edurne had a cough. For two hours the night was calm, and then suddenly temperatures dropped, the wind howled, and ice pelted their faces.

"What should we do?" asked Asier.

"Let's try to go a little farther," said Juanito.

Miss Go and her Sherpa, already descending, urged them on. Edurne's steps felt heavy, like rocks were strapped to each ankle. Fifteen hours after leaving camp, they topped out on May 18 in the late afternoon. Edurne's legs, heavy as granite, crumpled beneath her, and her cough had turned bloody. Frostbite nipped her feet and one finger. To reach Camp 3, she had to be carried.

During Edurne's recovery, Miss Go, the dark horse, astounded the climbing world again with her grueling schedule: first Makalu (April 30), then Kangchenjunga (May 18), then Dhaulagiri (June 9), and then Nanga Parbat (July 12). In a span of two years, she had summited seven 8,000m peaks, jumping her to 11, now in contention with the rest of the field. Though still behind, Miss Go's endurance gave her an edge in a sport that thrived on it. In fact, she considered climbing one more before the season's end. Super-human—that's what it was! But speed came at a cost. Descending that last mountain, Nanga Parbat, in an unroped section between Camp 2 and Camp 3, after thousands of righteous steps Ms. Go took one foul step, and that one step tumbled her head first down the mountain. She died there on Nanga Parbat. "She was such a good woman," said Edurne. "Funny and kind, not so serious like others. I will miss her."

Two days before Miss Go's tragic fall, Miss Oh had topped Nanga Parbat, bringing her to 12 climbs. She planned a 13th—GI—in October at the same time Edurne confronted Shisha Pangma, her old nemesis. Miss Oh succeeded on October 3, 2009, but Edurne failed at Shisha Pangma a fourth time. Her whole camp—tents, sleeping bags, equipment—were wiped away by Shisha Pangma's ferocious winds. "I cried almost the entire way down," she said. "It's over. We're going home."

Miss Oh moved into the lead with only Annapurna to go. Kaltenbrunner finished Lhotse, her 12th, leaving two colossals: K2 and Everest. Edurne needed Annapurna and the devil, Shisha Pangma.

Miss Oh attempted Annapurna in late 2009 hoping to clench the 14 × 8,000m title a year earlier than expected. On her first push, the death zone pushed her back with wind and bitter cold, her Sherpa suffering frostbite and fatigue. A day later, she pushed again only to be turned back. Her final mountain would not be conquered that season. She postponed the climb until 2010.

Edurne switched strategy. She targeted Annapurna in early April 2010, which required her to fix the route herself. She would risk exhaustion and a failed summit, but it would give her time immediately after to climb Shisha Pangma a fifth time. It was the only way she could out-climb Miss Oh and grab the title.

Arriving at Annapurna, her cousin Asier said, "Look, we have it all to ourselves." With the help of three Sherpas, Edurne and her team fixed the route over several days and then, heavily fatigued, set out from Camp 3 just after midnight on April 17. The death zone was still covered in thick ice. The picks barely stuck. By late morning, they reached the upper edge of Annapurna and saw not one, but three peaks. Which was the right one? "We'll just go to all three," said Edurne. She topped Annapurna—her 13th 8,000mer—at 1:00 p.m.

Quickly she and Asier descended to base camp where Miss Oh with her television cameras and army of Sherpas and porters was readying her final climb.

Edurne's team helicoptered to Shisha Pangma.

They arrived at base camp with adrenaline pumping. Their fatigue was surpassed by a desire to make history. Fully acclimatized, they planned to start immediately. Every second counted. Then clouds swirled in, and a dense fog, and snow and ice too. All the wretched misfortunes of weather conspired against a final climb of this devilish peak. For a clear path, Edurne waited a day, then two, then three. Twelve days in all she waited. The fog lingered.

As it lifted, finally, news came that shattered her. After 13 hours, crawling on all fours, Miss Oh had topped Annapurna, her 14th and final mountain. She claimed the title.

Undoubtedly sad, so close to a near impossible goal, Edurne put on the white shirt from Silvio, tucked her grandmother's prayer cards in her snowsuit, and pulled warm socks over her cold feet. With poise and confidence, she took her team up Shisha Pangma for a fifth go, leaving Camp 3 at 4:00 a.m. in howling winds to summit finally on May 17.

At the top of the mountain, she cried and cousin Asier cried. The tears celebrated as much the conquest as the whole 10 years of Edurne's journey with so much physical struggle and personal pain and death of friends.

When she returned to Kathmandu, her parents were there, her father bending a rare smile out of his stone face, and her mother hugging and hugging and talking wildly. Journalists swarmed her, punching out questions, asking about Miss Oh, about being the *second* woman to achieve the 14 × 8,000m challenge.

"If I am first or second, it is not important to me," she said. "Many times in

After summiting Shisha Pangma on her fifth attempt and completing the 14 × 8000m chal-
lenge, Edurne was joined by her parents in Kathmandu for a celebration. Photo courtesy of
Edurne Pasaban.

the bad moments of my depression, in moments on the mountain when I didn't
think I would make it, I didn't think about how many peaks I had climbed. The
important thing is knowing myself."

IÑAKI OCHOA DE OLZA, a Basque climber from Pamplona who died on Annapurna in 2008, once said, "You know the top of a mountain when every direction you go is down." Edurne knew this rule. Her photographs from each summit
show magnificent, breathtaking landscapes and the gleeful faces of herself and
friends.

In late 2010, doubts emerged that Miss Oh, surrounded by thick fog and
pelted by sleet, had actually reached the top of Kangchenjunga in May 2009.
Through the press, she denounced the rumors, claiming over and over that she
had reached the top and that she had proof. The climbing world asked her to
show the proof. After several weeks, she brought out a picture of herself standing on a bare rock and provided a statement from one of the Sherpas who was
on the climb to verify her claim.

The task of verifying the summit fell to one of the most unlikely referees,
an 86-year-old American woman named Elizabeth Hawley. She had moved to

Edurne sits with Elizabeth Hawley, the Grand Dame of Himalayan statistics, who determines whether a climb is successful, disputed, or unrecognized. In 2010, Ms. Hawley concluded that Oh Eun-sun ("Miss Oh") had not summited Kangchenjunga as claimed, and therefore the ascent became unrecognized. The crown for the first woman to climb the world's fourteen tallest peaks moved from Miss Oh to Edurne Pasaban. Photo courtesy of Edurne Pasaban.

Nepal in 1960 and ever since had met every team granted a license by the Nepal Tourism Board. Still to this day, she maintains the official database of successful and attempted ascents. A climber may lay claim to a true summit, but if Elizabeth Hawley with her hawkish eyes and beehive hairdo does not approve it, the climb really did not take place. She is the Grand Dame of the Himalayas, according to climbers, and all governments respect her authority in the matter.

Hawley reviewed Ms. Oh's evidence and concluded that the photograph "clearly" was not from the summit because "summit pictures of other people on the same mountain in the same season show them standing in the snow." Moreover, the picture revealed the end of a green rope that had lined the route but stopped at 8,350m. In talking with the Sherpas, Hawley discovered that one backed Miss Oh but several others denied her claim. Finally, a Korean flag was discovered about 200m below the summit. Judiciously, Hawley marked Miss Oh's ascent as *disputed*.

About four months later, a panel of seven mountaineers from the Korean Alpine Federation, after examining all the evidence, conceded that Miss Oh had "probably failed" to reach the top of Kangchenjunga. Pressured by the media and sponsors, Miss Oh admitted that she had stopped before reaching the top. In Hawley's database, *disputed* became *unrecognized*.

The crown moved from Miss Oh to Edurne. Not long after, *National Geographic* named Edurne its 2010 Adventurer of the Year.

Miss Oh never returned to Annapurna, at least not yet, but she ascended the tallest peak on all seven continents, an extraordinary feat.

Kaltenbrunner climbed Everest in 2010 and then K2 in 2011 to become the second woman to conquer the 14 × 8,000m Challenge. She returned home to the Black Forest of Germany and still climbs today.

Meroi returned to climbing with new climbing partners while her husband convalesces at home.

Silvio separated from his wife after the birth of their second child and now raises cows in the Italian countryside. He and Edurne never resumed their relationship as the Himalayan Couple, though they remain close friends.

Edurne began teaching classes on leadership at the university, giving inspirational speeches in the business world, and promoting a nonprofit for Nepali children. She still climbs with her cousin Asier, always looking for a new challenge. She and her father enjoy a comfortable detente, and her mother remains a best friend and confidante, though unwilling to make another trip to a Himalayan base camp.

Sometimes crossing the quiet white of a serac with only the wind rattling her snowsuit, Edurne thinks that her real achievement is not summiting 14 mountains, but 15, the last perhaps greatest of all: climbing from the depths of depression and emerging safe and whole with lots of oxygen. As snow reflects the sun and warms her face, she sometimes remembers Sir Edmund Hillary telling her on Everest: "Mountains are there to be enjoyed, and life is a beautiful thing."

Now she knows what he meant.

NOTES

1. Edurne had met Sir Edmund Percival Hillary in Kathmandu. A New Zealand mountaineer, on May 29, 1953, Hillary and his Nepali Sherpa, Tenzing Norgay, had become the first people to summit Mt. Everest. Born July 20, 1919, Hillary died on January 11, 2008, still making frequent trips to Kathmandu where he sponsored programs for Nepali children. Hillary was named by Time as one of the 100 most influential people of the 20th century.

2. The equivalent of 8,000 meters is 26,246 feet. Mount Everest, the tallest mountain in the world, summits at 8,848 meters or 29,029 feet. A commercial airline, depending on its size and flight duration, cruises on average between 28,000 and

40,000 feet. Throughout this profile, 8,000 meters is used to describe Edurne's feat because mountaineers refer to the challenge as the 14 × 8,000m.

3. Ms. Elizabeth Hawley, considered the Grand Dame of Everest statistics, reports that as of February 2014, the number of summits of Everest was 6,871 by 4,042 different climbers. Overall 248 people (161 Westerners and 87 Sherpas) have died on Everest.

4. In April 2007, the author traveled to Nepal to help oversee the first national election after this 11-year civil war, which Edurne Pasaban refers to in her expedition. While hiking to several villages in the Himalayas, the author encountered similar bands of Maoist rebels who exacted a bribe for the right to pass unmolested. Apparently, however, Edurne's negotiating skills were better than the author's, who had to pay $50 not once but three times during the trek, never receiving a note during the first extortion. That was smart!

5. Success and failure rates are difficult to calculate, though 8000ers.com does the best job in all mountaineering. By the close of 2010, Everest recorded 5,104 successful ascents by 3,142 people. During the same time, the number of recorded fatalities was 219, or about 4.3 deaths for every 100 successful summits. This number included support climbers such as Sherpas, those who never reached the peak, and those coming down from the peak. About one-quarter of those deaths (58) were people who reached the top and died on the way down.

On K2 through 2010, 79 people had died out of 302 ascents. About one in four people died for every successful summit. It's a daunting statistic, demonstrating why mountaineers consider K2 to be the "Savage Mountain."

6. The porters and Sherpas feared Kangchenjunga because of the Yeti whom they believed walked in a camouflage of white, cutting ropes, knocking climbers from rock faces, and then devouring them and picking his sharp teeth with their broken bones.

Afterword

URING A GAME OF WHIST in the Harvard dorms, our discussion one night settled on the Basque. My Danish roommate poked fun as he always did. I defended with the ferocity of Caesar.

Taking the last trick of cards, I said, "The Basque are stubborn and tenacious enough to take over the world."

"The Basque can't even take over Spain," he retorted.

I won whist; he won the argument.

The Basque have a big job. Usually, a citizen says I am from France, or I am from Spain, or I am from America, and he can stop at that point having conveyed, in the mind of an astute listener, the full heritage of his homeland, the art and literature, the songs and culinary delights, the native tongue and unique dress. A national boundary cordons off more than geography; it encapsulates the lifeblood and historical works of people inside the borders. Lacking a nation of our own, the Basque must answer another question: What is a Basque?

It's a good question, though it probably has several answers, perhaps too many to count. If so, this simple question loses value in the answering. I think a better question is, Who are the Basque? That question I can answer, and so can anyone else. This book answers it for seven Basque individuals who have contributed great things in science, education, geography, fashion, politics, and social good. Yet all have been shrouded in history or their achievements wrongfully claimed by other nations.

To be clear, these seven are not the only extraordinary Basque or Basque of note in history. Although I cannot enumerate every Basque achievement, as a traveler to over 30 countries now, a student of people and cultures, a business owner, and an appointee of two US presidents, I get a sense, at least anecdotally (and admittedly with a clear bias), that the contributions of Basque are not insignificant relative to other ethnic groups and cultures around the world. They seem hard working, strong willed, and motivated. Among them are doctors, lawyers, politicians, and business men and women, often entrepreneurs. They seek education as a means for achievement. For their numbers, they seem to have a disproportionate influence on the business, politics, and social fabric of the communities where they reside. In short, examples of extraordinary Basque people are likely replete in history, and some might even live right next door.

It seems odd, therefore, that the Basque might lose claim to important figures and events, and yet it does not surprise me in the least bit. The Basque have enjoyed a rich oral tradition. It really is wonderful. But no matter how good that tradition, it cannot capture all historical lessons, figures, and events within the Basque villages, towns, and now cities surrounding the Pyrenees, to say nothing of Basque communities spread across the world. Only the pen can do that, not the tongue. A robust written record plants a flag. It adds permanence to the richness of Basque heritage—the food and dance, the costumes and music, the stories and literature, the industry and invention, the politics and speeches. The Basque may never carve a permanent nation from each side of their mountain home, but they can recapture territory in history that rightfully belongs to them.

This point struck me as I wrote this book, and again the other day while telling a story. It was a story from my dad. He would tell me stories as a boy, stories that his dad in Spain had told him. I've shared those stories with friends and employees of mine, with US and foreign leaders, and even once with an Afghan warlord. Sometimes storytelling helps a listener swallow bitter medicine, think more deeply about a subtle point, or give context to an important moral lesson that a listener can chew on for days, months, even years. Stories from the Basque tell about who they are, why they are, where they come from. Until I settled down to write this book, however, I hadn't ever thought of writing those stories and leaving them as monuments to my dad and to his dad before him, and to Basque heritage more generally. I will have to do that one of these days. I hope other Basque will do the same. I would not want to lose them to history or to anyone else. They are too good and too important. If the stories are lost, we have only ourselves to blame.

Acknowledgments

A BOOK IS NOT THE PRODUCT of a single person, even if a solitary name appears on the cover. Many voices and talents contribute to it, and this book is no exception. I want to thank four groups of people, and a lifelong friend, who all contributed in big and small ways to the completion of this book.

First, I spent countless hours poring over autobiographies, letters, transcripts from interviews, photographs, scientific figures, and notes. Each archive was tucked away at a different location where overworked librarians and researchers helped me find the right material in the right place at the right time. Much thanks to the men and women of the Spanish Archives in Madrid, the Jesuit Institute in London, the Cajal Institute in Spain, the Mondragón Cooperative Corporation, the Balenciaga Museum, the Ronald Reagan Presidential Library in Simi Valley, California, the Ronald Reagan Foundation, and the archives of the University of Virginia and the University of Nevada Reno.

At each location, these guardians, who take on the colossal job of organizing and preserving historical records, helped illuminate key threads in the lives of the Basque men and women in these pages. Without them, we could not fully appreciate the past, and without knowledge of the past, none of us could understand how our future, by contrast, might soar to greater heights or go tragically off the rails. As the protectors of what came before us, these souls, in a very real sense, define the size and shape of our future. Among these guardians of history, I wanted to acknowledge specifically a longtime friend of mine, Mikel Lopategui, a graphic designer by trade and now a school administrator, who helped enhance several of the pictures, shoring up their pixel strength for clarity and brightness.

Second, I want to thank Edurne Pasaban and her team, who kindly met with me for hours, endured question after question, and then happily reviewed the finished work for accuracy and thoroughness to arrive at a story as she saw it and lived it. More than an historical figure, Edurne represents an inspirational role model for all people who want to think big, overcome adversity, and achieve great and seemingly impossible things. I enjoyed our time together, though I'm not prepared to accept her challenge for a "simple hike." My stairs at home present an adequate workout. When I think of challenge, I now think of Edurne. And when sleep pulls at my sleeve and I want nothing more than to sit and rest,

I know to take another step, to swim another lap, to lift another weight, to write another word, because just ahead there's a great reward, and maybe too family and friends waiting to embrace and comfort me.

Third, my teachers and editors over the years deserve acknowledgment. They are the ones who helped me write better, taught me to value language, to hear words and make them sing. Because of them, I try to avoid falsetto. In a way, I still write to please them, as if each sits with a red pen poised to tear at a sentence or scrawl in the margin: this could be better, more vivid, stronger, or clearer, they'd say. I know they're out there still with their red pen hovering like a sword of Damocles. It's a good motivator that forces me to think about every word, every phrase, every sentence, and to know that when I put ink to paper that it's as true as I can make it. Don't misjudge. I write for lots of reasons, but I'd be lying if I said my teachers weren't on my mind.

Similarly, the editors at the University of Nevada Press deserve appreciation for carefully reviewing every word of every paragraph on every page to keep the writing clean and tight, and for walking me through every stage of production. Too many moving parts spin my head. I'm thankful that the Press has stayed close to mitigate the dizziness.

Finally, I want to thank readers, Basque and non-Basque alike, for the flood of phone calls, cards, and emails, the kind words of appreciation, and personal stories following my first book. Anything that came of it, I donated to scholarships for kids in Nevada where I was born and raised. The support of readers has made it possible to help a bunch of kids go to college so far, and others will soon follow. They thank you, and most certainly, I thank you.

Eskerrik Asko!

Works Consulted

Juan Sebastián Elcano

"Account of the Mutiny in Port St. Julian." Presented on Wednesday, the 22nd of May, 1521, by a servant of Diego Barbosa, on behalf of Alvaro de Mezquita, to the Alcalde of Seville, dated April 26, 1520, which were the informations [sic] takend [sic] in Port St. Julian by martin Mendes, clerk of the *Victoria*; Sancho de heredia, king's notary; Gonzalo Gomes de Spinosa, Alguazil-mayor or chief constable of the fleet: he could not wirte [sic], and Domingo de Barruty signed for him. Eyewitness, 22 May 1521.

Albo, Francisco. Extracts from a Derrotero or Log-Book. Eyewitness, circa 1522.

Alexander VI, Pope (Rodrigo Borgia). Papal Bull Inter Caetera. Vatican, May 4, 1493. Amended by Papal Bull Dudum Siquidem, entitled Extension of the Apostolic Grant and Donation of the Indies. Vatican, September 25, 1493.

Barbosa, Duarte. *The Book of Duarte Barbosa.* Translated by Mansel Longworth Dames. New Delhi: Asian Educational Society, 1989 (originally published in 1812).

Brandt, Karl. *The Emperor Charles V.* Translated from the German by C. V. Wedgwood. 1939.

Columbus, Christopher. *The Journal of Christopher Columbus during his first voyage, 1492–1493, and Documents relating to the voyages of John Cabot and Gaspar Corte Real.* Edited by Sir Clements Markham. Hakluyt Society, First Series, Volume lxxxvi.

Correa, Gaspar. Gaspar Correa's Account of the Voyage. Eyewitness, circa 1522.

Guillemard, F. H. H. *The Life of Ferdinand Magellan and the First Circumnavigation of the Globe, 1480–1521.* London: George Philip & Son, 1891.

Lopez, Juan, de Recalde. Letter from Juan Lopez de Recalde to the Bishop of Burgos, of May 12, 1521, giving an account of the arrival of the *San Antonio* at Seville on May 6, 1521. Eyewitness, May 12, 1521.

Magellan, Ferdinand. Order of the Day of Magellan. Given in the Strait, which fell into the hands of the Portuguese, along with the Papers of the Astrologer Andres de San Martin, at the Moluccas: taken from Barros, Decade III, Liv. v, Cap. 19. This is the only known document written by Magellan.

Martir, Peter. *The Decades of the New World.* Translated from the Latin by Richard Eden. London: 1555.

Mitchell, Mairin. *Elcano: The First Circumnavigator.* London: Herder Publications, 1958.

"Narrative of a Portuguese, Companion of Odoardo Barbosa, in the Ship *Victoria* in the Year 1519." Unknown author. Eyewitness, circa 1522.

Navarrete, Martin Fernández de. Colección de los Viages y Descubrimientos que hicieron por Mar los Españoles desde Fines del Siglo XV. Vols. III–V. Madrid: 1825–37; Colección de Documentos Inéditos para la Historia de España. Vols. I, LXVI, LXXVIII. Madrid: 1841–95.

"Navigation and Voyage which Fernando de Magalhaes Made from Seville to Maluco in the Year 1519 (by a Genoese Pilot)." Eyewitness, circa 1522.

Penrose, Boies. *Travel and Discovery in the Renaissance.* Cambridge: Cambridge University Press, 1953.

Pigafetta, Antonio. *The Voyage of Magellan: The Journal of Antonio Pigafetta.* Translation by Paula Spurlin Paige from the edition in the William L. Clements Library, University of Michigan, Ann Arbor, including facsimile reproduction of the original Paris volume of 1525. Endmaps from the Agnese Battista Portulan Atlans, Italy, circa 1552. Maps in latter half from Bellin's atlas of 1781. New York: Prentice-Hall, 1969.

———. *Magellan's Voyage around the World: The Journal of Antonio Pigafetta.* Translation by James A. Robertson. Cleveland: Arthur H. Clark Company, 1906.

Vespucci, Amerigo. *The Letters of Amerigo Vespucci.* Translated by Clements Markham. London: Hakluyt Society, 1894.

St. Ignatius of Loyola

Genelli, Father of the Society of Jesus. *The Life of St. Ignatius of Loyola.* Translated from the German by M. Charles Sainte Foi. London: Burns, Oates, and Co., 1871.

Ignatius of Loyola. *Reminiscences.* In *Personal Writings.* Translated by Joseph A. Munitiz and Philip Endean. London: Penguin Books, 1996.

———. *Select Letters.* Translated by Joseph A. Munitz and Philip Endean. London: Penguin Books, 1996.

———. *The Spiritual Diary.* Translated by Joseph A. Munitz and Philip Endean. London: Penguin Books, 1996.

———. *The Spiritual Exercises.* Translated by Joseph A. Munitz and Philip Endean. London: Penguin Books, 1996.

Santiago Ramón y Cajal

Bentivoglio, Marina. "Life and Discoveries of Santiago Ramón y Cajal." Nobelprize.org. Nobel Media AB 2014.

"Camillo Golgi—Facts." Nobelprize.org. Nobel Media AB 2014.

Cannon, Dorothy F. *Explorer of the Human Brain: The Life of Santiago Ramón y Cajal (1852–1934).* New York: Henry Schuman, 1949.

"History of Neuroscience." Columbia.edu. Columbia University, School of Psychology.

"How Golgi Shared the 1906 Prize in Physiology or Medicine with Cajal." Nobelprize. org. Nobel Media AB 2014.

Kandel, E. R., J. H. Schwartz, and T. M. Jessel, eds. "Nerve Cells and Behavior." In *Principles of Neural Science.* 5th ed. New York: McGraw-Hill Professional, 2000.

Kandel, E. R., J. H. Schwartz, and T. M. Jessel, eds. "The Anatomical Organization of the Central Nervous System." In *Principles of Neural Science*. 5th ed. New York: McGraw-Hill Professional, 2000.

Morner, Count K. A. H. Nobel Prize commencement speech. December 10, 1906.

"Nervous System." In *Columbia Encyclopedia*. New York: Columbia University Press.

"The Nobel Prize in Physiology or Medicine 1906." Nobelprize.org. Nobel Media AB 2014.

Ramón y Cajal, Santiago. *Manual de histología normal y técnica micrográfica. Illustrated with 203 originals*. Valencia, 1889.

———. *Recuerdos de mi vida*. Madrid, 1901–1917. First published in English as Volume 8 of *Memoirs of the American Philosophical Society*, 1937. Reprinted, 1966 by the MIT Press. Translated by E. Horne Craigie with Juan Cano.

———. *Reglas y consejos sobre investigación científica: Los tónicos de la voluntad*. First published in English as *Advice for a young investigator*, 1999, by the MIT Press. Translated by Neely Swanson and Larry W. Swanson.

———. Address to Students after Receiving Grand Cross of Alfonso XII, and Made Counselor of Public Instruction. Madrid. 1897.

"Santiago Ramón y Cajal—Facts." Nobelprize.org. Nobel Media AB 2014.

Sotelo, Constantino. "Viewing the brain through the master hand of Ramón y Cajal." *Neuroscience* 4 (January 2003): 71–77.

CRISTÓBAL BALENCIAGA

Arzalluz, Miren. *Cristóbal Balenciaga: La forge du maitre, 1895–1936*. Translated from the Spanish by Carol Ungar. San Sebastián: Nerea, 2010.

Blume, Mary. *The Master of Us All: Balenciaga—His Workrooms, His World*. New York: Farrar, Straus, and Giroux, 2013.

Bowles, Hamish. *Balenciaga and Spain*. Fine Arts Museums of San Francisco and Skira Rizzoli Publications, 2011.

———. "The Balenciaga Mystique." *Vogue*, March 2006.

Breward, Christopher. *Oxford History of Art: Fashion*. New York: Oxford University Press, 2003.

Charleston, Beth Duncuff. "Cristobal Balenciaga (1895–1972)." Timeline of Art History, Metropolitan Museum of Art, https://www.metmuseum.org.

Domínguez Ortiz, Antonio. *Velázquez*. New York: Harry N. Abrams, 1990.

Emerson, Gloria. "Balenciaga, the Couturier, Dead at 77." *New York Times*, March 23, 1972.

Glynn, Prudence. "Balenciaga and la Vie d'un Chien." *London Times*, August 3, 1971.

Golbin, Pamela. *Balenciaga Paris*. London: Thames and Hudson, 2006.

Hartley, C. Gasquoine. *A Record of Spanish Painting*. London: Walter Scott, 1904.

"The King Is Dead." *Women's Wear Daily*, March 27, 1972.

Klensch, Elsa. "Balenciaga: Fashion Changer." *Vogue*, May 1973.

McDowell, Colin. "Balenciaga: The Quiet Revolutionary." *British Vogue*, July 1989.

Reuters. "Abre el museo Balenciaga, el primero dedicado a un modisto." June 7, 2011.

Snow, Carmel. "Editorial." *Harpers Bazaar,* February 1938.

———. "Paris Openings." *Harpers Bazaar,* September 15, 1938.

Snow, Carmel, with Mary Louise Aswell. *The World of Carmel Snow.* New York: McGraw Hill, 1962.

"A Spanish Night for Balenciaga in San Francisco." Women's Wear Daily, WWD.com, March 25, 2011.

"They Remember Balenciaga." *Women's Wear Daily,* March 27, 1972.

Vreeland, Diana. *D.V.* London: Weidenfeld and Nicolson, 1984.

———. "Evening Wear." *Harpers Bazaar,* September 15, 1938.

Walker, Myra. *Balenciaga and His Legacy.* New Haven, CT: Yale University Press, 2006.

The World of Balenciaga. New York: Metropolitan Museum of Art, 1973.

José María Arizmendiarrieta

"10 Great Companies to Work For." *Fortune (Europe Edition),* January 26, 2003.

Amsden, Jon. *Collective Bargaining and Class Conflict in Spain.* London: Weidenfeld and Nicolson, 1972.

Arizmendiarrieta, José María. *Reflections.* Translated by of Cherie Herrera, Cristina Herrera, David Herrera, Teresita Lorenzo, and Virgil Lorenzo. Bizkaya: Otalora, 2013.

Ash, M. "Reflections on Mondragón." *Town and Country Planning* 47 (1979): 11–14.

Barton, D. "Mondragón: Experiment or Prototype?" *Accountancy* 93 (1982): 125–126.

Clamp, Christine Anne. "Mondragón Meets the Recession." *Workplace Democracy* 10, no. 2 (1983): 10–11.

———. "Managing Cooperation at Mondragón." In *Proceedings of the National Employee-Ownership and Participation Conference.* Greensboro, NC: Guildford College, 1984.

Eitb.eus. "El papa reconoce las 'virtudes heroicas' de Arizmendiarrieta—Se trata del primer paso para la beatificación." *Sociedad,* Vatican, December 15, 2015.

Larrañaga, Jesús. *Buscando un camino: Don José María Arizmendiarrieta y la experiencia cooperative de Mondragón.* Bilbao, Spain: R&F, 1981.

Mondragón Cooperative Corporation. "Timeline of the Mondragón Experience." http://www.mondragon-corporation.com/eng/co-operative-experience/history/.

———. "Don Jose Arizmendiarrieta: Cause for Canonisation of Fr. Jose Maria Arizmendiarrieta." http://www.mondragon-corporation.com/eng/co-operative-experience/history/

Oakeshott, Robert. "Mondragón: Spain's Oasis of Democracy." *Observer (London) Supplement,* January 21, 1973.

Thompson, David. "Mondragon's Eroski as a Mass Retailer." *Cooperative Grocer Magazine,* November-December 2001.

"Trouble in Worker's Paradise: The Collapse of Spain's Fagor Tests the World's Largest Group of Cooperatives." *Economist*, November 9, 2013.

Whyte, William Foote, and Kathleen King Whyte. *Making Mondragon: The Growth and Dynamics of the Worker Cooperative Complex.* 2nd ed. rev. Ithaca, NY: ILR Press, Cornell University Press, 1988.

Paul Dominique Laxalt

"1980 Election Night." NBC News: Special Report, Decision 80. November 4, 1980.

"The 1994 Campaign: Virginia; Mrs. Reagan Denounces Oliver North on Iran Affair." *New York Times*, October 29 1994.

American Experience. "Reagan's Alzheimer's Letter." PBS.org, November 5, 1994.

———. "The Iran-Contra Affair." PBS.org.

Apple, R. W., Jr. "What Can Reagan Do?" *New York Times*, December 22, 1986.

Associated Press. "Iran Payment Found Diverted to Contras; Reagan Security Advisor and Aide Are Out." *New York Times*, November 26, 1986.

———. "Reagan Getting 'Steamed' at North over Reported Iran-Contra Remarks." March 18, 1994.

Conklin, Paul S. "'Sagebrush Rebels' Are Reveling in Reagan." *New York Times*, November 24, 1980.

Fahrenkopf, Frank J., Jr. "Remembering Ronald Reagan." American Gaming Association, www.americangaming.org.

Gibbs, Nancy. "The All American President: Ronald Wilson Reagan (1911–2004)." *Time*, June 14, 2004.

Kamow, Stanley. "Reagan and the Philippines: Setting Marcos Adrift." *New York Times Magazine*, March 19, 1989.

King, Larry. Interview with Paul Laxalt. "Ronald Reagan Remembered." *Larry King Live.* CNN. June 5, 2004. Transcript.

Knott, Stephen F., James Sterling Young, and Erwin Hargrove. Interviews with Otis Bowen, Secretary of Health and Human Services; A. B. Culvahouse, White House Counsel; James Kuhn, Personal Aide to the President; Stuart Spencer, Campaign Manager; and, Robert Tuttle, Director of Presidential Personnel. University of Virginia, Miller Center of Public Affairs, Ronald Reagan Oral History Project: Howard Baker's February 27, 1987, Entry into the White House. Washington, DC. October 2011.

———. Interview with Paul Laxalt. University of Virginia, Miller Center of Public Affairs, Ronald Reagan Oral History Project. Washington, DC. October 9, 2011.

Langdon, Dolly. "Will Reagan Ride Again in '84? His Blood Brother Paul Laxalt Is Saddling up the G.O.P." *Time*, April 18, 1983.

Laxalt, Paul. *Nevada's Paul Laxalt: A Memoir.* Reno: Jack Bacon & Company, 2000.

Laxalt, Robert. *Sweet Promised Land.* New York: Harper & Row Publishers, 1957.

Levy, Peter B. "Timeline." *Encyclopedia of the Reagan–Bush Years.* Westport, CT: Greenwood Press, 1996.

Lotshaw, Thomas. "Bi-State Compact to Preserve Lake Tahoe Turns 45 Years Old." Tahoe Regional Planning Agency, December 18, 2014.

Middleton, Drew. "A Fresh Look at MX Missile." *New York Times*, November 10, 1980.

Mydans, Seth. "Bidding Laxalt Farewell, Manila Seems to Bristle." *New York Times*, October 18, 1985.

———. "Marcos Reassures Laxalt on Rebels." *New York Times*, October 17, 1985.

Roberts, Steven V. "Politics Is Cited as a Key Factor in MX Decision." *New York Times*, April 19, 1983.

———. "Reagan's First Friend." *New York Times*, March 21, 1982.

Reagan, Ronald. *The Reagan Diaries*. New York: Harper Collins, 2009.

———. "Text of Reagan's Statement on MX Missile Basing." The White House, November 23, 1982.

Schmidt, William E. "MX Opposition Gaining in Utah and Nevada." *New York Times*, June 8, 1981.

———. "Political Leaders in Utah and Nevada Applaud Decision on the MX." *New York Times*, October 3, 1981.

Tower Commission Report. President's Special Review Board on the Iran-Contra Affair: John Tower, Chairman; Edmund Muskie and Brent Scowcroft, members. Introduction by R.W. Apple, Jr. New York: Bantam Books: 1987.

Turner, Wallace. "Laxalt's Power: Suits Focus Attention on Senator." *New York Times*, October 21, 1984.

———. "Laxalt's Road Ahead." *New York Times*, August 21, 1985.

———. "Laxalt Won't Run for Senate in '86." *New York Times*, August 20, 1985.

United Press International. "Excerpts from News Conference with Reagan's Cabinet Choices." December 23, 1980.

———. "Text of Resignation by Watt and Its Acceptance by Reagan." October 10, 1983.

Weinraub, Bernard. "U.S. Sends Laxalt to Talk to Marcos." *New York Times*, October 15, 1985.

Weisman, Steven R. "President Says He Needed to Relax Before Debating." *New York Times*, October 12, 1984.

———. "Reaganomics and the President's Men." *New York Times*, October 24, 1982.

———. "Reagan's Campaign Advisers Say He Would Face Tough Race in 1984." *New York Times*, September 18, 1983.

———. "Watt Quits Post; President Accepts with 'Reluctance.'" *New York Times*, October 10, 1983.

Edurne Pasaban

8000ers.com. List of Summits and Dates for Oh Eun-Sun, Edurne Pasaban, Gerlinde Kaltenbrunner, Nives Meroi, and Go Mi-Sun. 2010.

Associated Press. "Spanish Woman Reaches 14 Peaks." May 18, 2010.

Benavides, Angela. "Shisha Pangma: Edurne Pasaban Summits—Completes the 14x8000ers." ExplorersWeb.com, May 17, 2010.

Benavides, Angela, Brooke Meetze, and Tina Sjogren. "Oh Eun-Sun Report Final: Edurne Pasaban takes the Throne." ExplorersWeb.com, December 11, 2010.

Bradley, Ryan. "Adventurers of the Year 2010." *National Geographic*, December 9, 2010.

The Chosunilbo (English Edition): Daily News from Korea. "Mountaineer Oh Eun-Sun Meets Arbiter of Himalaya Ascents." chosunilbo.com, May 4, 2010.

Govan, Fiona. "First Woman to Climb World's Highest Peaks Stripped of Title." *Daily Telegraph* (Madrid), August 27, 2010.

"Edurne Pasaban: Queen of the Top of the World." *The Independent* (UK), March 23, 2015.

"Elizabeth Hawley, Grande Dame of the Himalayas." *The Baron*, April 29, 2010.

The Himalayan Database. AmericanAlpineClub.org.

Mulvey, Stephen. "Is Korean Oh Eun-Sun First Woman to Climb 14 Top Peaks?" *BBC News*, April 27, 2010.

———. "Korean Woman Climber's Himalayan Record Challenged." *BBC News*, April 23, 2010.

Pasaban, Edurne. Interview by Vince J. Juaristi. May 4, 2015. Amherst, Massachusetts.

———. *Tilting at Mountains.* Barcelona: Mountaineers Books, 2011.

Sharma, Gopal. "Elizabeth Hawley, World's Everest Expert." Reuters, May 9, 2011.

Sale, Richard, and John Cleare. *Climbing the World's 14 Highest Mountains.* Seattle: Mountaineers Books, 2000.

Sang-Hun, Choe. "Korean Is First Woman to Scale 14 Highest Peaks." *New York Times*, April 27, 2010.

"Stairway to Heaven." economist.com, May 29, 2013.

"The World's 14 Highest Mountain Peaks (above 8,000 meters)." Pearson Education On-Line.

Further Reading

IN WRITING A BOOK that relies so much on primary sources, I had to make choices about what to include or exclude from the final manuscript—what childhood story, what fragment of a letter, what singular episode in a career, what brush with death, or what moment of joy. Naturally, more was excluded than included. These choices were carefully balanced between tidbits that fascinated me and what I thought might fascinate readers of these Basque lives. I hope I did my job well. Still, I know that what interests me does not always interest others, a valuable point, I might add, for those prolific posters of mind-numbing drivel on Facebook.

Each of these profiles offered a glance into the lives of extraordinary Basque men and women, but in the end they are merely glances. Sniffing bouquets whets the palette for a glass of wine or maybe even a full bottle. For such eager readers with big appetites, I've compiled a list of additional sources that fascinated me and might help quench the thirst of other Basque enthusiasts.

JUAN SEBASTIÁN ELCANO. Although Antonio Pigafetta's journal of the first circumnavigation does not include a reference to Elcano, it still represents the only firsthand account of humanity's first entire voyage around the globe. Although flawed, it offers a descriptive step-by-step account of the trip. A book by Mairin Mitchell entitled *Elcano: The First Circumnavigator* offers a more comprehensive, though incomplete, treatment of the man. Finally, to understand a voyage during this age—aboard a wooden ship, at the mercy of wind and storm—consider *The Journal of Christopher Columbus during His First Voyage, 1492–93*, which made me believe that impossible feats may be overcome with hard work, courage, and just the right wind.

ST. IGNATIUS OF LOYOLA. St. Ignatius was a prolific writer of letters. He expressed himself best when offering guidance or defending his faith to others, as if he were sitting for a confessional at a distance. A good compendium of his letters is published by Penguin Books entitled *Select Letters*. A must-read for any Ignatius enthusiast is his work *Reminiscences*, which serves as an autobiography. It does not cover the whole of his life, but enough to show a clear trajectory toward his final days when the Society of Jesus came into being and education assumed a central role in his doctrine. It has been translated several times, but the most readable is a translation by Joseph A. Munitiz and Philip Endean.

SANTIAGO RAMÓN Y CAJAL. To understand Santiago, read his multivolume autobiography *Recuerdos de mi vida*, translated by E. Horne Craigie with Juan Cano. It chronicles every part of his life, sometimes in excruciating, exhaustive detail. The Nobel Prize Committee published the *Life and Discoveries of Santiago Ramón y Cajal* up to the point that he received his Nobel Prize in Physiology or Medicine. It is comprehensive, easily readable, packed full of personal and scientific details and explains why his work deserved recognition in 1906.

CRISTÓBAL BALENCIAGA. Among all the profiles in this book, Balenciaga proved to be the most enigmatic. He sat for only one interview during his life, which means that so much of what we know about him, and so much of what I gathered, had to come from secondary sources, mostly friends and fashion magazines. His one interview, conducted by Prudence Glynn, was published in the *London Times* on August 3, 1971, headlined "Balenciaga and la Vie d'un Chien." Though relatively short, it is worth reading if only because of its rarity. A more comprehensive view of the man comes from a work by Miren Arzalluz called *Cristóbal Balenciaga: La forge du maitre*, translated from the Spanish by Carol Ungar.

JOSÉ MARÍA ARIZMENDIARRIETA. Like St. Ignatius 400 years before him, José María was a prolific writer, first as a Basque journalist during the Spanish Civil War and then as a writer of economic, political, and social commentary in Mondragón. Many of his most popular and influential writings are collected in a book titled *Reflections*, translated from *Pensamientos de Don José María Arizmendiarrieta*, by a collaborative team made up of Cherie Herrera, Cristina Herrera, David Herrera, Teresita Lorenzo, and Virgil Lorenzo. To know what the man wrote is to know about the man. Proud of its history, the Mondragón Cooperative Corporation maintains a Timeline of the Mondragón Experience, which can be accessed on its website. It focuses more on the history of the company than Don José María, but the two are linked inextricably: to know about one is to know about the other. Finally, one of the father's students, José María Ormaechea, published *El hombre que yo conocí*, which was translated as *The Man That I Knew*. It offers an intimate look at a teacher through the eyes of a student.

PAUL DOMINIQUE LAXALT. Laxalt agreed to an interview with the University of Virginia, Miller Center of Public Affairs, to discuss his role in the Reagan administration. This interview is Laxalt in his own words, long after he had left the US Senate and years after Reagan had died. It covers candidly and clearly issues as far ranging as the Iran-Contra affair, Reagan's economic policies, and Marcos in the Philippines. It is a firsthand account of how Laxalt remembered Reagan, unfiltered by publishers, journalists, or political handlers. For a more comprehensive history of Laxalt's work related to Lake Tahoe, visit the Tahoe Regional Planning Agency and read "Bi-State Compact to Preserve Lake Tahoe Turns 45 Years Old." For treatment of the Iran-Contra affair, read the *Tower Commission Report*, compiled by President Reagan's special review board with John Tower, chairman; Edmund Muskie and Brent Scowcroft, members; and an introduction by R. W. Apple Jr. Finally, as a US senator, Laxalt received widespread coverage in the *New York Times*, the *Washington Post*, and other national newspapers and magazines that are easily accessible and searchable online. The *New York Times*, most of all, seemed to have deeper ties to Laxalt than the *Post* or the *Wall Street Journal*.

EDURNE PASABAN. Most of my source material for Edurne Pasaban came from interviews with her and her team. An author has no better source, in my opinion, than a one-on-one discussion with a subject to get a broad understanding of her nature, her habits, how she thinks, what she says and doesn't say, and how she says it. An author connects with people, and that connection affects the writing, mostly for the better, I think. To learn more about high-stakes mountain climbing, visit the site 8000ers.com, which lists all dates and summits of every climber and gives a detailed account of each mountain. To know Edurne better, read her autobiography, now available in English, entitled *Tilting at Mountains*, a wonderful reference to Don Quixote's tilting at windmills and the propensity of all humans to fence with imaginary enemies.

Author's Note

VINCE J. JUARISTI is the CEO and President of ARBOLA, Inc., a technology corporation in Alexandria, VA. Born and raised in Elko, NV, Vince grew up in a rich and proud Basque community. His Basque father came from Spain in 1948, and his mother is first-generation Basque-American. Vince still visits them regularly and remains active in Basque programs, often enjoying the fine dance and dining of Basque hospitality. He lives in Alexandria, VA, but home is still Elko.

.

Index